Praise for *Domesticity*

"Take M. F. K. Fisher's sublimely sensual writings on food, add a liberal dose of testosterone and a dollop of twisted humor, and you've got a good idea of the quirky style of Bob Shacochis's delicious *Domesticity*. . . . It is more than just the record of a passionate cook's culinary adventures. Mr. Shacochis uses food as a medium to investigate all sorts of human appetites, inventions and connections. He ponders the history of breakfast the social significance of ice cream, the relative value of table manners the pleasures of the dinner party. . . . *Domesticity* nourishes the se and the soul."
— *New York Times Book Review*

"By turns doting, curative, seductive. . . . Its celebration of the co greatest need—the significant eater—rings sweetly true."
— *Washington Post*

"Shacochis follows his nose to investigate such 'gastronomic rid nomenclature of pâtés and terrines and the aphrodisiac reputations or various foods. . . . Shacochis is literate, tough, romantic and the master of his kitchen."
— *Publishers Weekly*

"*Domesticity* is about the voluptuous pleasures of cooking for, and eating with, someone you love, about making meals a participatory rather than spectator sport. It is about excess and obsession. . . . Shacochis intends to reinvent our relationship to food—in much the same way that he has worked, over [the] years, to reinvent the notion of romance."
— *Los Angeles Times*

"The value of Shacochis' book rests in the best of its artful telling. When he describes food as 'one of the ways we have of locating ourselves, of telling ourselves where we are, both physically and emotionally,' the reader suspects that this is the secret key to his far-ranging essays."
— *Chicago Tribune*

"A modern autobiographical cookbook . . . Dedicated to the principle that the head, heart, and taste buds are all interwoven, the recipes go well beyond formulas—they are instead expressions of mood, setting, and lifestyle. A versatile addition to most collections, this book could just as easily be shelved next to Calvin Trillin as Julia Child."
— *Library Journal*

"Food, sex, and other thoughts. . . . The writing—polished, clever, and aptly targeted."
— *Kirkus Reviews*

"Scoundrels make good subjects, and though at times you might want to reach across the page and cuff Shacochis, you can't help but forgive him, and continue feasting on the light but well-seasoned fare he has to offer."
— *San Francisco Review of Books*

"These vibrant, offbeat, and sensual essays on the importance of food in the daily affairs of interesting, idiosyncratic men and women who know their way around kitchens combine an enthusiastic storyteller's love of narrative with an enthusiastic cook's love of fresh ingredients."
— *Entertainment Weekly*

DOMESTICITY

A Gastronomic Interpretation of Love

BOB SHACOCHIS

TRINITY UNIVERSITY PRESS
San Antonio, Texas

Published 2013 by Trinity University Press
San Antonio, Texas 78212

Copyright © 1995, 2013 by Bob Shacochis

Trinity University Press strives to produce its books using methods and materials in an environmentally sensitive manner. We favor working with manufacturers that practice sustainable management of all natural resources, produce paper using recycled stock, and manage forests with the best possible practices for people, biodiversity, and sustainability. The press is a member of the Green Press Initiative, a nonprofit program dedicated to supporting publishers in their efforts to reduce their impacts on endangered forests, climate change, and forest-dependent communities.

The paper used in this publication meets the minimum requirements of the American National Standard for Information Sciences—Permanence of Paper for Printed Library Materials, ANSI 39.48-1992.

Cover design by DVS Design
Book design by Anne Scatto
Illustrations by Richard Truscott
Cover illustration: Strawberries lying on sexy back, © iStockphoto.com/David Hiller

978-1-59534-191-4 paper
978-1-59534-190-7 ebook

"Thighs and Whispers" was previously published in *Vogue*; "Lost" was previously published in *Special Reports*; all other essays in this book appeared as "Dining In" columns in *GQ*.

CIP data on file with the Library of Congress

17 16 15 14 13   5 4 3 2 1

For my editors: Granger, Kathy, and Judy;
and the Big Guy, Art.
For my friends Scott and Captain Tay.

And for that Other Girl, what's-her-name.

CONTENTS

PART THREE

INTRODUCTION

Miss F. and I live together, and seem to have made a habit of it—for better or worse, but always under the obligation not to destroy each other, as is too often the style in the modern art of relationships. This all began in the mid-70s, when she first moved in with me. I was twenty-four years old. Miss F. had just turned an extraordinarily tenacious twenty-three, a miraculous age where she would remain for many years. I remember that, at the time, the air surrounding us felt pressurized with the understanding, held in common between us, that we had more or less been catapulted into love. Yet as far as I was concerned, this was not a big deal and certainly no cause for alarm. This happened on a regular basis among people our age—it was like still another dress rehearsal for the future, the time in our thirty-something dotage when we would weary of lust and romance and actually chance a commitment, essentially placing the gun of adulthood to our youth-crazed brains and pulling the trigger, leaving us with no other choice but to pursue that most dire and numbing of social acts called *settling down*.

Clearly, some men arise from their cradles as ready-made bureaucrats of love, and these are the ones who, at the earliest opportunity, march straight ahead toward the barn of domesticity, that hallowed shelter of tradition where they will be adequately fed and fattened, where the alluring scent of greener pastures gradually fades into oblivion. I could be appreciative of this breed—so vital to the preservation of what little's left of what used to be referred to as the American Way—without wanting to emulate them. As for myself, I held no intention of settling down or even simmering down: I much preferred life in proximity to the boiling point.

What were you supposed to settle down into anyway, I wanted to know. Tranquility? (What was that? I never even liked quaaludes in college.) Complacency? Boredom? Inertia? Brooding? A permanent state of annoyance?

Mowing the lawn?

Intertribal warfare among the neighbors?

Cornflakes? Canned soup? Iceberg lettuce? Tuna fish casseroles?

Just forget it. Boyhood gone to seed. No word in the domestic lexicon was more self-explanatory than wed*lock*. As I said, I loved Miss F. but wasn't about to throw out the anchor on our relationship since love, like a car built in Detroit, was not meant to last. Everybody knew that.

At the time, I did the right thing, or at least the only proper thing a gentleman could do, and promptly suggested to Miss F. that she was entering into an association with the wrong guy; that, by falling in love with me and moving in and then allowing the whole affair to canter along, week after week, she was making a mistake of a proportion that would ultimately have to be categorized as whopping. My caveat raised the issue of cake, that great euphemism for male appetites: I wanted to have my cake, of course, just as much as I desired to eat it, and if I had my ravenous way, I was going to be the one who baked it too, over and over again, experimenting with an epicurean variety of recipes, until I was cake-stuffed, blind with frosting, and could say in truth that I had had my fill—a process that one suspected, if not prayed, might take forever.

Settling down was deadly anathema to us boys with our cakes. Only the bourgeoisie ever really settled down, like flecks of precipitate drifting to the bottom of society's beaker to lie for eternity in sedimentary bliss, while the renegades, fops, aristocrats, pashas, brats, layabouts, and ne'er-do-wells who inhabited the upper and lower classes whirled around through the solution like radioactive paramecium, enjoying the libertarian currents of indulgence and selfishness and irresponsibility and having a lot of fun. In this regard, I took William Butler Yeats to heart, who once wrote, "I have certainly seen more men destroyed by the desire to have a wife and child and to keep them in comfort than I have seen destroyed by drink or harlots." I thought it for the best, then, that Miss F. detach herself from me and come back in ten years time. If I hadn't destroyed myself by then, she would be welcome to try her hand at it. And I believe I might very well have succeeded in my ambition to be a rascal, had Miss F. not been so unreasonably agreeable about my cake-ish declarations.

"We'll just have to see how it goes," she replied airily . . . which was not an entirely honest thing to say. Intelligent women know exactly how it will go, which is why so many of them can be found vomiting on the eves of their weddings. Miss F. knew perfectly well what sort of life she would make with me—precisely the one we have made—and I never have been quite sure whether to hold her clairvoyance against her, whether it was wise or wily or merely stoic of her to humor me in my boyish illusions. At least I can say this: Between lovers, seduction is neither a trap nor a trick; rather, it is the clarification of desire.

Settling down wasn't the point anyway, Miss F. explained. She herself had no interest in it. The point was being together.

"Yeah?" I said with no little skepticism. "What if you get in my way?"

"The way of what?" she wondered.

"My work, for instance. My writing."

"It will never happen," swore Miss F. (She was telling the truth.)

"Other women."

"Consider me already there," she answered resolutely.

"Well, I don't know about that," I groused. "What if I have to go on assignment to the Sudan for a year, and you can't come along?"

"That wouldn't be being together, would it?" she said. "You'd have to take your chances."

"I'll always be the restless sort."

"Of course you will," she replied. "You're an American and you're male. You'll probably always be coming and going. Just promise me that your concept of *coming back* means *coming back to me.*"

Apparently, this thing with Miss F. wasn't going to work out, I concluded. She was simply—impossibly—too level-headed, tolerant, and fair. After three months together, I sent her away. Just like that: *You have to go.* I suppose it was the most life-changing decision I ever made, because the worst happened, almost immediately. Her leave-taking made me wretched, utterly miserable; her absence was an insufferable pain. Three months later I quit my job and went to find her, thousands of miles away, already doing the unthinkable—starting a new life without me.

Now after eighteen years I have to face the fact that I have lived with one woman . . . and she's not my mother. I seem to have only a vague idea how all of this happened, and it flies in the face of some of my mostly deeply cherished fantasies, not a one of them having anything whatsoever to do with monogamy. On the male thermometer, fantasizing about monogamy registers about a half degree of heat above an Iowa farmer's dreams about corn.

I had once hoped that, should I ever be so foolhardy as to write a book of a deliberately autobiographical nature, I would first have had the good sense to live the life of a pirate, or a bon vivant, which would have allowed me to reflect shamelessly upon a career of grand debauchery or world-class caddishness, so that any account of my exploits would perforce bear a brash and manly title, something along the lines of *An Alphabet of Red-Hot Babes* or *Paris Redux: The Sober Years*; or something that had the heavyweight reek of my intimacy with power, like *Fidel and Me,* for example; or a paean to testosterone, like *Rafting the Buthalezi.*

Instead, here I am signing on with *Domesticity,* which is a book about relationships and food and dogs, about the gastronomic aesthetic and love and love's language, about friendship and laughter and anger and the distances that often separate us, about cooking and snobs and sorrow and writing and secrets, and about who's going to do the dishes, since it isn't going to be me. This is an unexpected right turn in my literary life, back toward the middle of the road, and, I must say, quite a terrible shock. In some ways, this is my personal tragedy as a guy, and the end of the fling others have imagined for me with the Cult of Ernesto, though I remain, as the *New York Times Book Review* once suggested, free, white, and hairy-chested.

Perhaps I should have anticipated the in-house response to my domestic meditations—they have, upon occasion, made Miss F. very nervous; they have made her gulp, made her furious, made her laugh at herself and me and us, and once in a blue moon, they have, I confess, hurt her, because, of course, my experience of *our* life has not always been hers—and yet she has never asked me to alter my perspective in order to paint a more comfortable public image of her or us, or who I think she is, or who I imagine we are, at any given moment. I suppose I also should have anticipated a certain out-of-house response to writing a book, however personal, with recipes in it, and yet when I've encountered it over and over again, I always found it baffling, and stupidly rude.

Take, for instance, the winter season, 1989–90. Miss F. and I were implanted among the self-anointed mandarins of high culture at the American Academy. Remembering them brings to mind Robert Hughes' phrase, "pale patriarchal penis people." Gilded incarceration would adequately describe the context of our tenure there—we were elite prisoners in the Palace of Negligence and Affectation—and it turned out to be the most horrible year of our lives, the only time, in time unending, that our relationship threatened to undo itself. (More about that later, although Miss F. advises me that my retelling of our unhappiness there is unfair to her—only half the story . . . and so it is.)

We lived at the mercy of the Academy's director, the Boring Meany, and his high-strung, vindictive French wife, Her Royal Awfulness, both of whom had dedicated themselves to winning the great class war of snobbery being waged among the Americans, and anybody else who got in the way.

On the nasty little occasion of which I speak, Her Royal Awfulness, in need of a project less tiring than her hourly harassment of the kitchen staff, was inspired to host something akin to a freshman mixer in the *salon,* and so invited over the snoots from the French Academy to rub vitae with the snots at our American one. It promised, as did most events at the Academy, to be an exquisitely cutthroat affair.

By the time I exited our freezing cell on the Academy's second floor, the soiree was in full dyspeptic swing. I paused on the marble staircase that led to the salon, so that from my temporarily elevated position I might survey the beautiful people below, inhale the genius they exuded, and tremble with anticipation at the prospect of my communion among them. Then, I descended, spotting Her Awfulness, who had also seen me; she made a summoning gesture, as is frequently the case among her tribe, and I obeyed, which is not always the case among the tribe of barbarians I call my own.

I weaved through the crowd, saying hello to this backstabber or that imposter; greeting the Marxist art historian wearing a $250 pair of designer shoes; the illiterate artist who, in his brilliance, created outrageously expensive prints of monosyllabic words after he had looked them up in the dictionary to learn how they were spelled. Finally, I stood side by side with Her Awfulness, herself encircled by a coterie of nattily dressed Parisians—three men and a young woman—each with arched eyebrows and that particular smirk of arrogance that makes the French so beloved by your run-of-the-mill gringo. These were the French writers, my counterparts, all four of them acclaimed novelists and recipients of the Prix de France, which I understand in France is actually an honor.

"Here is Robert," announced Her Royal Awfulness, meaning me. She could barely conceal the wicked pleasure she seemed to take in her identification of me. "He writes cookbooks," she said.

Perhaps it goes without saying that, after such a warm and generous introduction, and despite the gastronomic passions of the French, not a one of them had a word, kind or otherwise, to say to me throughout the evening. The anecdote is self-evident and requires no further interpretation, so I'll take my leave, for the time being, of the Academy's treacherous halls, to beg entrance into the infinitely more civilized and compassionate world of M. F. K. Fisher, whom I think of, would like to think of in all humility, as the guardian angel of this book. In her foreword to *The Gastronomical Me*, Fisher wrote:

"People ask me: Why do you write about food, and eating and drinking? Why don't you write about the struggle for power and security, and about love, the way others do?

"They ask it accusingly, as if I were somehow gross, unfaithful to the honor of my craft.

"The easiest answer is to say that, like most other humans, I am hungry. But there is more than that. It seems to me that our three basic needs, for food and security and love, are so mixed and mingled and entwined that we cannot straightly think of one without the others. So it happens that when I write of hunger, I am really writing about love and the hunger for it, and warmth and the love of it and the hunger for it . . . and then the warmth and richness and fine reality of hunger satisfied . . . and it is all one."

I plead guilty to both the sensibility and the hunger—literally. And my hunger, as it so often does with one's life, given the opportunity, changed me, made me both an exemplary wife and, I suppose, and to no one's surprise, a lousy husband. More significantly though, the hunger widened my literary horizon in a manner I never imagined or expected.

Five years ago, when the criminally inebriated editors at GQ magazine asked me to become their new "Dining In" columnist, when I stopped guffawing, I did what George Bush so frequently accused Bill Clinton of always doing—I waffled. The offer from GQ was actually a matter of coincidence: the fiction editor at the magazine had invited me to send him some of my novel then in progress. The chapter I submitted contained a scene in which the male character cooks an elaborate dinner, highlighted by a planked striped bass roasted over an open fire, for the woman he's romancing. At the same time, GQ's former Dining In columnist threw in his apron, and word went out around the editorial offices, "Does anyone know anybody who can write about food?"

The fiction editor believed he did. My dinner scene was photocopied and passed around; in desperation, the senior editors agreed the column was mine, if I wanted it. One of them telephoned to see what I'd say. I said, not quite emphatically, *No*. I said I probably wasn't the person they were looking for. The writing I had read about food, unless authored by the likes of Fisher or A. J. Liebling or Calvin Trillin, struck me as exceedingly boring, pea-brained, pretentious, faddish, rife with the worst sort of classism, devoted to the most anemic forms of *joie de vivre,* et cetera. It wasn't even lively enough, on its own terms, to turn my stomach.

The editor said, *Fine*. She said, Write about anything you want, in any style you fancy, *only tag a recipe onto the end of it*. I thought she was genuinely out of her mind and told myself maybe I should take advantage of this condition before she comes to her senses. She didn't seem to realize that I was a fiction writer, that I made things up out of thin air, that I embellished facts according to whimsy, plus I had political and social axes to grind, and that I had a sense of humor others found, to say it politely, inappropriate, or that I was the kind of guy who would likely use the column to thumb my nose at the insipid elitism embodied by gastronomic literature as it is standardly practiced. (It was the insipidness that riled me, not especially the elitism, since elitism in the service of creative excellence could hardly be called a vice.)

Or that I couldn't separate, intellectually or emotionally, how I cooked from how I lived, which was problematic, since how I lived with my common-law wife, Miss F., was not exactly natural material for mass consumption, and the text of the column, more often than not, would evolve out of the complexities of a contemporary though pointedly alternative life-style where the man remained at home (that is, when he deigned to be in town) and the woman went out into the world each morning (and wasn't allowed to return until after five). A column about the domestic landscape, as experienced by a couple with a very shoddily drawn domestic map, who were indifferent about orthodoxy and could care less, frankly, about the traditional roles society assigns to gender.

Miss F. and I had just moved from the Outer Banks of North Carolina to Florida, where she was to begin law school at Florida State University. We had sixty dollars in our pockets, no source of income other than my writing, no trust funds or bank accounts, an aging Irish setter named Tyrone, and a rowboat filled with all our earthly belongings, mostly books. For two weeks we camped out in a friend's backyard while sweatily searching for an affordable house to rent, but I had my garlic press and barbecue grill at hand and was determined to keep my dear Miss F. well fed while she swam up the academic stream through the currents of tort law and statutory interpretation. Then came *GQ*'s immodest proposal. I called them back the next day and said, in the immortal words of the Gumbo King, *Let the big dog eat.*

The book now in your hands is a result of that decision, five years ago—which is an extreme amount of time for a fellow like me to contemplate his domestic navel. In many ways, *Domesticity* is a prose stew, much like the commonplace books popular in the Middle Ages, a much-blackened iron kettle filled with extracts and essences—recipes, prayers, quotations, anecdotes, tributes and tribulations. In a way, it is the diary of our life that I never thought to keep. And as a document of self, it has taught me to value and remember the ordinary in the floodtide of an extraordinary world, where my attention most resides.

Bob Shacochis
June, 1993
Florida

PART ONE

DINING MISS F.

Miss F. and I live in a small city in north Florida, a place where cats and dogs are the favorite food of the local alligators. I'm sorry to report that we are many a league distant from a good delicatessen, yet close enough to the sea and year-round farmers' markets to assure ourselves that our existence is not at all deprived. Still, you can't find a first-rate roast beef sandwich within a hundred-mile radius, and so it was with great expectation and a sense of gastronomic deliverance that we travelled to Manhattan together last month when our schedules allowed us to be there together for the first time in a couple of years.

The first morning, we had our coffee and poached eggs at the Algonquin with a friend who'd been out of touch with us for a while.

"So what's up with you two these days?" asked she, a hyper-ambitious photographer permanently bivouacked in midtown. This woman lived a scratch-and-hustle life to stay afloat. Miss F. successfully barraged her with law-school war stories, having learned by now that everyone in the world enjoys hearing what innate sleazebags those occupied by the legal profession frequently are, as evidenced early on in their development during the tadpole stage of studenthood. When Miss F. finished with her cruel lawyer/rat joke, it was my turn.

"Well," I admitted with happy innocence, "one of the things I'm doing is writing the 'Dining In' column for *GQ*."

"Restaurants!" she enthused. "Lucky you!"

"No, no, no," I corrected her, "It's not about restaurants, it's about dining in. You know, staying home."

"Dining *in*?" She looked puzzled, even alarmed, as if since she last saw me I had become a fellow who spoke only in nonsense riddles. Then her face brightened with revelation, and finally her expression was one of incredulity.

"You mean to tell me," she gasped, "that you're writing a column about *take-out*?!" Her confusion was familiar to me, and entirely justifiable seeing as how never once, invited into a New Yorker's apartment, had I opened a refrigerator and observed actual, verifiable food in the box. Always, the freezer would contain a frosty bottle of vodka and a misshapen berg of ice. The lower compartment would invariably house a jar of Dijon mustard in the door, a quart of milk, mineral water, or juice, or perhaps a supply of medication requiring cool temperatures; and occasionally, but not as often as you might think, a white paper sack or tin-foiled lump of something meant to be eaten last week, when it was fresh, in some more exciting part of the metropolis than one's own place of residence.

Why does the sight of a barren refrigerator evoke in me a sense of culture shock? I'm not sure I understand it at all, the typical urbanite's aversion to preparing a meal, eating at home a refined version of what has been thoughtfully foraged from the outside. Sure, Miss F. and I were playing along—we were in the Very Big City for business, to have a fast time and, yes, to eat: to eat, extravagantly, intemperately *well*. Still, after 72 gourmanding hours, I'd had it. The idea of dining out night after night—even just several times a week—seems a bit rigorous to me, akin to camping out, an activity that I have determined to be the essence of the New York City life-style, high or low. People drop by their own digs to brush their teeth and pick up mail, and to sleep or commit variations on that theme. And that's about the extent of their domestic downtime, except on Sunday when they might nod at a ballgame on tv while they scan the *Times*. Any other aspect of home life for anyone not awash in babies is too tedious: it seems irrelevant, unproductive, unprofitable and—here's the clincher—boring. Nobody in the world has a lower boredom threshold than New Yorkers, and it makes their kitchens lonely, forgotten places.

Okay, so one fellow's domesticity is another fellow's shackles. I too am seduced by cosmopolitan restaurants and trendy bistros, menus indecipherable except to a graduate degreeholder in the Romance languages. Ultimately, however, these establishments can become bordellos of endless gastronomic affairs with the appetite prowling and carousing, lascivious and transient. Little more is generated here but an ephemeral commitment that applies only to the glamor of the moment. I am no more immune to these moments of escape than anyone else but I know I'll always come home, with a sense of relief, to my own table, convinced that home is the setting of something better, where meaning and satisfaction are anchored firmly into the foundation of our private lives and don't drag off in the tide of yet one more inflated transaction added to the commerce of the day.

What I mean to describe in these pages is the fundamental difference between the process of creating and the process of consuming—a dichotomy much discussed in the current state of the union. The balance, the equilibrium—you could argue that it begins in the kitchen, a most encouraging environment for the evolution of values and temperament, where we learn what is too little and what after all is too much. As best I can tell, there are no Mozarts of cooking, child geniuses born with whisks in their hands, whipping up immortal *creme au beurre* at age five. Instead, we begin with grilled cheese sandwiches and spaghetti every night of the week until, after years of trial and error, we graduate to cassoulet. Very often, it isn't talent that makes a good cook; most often it is the maturation of standards, the determined old-fashioned momentum of love. Let's face it, gentlemen, the kitchen, not the bedroom, is the part of the house where we make ourselves grow up.

•　•　•

On the return flight to Florida, Miss F., a bit soporific from her annual dose of the Very Big City, yawned and wondered out loud what we were going to do about dinner when we got back home.

"I've been thinking about that," I admitted.

"Poor Mary," sighed Miss F., but with ambivalence, when I told her what I'd planned. Miss F. is grateful that we no longer live in a hunter-gatherer society but she likes her lamb nevertheless. Being a cook, though, you can't kid yourself about where the chops come from, and that's for the best, because something vital is preserved in that knowledge. Halfway between the abattoir and the dining room of the Hotel Athenée is where I try to live.

BUTTERFLIED LAMB ESPRESSO

This recipe may be grilled or broiled.

1 leg of lamb, boned and flattened, trimmed of excess fat

Marinate overnight, refrigerated.

MARINADE:

2 cloves garlic, minced

½ cup tawny port wine

½ cup brewed espresso coffee

¼ cup vegetable oil

1 tablespoon dry mustard

1 tablespoon grated ginger

1 teaspoon each dried thyme, salt and pepper

Skewer the meat at right angles so it doesn't curl inward while broiling. Broil six to eight minutes on each side, brushing once with the marinade. Slice across the grain and serve with kohlrabi in a sauce bechâmel, and endive salad.

SERVES 6.

CUISADO DE CARNERO

This is a celebrated style of preparing lamb in Puerto Rico.

3 pounds lamb shoulder, trimmed of fat and cut into 2-inch cubes

Heat 3 tablespoons oil in a large pan, sprinkle lamb with 1 teaspoon each salt and pepper, and brown a few pieces at a time. Remove the meat to a side plate. For the rest of the recipe you'll need:

1 cup dry white wine

10 tablespoons fresh orange juice

3 tablespoons fresh lime juice

2 tablespoons seedless raisins (optional)

2 fat, stuffed green olives, chopped

2 cloves garlic, minced

2 whole cloves

3 teaspoons capers, chopped

1 teaspoon fresh, hot chilies, chopped fine

1 bay leaf

12 boiled new potatoes

Pour off oil from pan and add wine. Bring to a boil, add the other ingredients, stirring constantly, then return the lamb to the pan. Cover and simmer for about 90 minutes until lamb is tender. Center braised lamb on a heated dish, encircle with potatoes, then pour the sauce over the meat.

SERVES 6.

LAMB SCHEHERAZADE

This is a Middle Eastern–style leg of lamb. You can roast it, if you wish, for 50–70 minutes at 350 degrees, but it's much better grilled with indirect heat for about 2 hours.

1 leg of lamb (4 pounds)

4 cloves garlic, slivered

4 teaspoons pepper

Crosshatch lamb with a sharp knife, insert garlic into slits, and rub with pepper. As it grills or roasts, baste with the following sauce:

1 cup white wine vinegar

1 cup soy sauce

½ cup olive oil

2 tablespoons fresh lemon juice

1 small onion, grated

1 teaspoon fresh grated ginger

½ teaspoon ground nutmeg

½ teaspoon ground cloves

When the meat is done (145 degrees for rare; 155 for medium), slice from bone and serve with cucumber-yogurt sauce:

2 cups plain yogurt

1 cucumber, peeled and shredded

½ cup green onions, chopped

1 package frozen sweet peas, thawed

½ teaspoon ground cumin

½ teaspoon each salt and sugar

½ teaspoon chili powder

Stir ingredients together in a bowl. Cover and refrigerate overnight. Stir before spooning on lamb. Serve with tabouli.

SERVES 6.

BOZBASH
(Lamb Stew with Sour Fruit)

1 handful of chick peas (soaked for 24 hours)
1 pound stewing lamb, cut into chunks
3 cups water
2 onions, chopped
4 damsons or stoned prunes with a squirt of lemon juice
1 tablespoon tomato paste
2 potatoes (or 5 chestnuts)
1 tablespoon coriander
1 tablespoon fresh parsley, chopped
½ tablespoon fresh thyme, chopped
2 pinches saffron or tumeric
6 black peppercorns
Salt and pepper to taste

As Leslie Chamberlin will tell you in her wonderful book, *The Food and Cooking of Russia*, cook the chick peas in unsalted water for 3 hours. Drain and reserve the liquid. Place the lamb in a saucepan with the water, bring to a boil, then simmer covered for an hour. Add the chick peas, onions, damsons, and peppercorns and cook over low heat for 30 minutes. Add tomato paste, chopped potatoes or chestnuts, season to taste with salt and pepper, and cook for another 30 minutes, adding the reserved liquid from the chick peas if necessary. After a half hour, add the fresh herbs, saffron, more salt and pepper if needed, simmer for three minutes more, let cool for about 5 minutes and then serve.

SERVES 4.

THE SCALLOPING
GOURMET

One of the great nostalgias of my life is the seafood market of the eastern seaboard, especially the ones you find on the edge of a cornfield, those questionable looking but godsent roadside concerns located on the western boundary of the tidelands, backdropped by a spine of mountains running from North Carolina and Virginia through Maryland and into Pennsylvania. Reminiscent of the Fifties, the structures possess the same habitual shabbiness and temporary character: as often as not the naive fastidiousness of a ma-and-pa enterprise or the ethnic humbleness and insularity of an Old World cottage.

Inside there are outmoded deli display coolers with noisy refrigeration systems or, better still, long plywood trays painted white, shoveled full of crushed ice. Laid out in the snow like avalanche victims, the day's catch has been trucked in from the docks of Philadelphia or Baltimore or Maine Avenue in D.C. or hauled from Norfolk and Hampton Roads. I love any grocery or restaurant that handles a bulk of crushed ice, keeping it out front so you can walk up and feel the tendrils of its vapor, for the presence of ice seems like a real guarantee, a basic old-fashioned and true aesthetic. I stop at these shacks for the simple reward of a whiff of oceanic brine and, when the seasons commence, to smell the Old Bay spice and vinegar of a fifteen-gallon cooker steaming blue crabs, the slough-mud fragrance of the bushelled Chincoteague oysters, the cold bone scent of little neck clams, and the trace of iodine in the eelgrass clinging to the shrimp dragged from the sounds. And the fish, fresh Atlantic fish, their scent the strange olfactory equivalent of being underwater. A little chill, a little blood and salt, a little Darwin. When I'm on the road I stop, even with no money in my pocket, if only for a glimpse of the entrepreneurs who understand about the rest of us lubbers, that no matter who we are, we couldn't be living all that well without fresh *fruits de mer* for our tables.

Long before I met Miss F., I lived in northern Virginia and courted a girl in college, two hours south in the mountains. After every weekend visit, on my way north back toward Washington, I would pull over at a clapboard seafood shack on Route 29 to provision myself for the following week. The business was named forthrightly, "Jimmy's Seafood," with another improvised sign beneath the first bearing the important message "Crabs, Live or Steamed." Jimmy was a round black man in denim bib overalls and a clean white shirt who had a weakness for croaker and shad roe and could not be wooed from these pleasures. I held in esteem the hygiene of his ice, the sawdust sprinkled on the bare wood floor, the surgical evenness of his gut lines on the pale hollow bellies of gray trout and blues, the fact that you never saw a bivalve in his shop with a yawn to its shell. As a rule, he corned or smoked his own surplus after three days, and there were translucent dice of mullet or mackerel to sample, covered with a sheet of wax paper, on a plate near the cashbox. The shack was torn down about ten years ago and replaced by a gas and convenience store. The good news, from Miss F.'s point of view, is that I miss Jimmy and his stock much more than I miss the old girlfriend.

Now, approaching the middle of my so-called adulthood, after too many years spent slogging through the mud of the ocean-lonely prairies of the Midwest, seeking some form of higher education, I hold these truths to be self-evident: 1. Life is too short not to eat seafood as often as possible; 2. Life is too short not to live it by the glorious sea; 3. Life is too short not to go offshore at least once a year; and 4. Life is too short, period; yet living on the coast and grilling yellowfin tuna you caught yourself that very morning out on the Gulf Stream are terrific palliatives for the cruelly transient nature of your dear self. This experience will help you stop obsessing about it to the point where you will recklessly endanger your well-being by going out to the stream again, despite gale force winds, the next day, until someone more sensible than yourself reminds you that life, after all, is too short to live it as a fool. At this point, the fifth self-evident truth is operative: that life is a confusing cycle of both flaunting and fearing the knowledge that one's ass is sooner or later grass—so screw it, let's go fishing.

In 1986, Miss F. and I decided we had lived wisely and frugally in the year 1985, counting our pennies and even saving them, so, telling ourselves we deserved a seaside life for as long as our bank account held out, we moved from an Iowa pig farm to the Outer Banks of North Carolina, arriving at Cape Hatteras the same day as Hurricane Charlie. Damn the storm—we were happy to be there. Hatteras was a place I had dreamt of moving to ever since I was a surfstruck, fish-crazed child, imagining myself a year-round resident in a beach bum's cottage, battered by nor'easters and blitzed by bluefish.

We moved into a double-wide trailer on stilts, furnished with plastic couches and chairs that your skin stuck to in the humidity. When the wind blew over fifteen knots, the house rocked and pitched; lamps would teeter off end tables, water would slosh out of the toilet. Miss F. studied diligently for her LSATs and pumped fuel at the local marina. I worked on a novel, freelanced articles for magazines, fished commercially for tuna offshore and for trout inshore, hired on as a culler on the shrimp-boats (employment best described as an insomniac's rampage), raked scallops and clams in the sound, tonged oysters, surfed, jogged on the beach daily with Tyrone, our dog. All of this was a more athletic and physically vigorous life than I had lived in a decade, and yet, no surprise, my weight ballooned by eleven pounds as I devoured anything I could coax out of the water.

I kept four crabpots about a mile offshore in the sound in back of our house, paddling out each morning to gather my catch and rebait the pots, dumping an average of about three dozen crabs into the bottom of my canoe.

I would steam the crabs immediately, eat three or four for lunch, pick the rest during the evening news for future crabcakes. During April and May I'd usually find a couple soft shells in the pots, and these would be sauteed for breakfast. As for crabs, it is my opinion that civilization started in the United States the miraculous day a bushel of live Chesapeake Bay blue crabs were delivered to Thomas Jefferson at his mountain home, Monticello, a long wagon-ride inland from the water.

Every two weeks or so Miss F. would announce that she couldn't go another day without a tray of clams casino, so I would fourwheel down to the southern end of the island and spend an afternoon wading around the shallows, waiting for the tines of my rake to tick across the shells of cherrystones and little necks, planted like tulip bulbs in the sand. In the cooler weather the scallops had migrated up to Hatteras, and for every clam you raked, a dozen mossy chattering scallops came with it. Entire families would be out roaming the water, their buckets floated in inner tubes, and at the end of the day the crews would be circled up on shore, shucking the scallops into plastic five-gallon tubs to wholesale, but eating raw scallops too until even tasting them became too much like work. These days and these scenes were timeless, and their beauty escapes the telling.

Even the people who fished all day for a living could think of nothing on earth more fun than to relax fishing on a day off for their kitchens. Up on Diamond Shoals, the surf casters would drag in red drum (redfish) and chopper blues as big as torpedoes. Skiffs would be hauled out to the point by four-wheelers and launched for Spanish mackerel and kingfish. When the Spanish were running in the late spring, you couldn't reel them in fast enough, after a hundred or so your wrist and fingers would swell, but the price per pound kept fellows fishing until they lost the school, the wind shifted, or the sun went down. Less ambitious anglers would set up shop down the length of Frisco beach, lines out in the surf, idly waiting for croaker and sea mullet, sitting on coolers of ice cold beer.

To go offshore for sport is an expensive proposition, but one day in May I organized a trip with six friends and out we went, leaving Oregon Inlet to motor forty miles out to the stream, where the water is summertime and forever blue, where the water is as much of a wilderness as you're bound to find left on this earth, where the wind smells like the islands thousands of miles away. As we entered the stream we passed through an enormous school of dolphin that went as far as the eye could see. Hammerhead sharks and hundred pound sunfish cruised the surface. We idled down to trolling speed and put our lines out, baited with ballyhoo. You can fish six lines if you're quick enough; drag through a school of yellowfin and it's not unlikely you'll take six fish on at once. This day, though, our luck was bad. We chugged miles and miles and couldn't find what we were looking for, nor could any of the other boats

in the fleet. Finally we happened upon a school of twenty-pound blues, caught what we wanted, then, serendipitously hooked into a yellowfin tuna just as we were calling it a day. The six of us and Miss F. grilled the yellowfin that evening for dinner. The next day my fishing mates headed back to the mainland, leaving me with about a thirty pound surplus of bluefish filets. They really didn't care for the fish: liked to catch it, didn't like to eat it. Now that's something I can't well understand. If you've ever fried bluefish like you might do a trout, gotten it crispy and salty on the outside, sprinkled with a little malt vinegar, then you know what I mean.

Miss F., I said, you just tell me when you get tired of eating fried bluefish for lunch and dinner and I'll fix you something else, fix you a steak or something.

Maybe she got tired of it, but she didn't speak up. It took us awhile, took us about a week or so, but we ate that bluefish and couldn't think of a thing to complain about in our lives, except perhaps that the closest liquor store was sixty miles away, but even that seemed more like a luxury than anything else we could call it. As the gastronomic calendar goes, it was the best year of our lives.

COBIA CEVICHE

The firm, snow-white flesh of cobia makes a most excellent ceviche, but if your local seafood market can't find it, or get it to you the same day it's caught, try using *fresh* Spanish mackerel, flounder, or tuna. Though the mackerel isn't as firm as the others, they're all exquisite raw. Small bluefish are fine too, though certainly fishier; diced scallops and conch also make terrific raw salads.

Juice of two limes

1 teaspoon Worcestershire sauce

1 tablespoon red-wine vinegar

1 tablespoon water

½ teaspoon salt

1 teaspoon fresh ground pepper

1 cup diced red onion

1 cup diced green pepper

Splash of hot sauce

1 tomato, diced (optional)

Mix ingredients and marinate one pound diced raw cobia for an hour in the refrigerator. Serve on a leaf of Bibb lettuce as an appetizer.

SERVES 4.

MISS F.'S CHAMPAGNE SCALLOPS

2 pounds scallops

2 cloves garlic, halved

4 chives, chopped

½ teaspoon parsley

½ teaspoon thyme

2 whole cloves

1 teaspoon salt

1 teaspoon pepper

2 cups champagne

1 cup onion, diced

4 egg yolks

2 tablespoons half and half

1 teaspoon arrowroot starch

In a large pot, simmer scallops for four minutes with parsley, thyme, chives, onion, cloves, salt, pepper, and champagne. Remove scallops and boil the remaining broth for eight minutes. Remove and discard garlic and cloves. In a mixing bowl, beat remaining ingredients. Pour contents into broth and cook at low heat, stirring constantly, until sauce thickens. Serve scallops on rice, smothered with the champagne sauce and sprinkled with paprika.

SERVES 4.

GRILLED TUNA, HATTERAS STYLE

Marinate four yellowfin tuna steaks (portions can range from 8 oz. to a pound, depending on appetites) in the following vinaigrette, for ten minutes. (I hate to tell you this, but truly lazy cooks and plenty of seafood restaurants use Italian salad dressing to marinate the tuna in. Go right ahead—I just don't want to hear about it.) Grill the tuna over charcoal (filets should be about an inch thick) five minutes to a side. Or broil for the same length of time. Serve with a basil/tomato salad.

MARINADE

Juice of ½ lemon

¼ cup olive oil, with a splash of sesame oil

1 tablespoon red-wine vinegar

1 teaspoon dry mustard

1 clove garlic, minced

½ teaspoon tarragon

½ teaspoon thyme

Salt and pepper to taste

About seven minutes into cooking, take a fork and flake one of the filets to test for doneness. As soon as the middle of the filet turns white, pull the steaks from the heat. Tuna that's too dry is a terrible disappointment.

SERVES 4.

BAKED RED SNAPPER WITH ONIONS
AND ALMONDS

1 3-pound red snapper, cleaned (leave tail and head on)
1 large onion, cut into paper-thin rings; plus ¼ cup chopped onion
¾ cup blanched almonds
6 tablespoons olive oil
1 large clove garlic, chopped fine
1 tablespoon chopped parsley
½ teaspoon chopped thyme
1 bay leaf, crumbled
1 cup fish, chicken or vegetable stock
4 tablespoons fresh lime juice
Salt and pepper to taste

Preheat oven to 400 degrees. Toast almonds until golden brown, remove from oven and grind into crumbs in an electric blender. In a large frying pan, heat 2 tablespoons oil and sauté chopped onions, almonds, garlic, and parsley for five minutes. Add 6 tablespoons of stock, a little salt, and remove from heat. Into a large, open baking dish, pour the remainder of the oil, spreading it evenly over the bottom. Layer the sliced onions in the dish and sprinkle with bay leaf and thyme. Put the fish in the baking dish, drench it with lime juice and salt and pepper to taste, then coat the top side of the fish with the onion/almond mixture from the frying pan. Pour the remainder of the stock into the dish and bake uncovered for 30 to 40 minutes, or until the flesh is firm when pressed lightly with a finger.

SERVES 4.

SAUCED

There's a liquor ad making the rounds lately—I've seen it among the pricey fashion catalogues and magazines that arrive by the ton in Miss F.'s mail. Two thirtyish, jock-muscled, reassuringly groomed, slim-hipped studs have shed not only their wingtips but their machismo as well and are a-jogging in bathing suits at the sunny shore. Their pumping legs are all blurry with speed. Their heels splash diamonds of water off the tide-swept sand as they gallop ahead, vying for the lead, presumably toward the rewards implied by the caption that elaborates this deceivingly manly scene, this exuberant charge of testosterone from our would-be Olympians, an astonishing proclamation from the sensitivity-addled male navigating the cultural waters of the late 80s:

"She loves my cooking. And she drinks ———."

Gushing copy annotates this smarmy confession: "There's a way to show your admiration for his cooking—and everything else you like about him." (Like what? I ask myself. His big whopper?) The ad urges female readers to reciprocate the culinary charms of their lovers with a bottle of whiskey.

Well, I have to say, gentlemen, that we've come quite a long way when we race each other for the chance to have our old patriarchal selves disrobed by a little fanny-patting flattery. Use the strategies of feminist rhetoric to interpret this advertisement, and what you can't help but see are two exploited hunks of boymeat, eagerly battling one another to the stove to compete for the honor of indentured toil amid pots and pans, nursing the pathetic hope of being blessed, come bedtime, by the mistress of the house with a little nookie and a lot of scotch. Are these guys supposed to be tender warriors or yuppie wimps? Either way, I am mystified by the mentality being promoted.

I can't bring myself to applaud how progressive or "politically correct" this ad might very well be. There's something innately feeble about one guy (or gal, for that matter) boasting to another that his lover loves his cooking. This enlightened role reversal is dopey. Sociological backsliding. Restore the traditional sexual order and see what happens: *He* loves my cooking. The fawning insecurity is immediately apparent, as is the nausea summoned by such a stereotype. Yeah, honey, he adores your cooking, and after he gets a few drinks in you, your booty drives him crazy. No matter which sex is doing the cooking here and which one's doing the loving, we're most certainly dealing with Birdbrain Bimbo Homemakers, gender irrelevant.

As with most—strike that to read: *all*—examples of it-hurts-to-be-this-hip Madison Avenue marketing, the ad manufactures its own la-di-dah reality, rather than reflecting the more complex lives of everyday folks. In the domestic universe of any contemporary couple, the partner who has little desire to cook, or doesn't feel like operating in the kitchen on any given night, is invariably going to love the fact that the other one wants to, regardless of whether the food arriving tableside might make a rioting mob out of the gentlemen lined up for chow at the federal pen.

Indeed, the advertisement seems to encourage a scary Andrea Dworkin–type matriarchy, where the sexes have no more hope of parity than they had on *Father Knows Best*. The juicier, more intriguing and inevitable issues are—can you imagine!—dodged. What if *she* considers it *her* kitchen and doesn't want him mucking around in there? What if one cook's talents are vastly superior to the other's? Then what? Do schedules have to be worked out? A nightly coin toss? Gastronomic war?

Whose kitchen are we in anyway? Hers or his? Have they worked out a
civilized arrangement yet, or should the caption in a revised ad read:
"She loves his cooking, but says *hers* is better, and would prefer he stay
the hell out of the kitchen if he's not going to clean up his mess afterward." To which the second runner huffs sympathetically, "*Bitch.*"

In the relationship between Miss F. and myself, our first serious dis-
agreement came quick, only a month after she had moved in with me on
a West Indian island, and naturally it took place in the kitchen—*my*
kitchen, at least up until that day. Thirteen years ago, but Miss F. still
has a vivid recollection of the dispute.

Before Miss F. recites the anecdote—for the life of me, the incident
escapes my memory, though I vaguely recall an urgent but altogether
innocuous discussion between the two of us those many years ago—I
would like to admit that I have, upon occasion, been somewhat rude in
the kitchen. My sense of the culinary environment mirrors a pilot's
notion of a cockpit: if you have no good reason to be in there, or don't
know what you're doing, better get lost fast. This isn't hubris, just simple realism.

While some cooks are most cheery when the kitchen doubles as a
salon, I approach the room primarily as a workshop where sweat, and
occasionally blood, shall be spilled. If there's adequate space, guests are
permitted to socialize on the perimeter, but woe to them who wander
between the stove and the refrigerator, interrupting the chef's mobility.
Anyone who repeatedly asks if there's something he or she can do must
be taken outside or tranquilized. Likewise, overnight guests who insist
on giving the cook the evening off so that they might throw together a
specialty dish for you, then serve up some pastey or sweet horror with
gumball rice or pineapple rings, deserve to be blindfolded, stood up
against the garage, and shot. I keep a spoon glowing on the burner for
those who sidle up, begging for a little taste. The best men are cooks, the
old saying goes, but when some men are in the kitchen, it's Old
Testament time—Jehovah at the stove.

On the evening in question, Miss F. reminds me, sailing friends had
come off their sloop, invited to dinner ashore. The island was a poor

place but I had been lucky enough to secure two pounds of something resembling fresh medallions of pork, perfect for simmering in a marinara sauce and ladling over pasta—glorified spaghetti is what I'm talking about. Earlier in the day, it became clear that my work at the Ministry of Agriculture would take me longer than I had foreseen, so at noon I drove out along the coast to warn Miss F. I'd be late and that she'd have to do the cooking herself. We really hadn't known each other very long: Miss F. made a satisfactory breakfast in the morning, but as to the extent of her culinary skills, I had no idea. I divulged the menu and explained how I wanted it prepared.

No problem, Miss F. told me, and I drove back, relieved, to the Ministry. Unfortunately, I arrived back home in plenty of time to offer my assistance to the chef. When I walked in, Miss F. was stirring a pot of sauce that, naturally, I felt compelled to sample, and bit down into a mushy clove of garlic.

"Why isn't this garlic minced?" I asked, spitting it out into my palm.

"Get away," she ordered, nudging me backward with her elbow, but I pushed forward for a second taste.

"Not enough salt in there," I advised.

"Bugger off," she said, having picked up some of the common-wealth's ex-pat idiom.

"And where's the meat?" I sputtered (or so says Miss F.). "Why aren't my medallions in here simmering succulently, eh?"

"I am not putting pork in my marinara sauce," she said, with a stubbornness that rivaled my own. "No way, buster."

"Come on," I persisted, "let's put the goddamn meat in there." I turned toward our pint-size refrigerator. "The medallions are fairly thick. Do you think I should quarter them first?" I asked, trying to be democratic.

When our guests knocked, Miss F. tells me, we were by then shouting at each other. The confrontation continued for years, both of us claiming bragging rights to the Better Sauce. Mine was lumpy and spicy, hers smooth and subtle. The issue faded a while back, not only because Miss F. enrolled in law school and had zero time for cooking, but because, in my opinion, her marinara sauce slowly became more and more like mine—though I'm sure if you asked her she would say this is merely the delusion of a gastronomic imperialist.

At a dinner party last year, while I stood in the kitchen frying plantains, I overheard Miss F. agreeing with a well-meaning friend that, yes, it was wonderful to live with a fellow so devoted to cooking, one who took the art seriously. I could actually feel the irony gathering in the air before it sounded from her tongue. Yes, he takes it seriously, she added—too seriously if you ask me. For instance, Miss F. continued, "even when he takes the night off and I cook, he always has to meddle, even before the cooking starts. He still wants to have everything to say about it, and he's obnoxious."

Aw, honey. What she really meant to say is that I'm a perfectionist, with a perfectionist's mildly annoying habits, like turning the heat off under her veggies when I have inadvertently discovered they've been steaming long enough. It's a situation that's been more or less resolved this way. Miss F. has her excellent specialties, her triumphs: French beef salad, shrimp creole, a beautiful flan, anything Chinese; and her experiments: anything she grills, anything Italian, a variety of weird soups. I may only comment enthusiastically about her specialties, but her experiments are fair game. In return, Miss F. abstains from direct verbal comment, favorable or otherwise, on my own efforts, though she will often widen her eyes with joy, or frown maybe once or twice a year and put the plate on the floor for the dog. I try to pump her for feedback but her lips are zipped. *You didn't like it?* I say. *What? Honest? Too much crushed pepper, is that it? Not enough marsala? What? What? Tell me, please.* She won't come clean, so there I sit, rocking like an autistic child, my imagination sprinting down the four-color glossy beach with a chum whose stoveside manners are just too good to be true:

"She loves my cooking," I gasp out, short of breath. "At least, I think she does."

My running companion grins at me and pulls three or four paces ahead.

"And she drinks ——— by the tumbler," I say, "and screams, when I interfere with hers."

In the spirit of spirits, and reconciliation with the liquor industry, let me recommend to you that this summer you soak your meat in booze. This is not to suggest intemperance at the family cookout on the Fourth, a chugging contest in salute of the flag, or that you should be swilling martinis to fortify your nerve when you reenact the Battle of Midway, using illegal bottlerockets you plan to fire at your passed-out brother-in-law. I recognize these are all well-loved and patriotic traditions, used to celebrate forms of independence both national and domestic but—the pleasures of self-marinating aside—what I'm saying is that alcoholic spirits make superb marinades for summertime grilling, each liquor providing a unique and worthy flavor to the object of your appetite. Here are three recipes to make even the most saintly family teetotalers forgo their abstinence.

CHICKEN MARGARITA

4 cups tequila

1 cup water

¼ cup each fresh squeezed lemon and lime juices

¼ cup olive oil

Mix liquids in a glass, porcelain or earthenware dish and add:

1 cup fresh coriander, chopped

1 cup mixed peppers (cubanelle, jalapeno, Hungarian waxed, sweet red), diced

2 cloves minced garlic

1 tablespoon mace

1 tablespoon achiote seed

1 tablespoon salt

Submerge 6 chicken breasts in the liquid and allow to marinate, chilled, overnight.

SERVES 6.

CAPTAIN KEITH'S COCONUT-GIN MARINADE FOR FISH

In a glass dish, mix 2 cups of gin with one cup coconut milk—not coconut water.

Here's how to make coconut milk: empty the water out of a coconut (this sweet, refreshing liquid makes a great cocktail, mixed with gin or vodka); break open the shell, extract the nut meat and grate it into a bowl. Soak the gratings in two cups of water for fifteen minutes, stirring occasionally, and strain off the milk.

Add ¼ cup fresh basil leaves, chopped; 1 clove of garlic, minced; and 1 teaspoon each salt and pepper. Swordfish, kingfish, red snapper, and grouper are well-suited for this marinade.

Marinate four filets or steaks for a half hour each side.

For one-inch filets, grill five minutes to a side. Captain Keith, a professional sport fisherman down in Hatteras, will serve you wahoo cooked this way, if you charter his boat and happen to hook one.

SERVES 4

RUM RUNNERS COUNTRY RIBS

Whatever you steep in rum will be imbued with a rich, faintly sweet aftertaste of molasses. Both pork and beef marinated in rum develop a fuller-bodied, gamelike flavor similar to venison.

4 cups dark rum

2 cups water

½ cup malt vinegar

¼ cup light soy sauce

¼ cup sesame oil

¼ cup fresh squeezed lime juice

Mix marinade in a non-metal bowl or dish and add:

1 large onion, diced

2 tablespoons crushed red pepper

3 cloves garlic, minced

¼ cup fresh parsley, chopped

bouquet garni (a sprig of thyme, two bay leaves, celery seed, rosemary, 4 whole cloves)

1 tablespoon each salt and fresh ground pepper

Marinate country ribs (1 pound per person) completely submerged for six hours. Grill slowly for 45 minutes. Refrain from drinking marinade when the beer runs out later in the evening.

SERVES 4 TO 6.

BEAN THERE

Of the gastronomic truths that help illuminate human existence, perhaps the most tantalizing is that each life can be identified and tagged with a single edible entity—I hesitate to say food—that embodies the personality of an individual. For the author and celebrated eater Calvin Trillin, the centerpiece of his gastronomic crest would be—presuming he could possibly make up his mind about such a portentous emblem—a slab of barbecue ribs. The culinary flag of my vegetarian friend Sarah would therefore be embroidered with a bowl of mush or a bowl of any non-animal substance that is warm, squishy, and pale. Don, a roadside entrepreneur who vends fireworks and Christmas trees, would be required to sport a bill cap bearing the Ding Dong logo. Likewise, my gastronomic mentor Captain Tay would have his maritime license stamped with the image of a chili pepper. In the wisest of New Age societies, we would abandon the celestial interrogative, *What's your sign?* and replace it with the more vital, revealing, and intensely serious question, *What's your food?* To which my dear, snacking Miss F. would have to respond, "Goldfish crackers" or "Granny Smith apples," which are what she appears to survive on when I'm not around.

Actually, what we eat or refuse to eat is as clear a window as you're going to find, on short notice, into a person's culture, race, religion— even, it could be argued, into their intelligence and education. And, as often as not, we use this information against each other. Sweet summer melons become a derogatory symbol for black Americans; fish for Catholics; curry for Indians; potatoes for the Irish; rice for Asians; tortillas for Mexicans; blubber for Eskimos. Where I used to live on Hatteras Island on the Outer Banks of North Carolina, calling someone a mullet-eater was the same as saying he was as dumb as a jar of dirt for eating a trash fish only good for bait. On Ocracoke, the next island south, the words "fried mullet" would make local mouths water; in their opinion, Hatteras islanders were just too prissy for their own good when it came to eating what was in the ocean. Here then, in the channel between the two islands, was the dividing line between north and south. From the channel all the way down to the Florida Keys, folks for centuries have considered mullet one of the better-tasting fish in the sea, not to mention one of the most abundant. North of the channel, though, mullet was as unloved as the poverty and ignorance it was associated with.

No doubt about it, if you want a pure insight into peoples' lives, find out what they most enjoy eating, and what they would never eat, even if it meant starvation. It's a good idea never to cook for somebody without knowing this information. More importantly, it's romantic suicide to live with somebody until you're sure your gastronomic stars aren't crossed. When I'm planted in the kitchen, Miss F. will clamor for all manner of extravagance and exotica and reciprocate my efforts by eating anything I put on her plate. Still, although my conch chowder can go bowl to bowl with the best in the world, Miss F. doesn't particularly care for my version, which has barley in it, for she has an irrationally poor regard for that marvelous grain, associating it with nineteenth-century gruel. At the worst of times, when I have no patience for such things, I consider Miss F.'s aversion for barley to be a latent character flaw, some inner demon that might one day rise up and show itself as a true incompatibility, like, say, a dislike for red beans and rice.

If I'm to be wholly honest, however, I must admit that I rarely give a damn what people eat or don't eat. Whatever you're having for dinner— from armadillo stew in Texas to zucchini casserole in Vermont—I'll be delighted to have it too, yet in seeking genuine gastronomic fellowship, I divide society into readers and writers, and you'll know what I mean. Writers love to read too but their quintessential activity is pounding out the prose. Which is to say that on my gastronomic flag of identification you will find not a garlic bulb but a garlic press. In a recent conversation with a friend I was made acutely aware of this difference I'm describing, the disparity in both perception and life-style between those of us who merely eat and those of us devoted to cooking as well.

We were talking about travelling—spring vacation was coming up. I had cause to mention that an eater travels differently than a cook. "I don't believe that's true," my friend replied, and I argued my case as follows.

As best I can figure from published evidence, the gourmand Calvin Trillin rarely if ever misses an opportunity to stuff himself. Fearing he might be disappointed or worse by airborne cuisine—an anxiety that seems entirely reasonable to me—he often packs himself a haversack of tasty gourmet provisions to be relished on his flights to and fro in search of the perfect bite. Trillin of course isn't a cook but rather a distinguished chowhound. To become a distinguished chowhound you have to be ready and willing to put whatever organic matter you find on your plate into your mouth and chew . . . at least twice. You don't necessarily have to swallow to be a distinguished chowhound and, more to the point, you never have to set foot in the kitchen unless you wish to congratulate or threaten the chef.

As for myself, I am as fulfilled by the saucepan as I am by the sauce. Like Trillin, I too am a peripatetic person and, en route to a destination, I too make the effort to travel with my gastronomic bags packed. Not titillating treats for the flight itself—I prefer to drink exclusively at elevations higher than the invisible 13th floor—but gear appropriate to my impending culinary circumstances.

For example, boarding a plane in Miami to a remote South American island where I once resided, my companion and I checked in an excess of a half-ton of baggage. His portion of the overweight consisted of scuba tanks, an air compressor, and an outboard motor. My contribution, I am proud to say, was a refrigerator, a stove the size of a console tv, a meat grinder, and a niggling few kilos of spices and condiments. All of this would be jetted to the main island in the archipelago and then ferried by work boat to the more primitive island where I lived at the time.

Now, we could have saved ourselves a lot of trouble by simply eating at any of the four Creole restaurants on the island, all very good, but that's not the way a cook thinks. Thanks to my imported refrigerator and stove, I could now spend my days out on the reefs instead of roaming the bare markets, the self-proclaimed *chef de maison*. And so our meals improved from a pot of sticky rice and salt pork cooked on a smelly, smokey kerosene burner, to turtle stroganoff, red snapper creole, and pasta with conch marinara.

"Okay," my friend agreed, "but that's an isolated incident."

"Extreme," I answered, "but not isolated. For instance, I rarely go anywhere overnight without my garlic press, in case the opportunity arises to secure a kitchen. When I visit new places, it's the markets I head for first, to see what can be discovered, and then the museums. And I am reluctant to go on any vacation where I can't take my portable barbecue grill."

My friend shook her head, thankful that she never had to travel with me.

"Oh, you don't have to travel with a cook to be affected by a cook's agenda," I explained, "you just have to be going the same place to end up being enlisted in their schemes." I told her about last year's April ski trip to Colorado. Miss F. and I had not yet had our annual conch fritter fix for 1988 (Miss F. wants her tombstone engraved with a conch shell), so I cajoled my sister, who lived in San Francisco at the time, to swing by a Chinatown seafood market on her way to the airport and pick up five pounds of conch to bring along to the Rocky Mountains for some *apres-ski* feasting.

Maybe you know that cleaned conch meat, as it sits, sort of drains a clear, viscous fluid, entirely acceptable to the nose as long as the meat stays chilled. Unfortunately, my very proper sister had not brought along a carry-on container for the flight and, consequently, boarded the plane with five pounds of warming conch wrapped in butcher's paper and dropped in a brown paper sack. The bag was beginning to leak, and become a bit whiffy, so she further wrapped it in her ski jacket and stuffed it into the overhead bin. Halfway through her flight to Denver, the attendants were holding their breaths when they passed by her seat, her travelling companions had moved to the rear of the plane, and the entire manifest of passengers was wondering out loud why they seemed to be aloft with a whale breaking such rich wind.

Nevertheless, the conch arrived on the slopes in good shape, unlike the condition of my sister's ski jacket, which I think she threw away. While she had flown east, Miss F. and I had driven west with our dog, Tyrone, my meat grinder and garlic press, the portable barbecue grill, and eighteen bags of eclectic groceries, including a package of smoked andouille sausage to cook with red beans and rice, another of Miss F.'s most loved dishes but almost impossible to find done right in a restaurant: Cajun, Creole or otherwise. Even the chefs of New Orleans will tell you you have to go to someone's house if you expect to eat a memorable dish of red beans.

My friend implied that I was a tad obsessive about cooking, and I finally had to tell her the one thing I wouldn't do in my gastronomic vision of the world. When I've had to live by myself for one reason or another, I won't cook for myself. I'll *fix* things to survive on, or order out, but I won't cook if I'm the only one there to eat it. Just like writers and writing, what's the point of doing it if there's no one to share the pleasure of the results? That's when you'll find my life-style accurately represented by a tiny carton of Chinese carryout. Otherwise, look for a bright red banner, flying the sign of the garlic press.

RED BEANS AND RICE

2 pounds red beans, soaked overnight

1 ham bone

1 pound baked ham, cubed

1 pound andouille sausage

1 large onion, chopped

½ green pepper, chopped

2 cloves garlic, minced

2 tablespoons fresh parsley, minced

2 bay leaves

½ teaspoon crushed red pepper

⅛ teaspoon cayenne

1 teaspoon thyme

1 teaspoon basil

Salt and pepper to taste

Drain the beans, put all ingredients into a large pot, add enough cold water to cover everything, and bring to a boil. Lower heat and simmer for 3–4 hours until beans are tender, adding water if the mixture is too dry, stirring every half hour. Ladle over cooked rice.

SERVES 6.

MISTAH BOB'S SOCKLESS CONCH FRITTERS

2 pounds ground conch

15 generous tablespoons flour

1 teaspoon baking powder

5 eggs

¾ stick melted butter

4 teaspoons salt

4 teaspoons pepper

4 shakes tabasco sauce

½ large onion, diced

½ green pepper, diced

½ red pepper, diced

2 cloves garlic, minced

Splash of lime juice

Dash of Worcestershire

Stir everything together until the mixture has the consistency of pancake batter. Fry hot-hot in ¼ inch of vegetable oil, spooning the fritters from the bowl into the pan. Drain on paper towels. Serve with a dipping sauce of Creole mustard, sour cream, tabasco and lemon juice.

MAKES 25–30 SOCKLESS FRITTERS.

CLAM HER UP

What could be more emblematic of the bachelor's domestic stoicism than the fiercely burned pan and unwashed platter, the Spartan interior of a refrigerator? Yet the day comes, as the old story goes, when the single guy marries or moves in and the miracle unfolds. The crisp pages of his well-intentioned shelf of cookbooks are transformed, saucily splattered, worked loose from their bindings. Incredibly, home becomes a place where actual meals are prepared, sometimes with loving forethought. A new nostalgia gathers in the wings of his adult life: The boy has found someone to feed him. He has married a restaurant, a personal catering service—a girl.

Well, not in my life. Mine is a deskbound existence with a delinquent feel to it on the one hand, and yet so blissfully mired in domestic ritual as to be outright housewifey. I do all the cooking within these walls, all the grocery shopping without, and I'm a serious practitioner of the dining-in routine. Here's what I mean.

Suppose I were to tell you that last month I slapped Miss F. because she wouldn't come to dinner when she was called. In most cultures on this planet, a mere slap delivered under just such an aggravating circumstance would be cause for ridicule. And all because it is generally considered an aberration or even a threat to the social order for a fellow to cook for his spouse, night after night, year after year. Throughout his miserable, wussy life, a real man may, on rare occasion, compose a manfully complicated meal for his guests, and anytime whatsoever he desires to earn a living in the kitchen, he may cook eight hours a day for strangers. And it's okay to help out, but only in little ways. For instance, he may tear a recipe from a magazine and Scotch-tape it to his wife's diaphragm case. Or, on a weekend picnic, he may barbecue her a side of beef, and, when he wishes, he has the right to bellow for condiments. And cold beer.

Anyway, I never laid a hand on my darling, of course. I had spent a devoted hour grilling lamb chops, steaming asparagus, fluffing a Caesar salad, and when I summoned her, across the house, there came from within the uncustomary madness of her study an unexpected and I must say shrill response: *"I'm too goddamn busy!"*

I promise you I am not a choleric companion, but, really, I didn't care if she was in the middle of open-heart surgery. I wanted her to come eat, and—on the same schedule our tyrant mothers once kept—*now*. Like Castro, though, she couldn't be dislodged from office. I covered her plate to keep the grub warm; I took my own portion in hand, turned on the evening news, sat in my rocker, ate and listened . . . for her footsteps. The fare may well have been splendid, but just let me tell you, your own food can never taste as great as the exact same thing cooked by someone else. Which is the real point of cooking: an act meant to please yourself by pleasing another.

When Miss F. emerged some fifteen minutes after Peter Jennings had already been there and left, I refused to talk to her.

She was a nervous wreck anyway, in her first year of law school at age thirtywhatever (after earning a degree in pottery ten years earlier) and studying for final exams. Big deal. Understanding? Oh, sure. But, hey, Miss F. was out there on the panicky edge. She didn't want to be fed—at the moment, all she wanted was sedation. From my point of view, the meal had been carefully designed to soothe her from the convolutions of torts, to fortify her for an assault on the barbed wires of property. I vowed to not so much as glance in her direction until she'd admitted that dinner was wonderful, that it offered respite from a cram diet of statutes.

She didn't make a sound, however, except to wearily recognize that I had stopped speaking to her. Undaunted, I conversed with Tyrone about recent climatic patterns and who's who in the city park. She trudged back to her little hell. Afterward, I found her dish by the sink. The lamb chop had been listlessly stabbed, the tips gnawed from the asparagus spears. She had fussed with the salad, eaten only the croutons.

The indecent sight of forsaken food hardened me. I marched to her room, sidestepped mounds of briefs and litigative histories. She was hunched over her desk, memorizing line by line a book big as a truck tire. I massaged the tension in her shoulders and delicately warned:

"If you don't eat the beautiful food I made you, you're going to flunk crim law."

That fine and much-honored domestic tradition—food as reproach and intimidation—also failed. She was beyond orthodox tactics. I was downcast, demoralized, bruised by a feeling of loss; good food, after all, is a cradle of communication for lovers. I felt betrayed in our covenant: I

would stay home, walk the dog, write stories, make sure she was well fed; she would visit the academy for three years to become skilled in how the party of the first part totally and forever screws the party of the second part, thus ensuring an income for the household. But there'd be no payday if she first died of starvation. My duty was clear: Mount up and speed to my favorite commercial environment, the supermarket. (You can take your stereo warehouses and sports shops and dump them into a big hole as far as I'm concerned. I'm infatuated with groceries.) Up and down the aisles I heard the poor girl's silent appeal: *"Help, save me, fix me something irresistible."*

The following evening, I created a masterpiece straight from Little Havana: a pot of black beans, rice, pork tenderloin marinated in mojo criollo, cucumber salad in a lime vinaigrette. At suppertime, the phone rang. She was in the library and would be home around 1990. At 2 A.M., she crawled exhausted into bed, puppies whimpering in her stomach from malnutrition.

The next day, as she dressed for her six-hour-long criminal-law exam, I looked at the dark lagoons under her eyes, her pallid and fatigued demeanor, looked out the window at the cloudy, cold, wet weather, looked back at this woman and thought, Soup. Not just any soup but chowder, one both hearty and elegant, especially something seafoodish, her greatest gastronomic weakness, and not just any old standby recipe but something with an originality that would seduce the iron pants off any preoccupation she brought home, and something, finally, that would utilize the previous night's black beans.

She trudged home from the exam-without-mercy, with barely enough strength left to lift her sneakered feet. I made her sit on the couch in the living room and ponder the aphorism that love, like food, is a source of energy. "I'm just not hungry," she moaned. "Food seems so trivial these days." Ten minutes later, I fetched her a hot bowl. She circled through it with her spoon, watching the blend of contradictory colors, her interest slowly kindling, and finally tasted.

"God. God," she said, and then, after another mouthful, "God!" She wondered out loud where she had been for the past two weeks. Her spoon clanked the bowl's bottom.

"Seconds?" I queried.

"Please, sir," she nodded. "It's fabulous." Law school, I've noticed, is very good at drumming a strict etiquette into its more terrorized rookies.

EARTH, FIN, AND FIRE CHOWDER

1 dozen littleneck or cherrystone clams (or 1 6 ½-ounce can minced
clams and 1 cup bottled clam juice)

2 strips bacon, chopped

1 large onion, chopped

1 stalk celery, chopped

½ cup chopped parsley

2 cloves garlic, minced

1 pound bay scallops

1 pound medium shrimp, shelled and deveined

1 bay leaf

¼ cup chopped fresh basil or ½ teaspoon crushed dried basil leaves

1 cup cooked black beans

1 sweet red pepper, chopped

1 to 2 cups half and half

Salt and pepper

Butter

Crushed red pepper (optional)

Steam clams, remove from shells, mince and set aside with 1 cup broth. In a big, heavy pot, fry bacon until it's cooked but not crisp. Remove and set aside. In bacon drippings, sauté onion, celery, parsley, and garlic until tender. Pour reserved broth (or clam juice) over sautéed vegetables, add 6 cups water and raise heat. Add bacon, clams, scallops and shrimp. Stir in bay leaf and basil. Bring to boil, then immediately reduce heat. Skim about half the scallops and shrimp from pot, purée in food processor and return paste to pot. Purée black beans, then sweet red pepper, and add both to soup. Simmer for 15 to 20 minutes. Turn heat down and add 1 cup half and half. Your chowder, which up to this point resembled dishwater, will become a gorgeous velvety tan, with swirling bright-red flecks. Taste it. If it seems too thin, add more half and half until the texture's right. Season with salt and pepper to taste. Heat through, stirring occasionally, but don't allow chowder to boil. If soup is being presented hot, ladle a serving into a bowl, float a dollop of butter on top and sprinkle very lightly with crushed red pepper. Or serve chilled without butter, but with a sprinkling of minced green onion or fresh coriander.

SERVES 6.

The chowder, by the way, is a perfect overture for Spanish mackerel in foil. For each serving, set a filet of Spanish mackerel (bluefish, sea trout or sea bass will do as well) skin side down on an ample rectangle of aluminum foil. Season with salt and pepper or soy sauce. Put a pat of butter in center of filet and a slice of onion at each end. Sprinkle with minced garlic. Place atop the filet any vegetables you want as a side dish, such as corn on the cob, and fold the foil into a sealed packet. Bake in a very hot oven (400 degrees) for 15 to 20 minutes. (In the summer, put it on the grill.) While the fish cooks, the vegetables steam *al dente*.

MACHINE DREAMS

Lately I've been questioning friends as to their ideas about what might constitute a well-equipped kitchen. "A well-equipped kitchen," said a pal in the restaurant business in North Carolina, "is an intelligent woman who likes to do dishes." In the spectrum of culinary resources, I suppose this standard falls somewhere in the cool range of indigo.

Other chums have told me I shouldn't even attempt to go over-easy on an egg without a complete set of Calphalon cookware; a Kitchenaid infinite-heat no-drip glass-surface cooktop; a flaming Jenn-Air grill; and a Brother three-in-one microwave, convection and high-speed oven with auto-cook and splash trivet. If I don't stop these high-tech apostles of kitchen affluence, they lull me into a stupor with their blissful postmodernist gadget poetry, until they're certain they've converted me to their brand-name religion. Elkay Eurostyle sinks. KWC Neodomo Swiss-precision faucets. Poggen Pohl cabinets. Corian countertops. Amana refrigerators that do everything but tango and give birth. Leicht total-system kitchens. Okay, all splendid products, probably, but not the stuff that occupies my mental space when I think about kitchens. Nor the space of any kitchen I've had the opportunity, shared with landlords, to briefly

pretend was mine. I've been plumbing the knowledge of my fellow kitch-
eneers for good reason. For the first time in fourteen years, Miss F. and I
have become homeowners, ending a seemingly interminable era of ten-
ant wistfulness. Ever since a few months ago, when Miss F. announced
her unilateral decision, "We're buying a house. Do you want to go look
at it?"—I imagine if we ever have a child, she'll report the event in
much the same way—our daily mail has been fattened by subscriptions
to magazines with names like *Metropolitan Home, Architectural Digest,
Bathroom Monthly*, and the lively *CrawlSpace!* While Miss F. has secretly
been surveying which walls she can knock out without collapsing the
superstructure, I've been scanning articles with such wallet-itching titles
as "Bitchin' Kitchens," "Hot News From the Kitchen," "Really Hot!
Hot! Kitchens" and, my favorite, "Blazing Hot, Dizzily Expensive
Kitchens."

What I rediscovered from these tony paeans to the gastronomic environment—though the message may well cut across the grain of more
materialistic personalities like, say, your Donald Trumps—was that,
unless you're running a public eatery, how you outfit your kitchen has
everything to do with convenience and nothing whatsoever to do with
the quality of your cooking. (Who cares what Trump's kitchen looks like
anyway, considering it has nothing more to say about the man's identity
than the obvious fact the guy once made more cash in a week than the
annual GNP of most nations.) Reading the design magazines, I realized
I did not want any kitchen I was paying the mortgage on to be a showcase—an achievement based more on buying power than ingenuity. I did
not want a kitchen that was a computer age marvel, requiring a thick
operator's manual and six weeks of training seminars, vulnerable not
only to power outages but inclined to moody funks during perils of
intense sunset activity. I did not want NASA in my kitchen, nor IBM,
nor did I really need I. M. Pei in there with me making sauces, nor a
minimalist in a lab coat, nor the lighting directors for Lincoln Center.

"Kitchens have come into their own as *real rooms*," I am advised by
one of the bright-eyed publications Miss F. has gathered to our domestic
bosom! All I can figure is that these oracles of the hearth must have

been raised by B. F. Skinner in the laundry room of a Medici villa. The hippest, newest, *funnest* cutting edge in culinary esthetics, it seems, is the simulation of what we once knew and loved but have since, in our boomer feeding frenzy, forgotten.

Well, shoot, count me in on this brilliance. Because the only childhood room my memory turns to with profound pleasure is my grandmother's now-extinct kitchen, with its step-down outside entrance shaded by an enormous cherry tree, its dill fragrance blending with a sour but not unpleasant trace of cabbage and the old-world scent of a coal furnace. The house's root cellar and coalbin were separated at the back of the kitchen by flowery curtains; a stairway leading up to the parlor and living rooms was always crowded with kids not old enough to sit with the adults playing pinochle and gossiping at the large square maple table centered in the room. Outside the windows, the view behind the house was brambley—my grandmother's raspberry patch—and beyond, the Allegheny Mountains were close by, waiting for us to organize a mush-room-picking excursion. My coal-miner grandfather had dibs on the chaise longue, its painted upholstery cracked like safety glass, and there he would sit whittling into a pail, mumbling at the swarm of grandchil-dren in a language none of us kids understood but certainly found threatening. From her station at the stove, my hefty grandmother gently ruled, even as she stirred an omnipresent stewpot of spaghetti sauce or cut potatoes into a soup. If the rest of the house had been torn away by a storm, I don't think anyone would have noticed, or have cared.

On the other hand, the suburban kitchens of our mothers' genera-tion were, as often as not, test sites for the fission of the nuclear family. These postindustrial kitchens shrank, became less significant in our daily schedules as technology transformed them, were left empty and inscrutable by parents off working, were subordinated as a gathering place by wherever the television was plugged in.

Not to say our mothers' grub wasn't good—it was, and even occa-sionally surprised us when it flirted with experimental motifs. Yet I can't help but feel it's time to reclaim our grandmothers' kitchens as our own. Start from the outside. Front doors are for guests and strangers; kitchen doors are for family and friends, an access to the toasty heart of a home. No fooling around with formalities. "Come on in," we say, "get yourself something to drink. Taste this." In the best of all possible kitchens, the outside door would lead to a mudroom for kicking off footwear, or toweling off a wet dog; then, a glass-paned interior door would swing open upon our savory trademark gastronomic aromas. Rag rugs on wooden floors; bare ceramic tiles; Depression-era linoleum, old and warped but caringly maintained: anything on the floor but the anonymous betrayal of wall-to-wall carpeting. Colors aren't as important as natural light from windows framing surrounding vistas. Pots and cutlery out in the open, hung from hooks, shelved. Whatever art or mementos or kitsch you need on the walls to express, not your bank account, but your humanity—your affections, not your affectations.

If you're lucky, there's not only an abundance of countertop space in your kitchen, but room for a real table so that all but the most formal meals may be served here, in the atmosphere of creativity rather than in the isolation of a dining room. My kitchen in Florida won't have such spatial wealth, so until I graduate to bigger digs, there won't be a place for the feature that typifies all the kitchens in heaven: a fireplace, with an overstuffed chair and ottoman set before it. Am I awash in nostalgia? Maybe, but the amount of gadgetry and gizmos and futuristic appliances you employ while cooking has no special qualitative effect on the food you serve, and demystifying the kitchen is a rite of liberation for dilettante cooks. The best chocolate cake I have ever eaten was made from scratch and baked on a kerosene burner in an aluminum pie plate. If you're really looking to test your mettle as a chef, try concocting a velvety Normande sauce or a sauce Barris, which, I assure you, if you get them right, has virtually nothing to do with the fact that your kitchen might be as technically sophisticated as a jet cockpit. The credit goes to you alone.

BLUEFISH A LA NORMANDE

Sole is the traditional choice for this dish, its light, delicate filets braised in cream sauce or white wine. Feel free, however, to substitute your favorite fish, or to forgo seafood altogether in favor of chicken or veal, using the measurements in the recipe below. Bluefish cooked à la Normande will surprise you with its unaccustomed subtlety. (To start, you will have to prepare the fumet, or fish stock, and the velouté, a basic white sauce that provides the foundation for the Normande sauce.)

FOR THE FUMET:

1 3- to 4-pound whole bluefish

4 cups water

2 cups white wine

½ cup sliced onions

½ cup sliced shallots

1 cup sliced mushrooms

Juice of half a lemon

1 tablespoon salt

¼ cup parsley

¼ cup watercress

1 bay leaf

FOR THE VELOUTÉ

2 tablespoons butter

¼ cup flour

2 cups fumet

Calvados

FOR THE NORMANDE SAUCE:

1 cup velouté

1 cup fumet

4 tablespoons cream

2 egg yolks

¼ cup butter, cut into small pieces

FOR GARNISH:

1 avocado, sliced

Fresh basil leaves, chopped

2 to 4 1-pound bluefish filets

To make the fumet, clean the whole bluefish and steak it—bones, fins, flesh and all. Put fish in stewpot; add water, white wine, onions, shallots, mushrooms, lemon juice, salt, parsley, bay leaf, and watercress. Reduce heat to low and cook gently for an hour, stirring every 10 minutes to separate fish flesh from bone. Strain through a sieve or a piece of cheesecloth; set aside to cool.

To make the velouté, first make a pale roux: Melt 2 tablespoons butter in a saucepan over medium heat; add flour, stirring constantly, until mixture bubbles but doesn't brown. Blend in 2 cups of the fumet and a splash of Calvados; bring to a boil, cut heat immediately and simmer 25 minutes, occasionally skimming the surface and stirring. Remove from heat, strain through cheesecloth, and stir until cool.

To make the Normande sauce, heat together 1 cup of the velouté and 1 cup of fumet in a heavy saucepan. Blend 2 tablespoons cream with 2 egg yolks and add to pan; simmer mixture on low heat. While making sauce, cook filets—braise, bake or grill, as you prefer. A few minutes before serving time, add the ¼ cup butter and remaining cream. Stir until smooth.

Arrange cooked filets on platter, smother with sauce, and garnish with avocado slices and chopped basil leaves.

SERVES 4 TO 6.

FETTUCCINE BARRISIMO

This terrific easy pasta dish was inspired by friends in Buxton, North Carolina, who have housed Miss F. and me plenty of times when we've come unmoored, and who have endured my hurricane presence in their serene, island-style kitchen.

FOR THE SAUCE BARRIS:

1 stick butter

¼ cup flour

1 pint half and half

1 pound raw shrimp, peeled and deveined

1 pound fresh raw tuna

1 cup parmesan cheese, grated

1 pint whole milk

1 pound fettuccine noodles

1 cup lump crabmeat

Red caviar

Pepper to taste

Make a roux; melt butter in a saucepan over medium-high heat; add flour, stirring constantly, until mixture bubbles but doesn't brown. Add half and half slowly, blending thoroughly, and bring to a boil. Reduce heat. In a food processor, purée shrimp and then tuna; add to cream sauce, stirring frequently. Add parmesan, stir until melted, adding milk as needed to prevent sauce from becoming too thick. Cook fettuccine according to package directions; while it cooks add crabmeat to sauce, and more milk as needed. Drain fettuccine, rinse in cold water. Place individual portions on dinner plates; ladle sauce on top. Sprinkle with red caviar. Add pepper to taste.

SERVES 4 TO 6.

FAMILY FUEL

The holidays. For better or worse, everbody's home.

Blood may be the tie that binds; at the same time, it doubles as the knot that baffles. Ever since Eden's door closed on Adam and Eve, families have struggled to fortify themselves against a simple truth: It's a mixed blessing to be related to another human being.

Perhaps the most vital gastronomic role at holiday gatherings is this: Without food, plenty of it and lovingly prepared, we might kill one another. In the volatile clump of the assembled clan, killing one another over the holidays is a time-honored tradition, second only to eating your own weight in food between Christmas and New Year's. Even if we can't agree on which of a dozen names to call God, which profession is honorable or how much money is enough, why Sally married such a ne'er-do-well or how Harry's kids came to be such spoiled bastards, or if retiring to California made Mom and Dad ditsy, it is incumbent upon every member of the flock to admit that the grub was good, then join in the consensus that seconds are in order. A baked ham inspires truce. A turkey levels dissent. The emblem of harmony and goodwill is manifested in a leg of roast lamb. Indeed, a holiday meal opens a window into the true spirit of kin.

Reading my *Larousse Gastronomique*, I'm reminded that throughout the Western world, traditional Christmas dishes are handed down from generation to generation, especially on the most important day of Yuletide, Christmas Eve. In France, the feast is *le reveillon*, with its oysters, white sausages and tourtière (meat pie); in Italy, a meatless banquet; in Poland, the traditional supper called *Wigilia*, with three soups, three fish dishes and noodles, cabbage and cheese pierogi; in Armenia, the same supper Mary supposedly ate the night Christ was born: fried fish, lettuce, boiled spinach; in Denmark, roast goose stuffed with fruit, served with red cabbage and caramelized potatoes; in Greece, roast lamb and *Christopsomo*, sweet glazed bread decorated with the handprint of the chef; in Germany, carp and stollen; in Mexico, the fiesta of *Nochebuena* with its fruit salad, empanadas and buñuelos (fried dough). It was apparent to me, even as a child, that Christmas Eve was a paradox of intimate mystery, an evocative ritual of ancestors, and through it, I would be given a taste of a past as foreign as a czar. Both sets of my grandparents emigrated from Lithuania at the turn of the century, and my father's mother brought with her a family culinary treasure that survives, a recipe for terrific homemade kielbasa. When my parents followed the American Dream from the coalfields of Pennsylvania to the environs of Washington, D.C., my mother shared the recipe with a local butcher in Virginia. It was a disaster, that first suburban batch of my grandmother's Baltic sausage. The recipe was elementary, a *babushka*'s instructions—a handful of this, a handful of that—but the grandmatriarchal hands were dainty, whereas the butcher had a proletariat's paw broad enough to cup a plucked chicken. Sampling his original fifty pounds of links, he couldn't believe Lithuanians had such an inhuman fondness for salt, yet once the recipe was adjusted, the butcher made perfect fresh old-country kielbasa for my family for the next thirty years.

Poached kielbasa, eaten with horseradish and mustard, rye bread and hard-boiled eggs, was surely the most exotic of my favorite childhood meals, given my second-generational dread of anything not fully mainstream, and never so enjoyed as after midnight Mass on Christmas Eve, a nocturnal feast in the European tradition, meant to revitalize cele-brants after the duty of worship.

In contrast to this lusty post-church fare, our Christmas Eve suppers before the service respected abstinence and somber devotion—nothing to suggest assimilation into the culture of the New World—although potatoes, the infantry of Litwak cuisine, were there in dismal abundance. My father would inaugurate the supper with his prayer, the whispered platitudes of the season, and each year an upwelling of emotion would choke his throat. After a sip of white wine, he ate from and passed to his right the *plotkelis*, an unleavened bread made in Lithuania in an iron mold and stamped with Nativity scenes. Then on to the meal itself: aus-tere filets of fish, an unadorned vegetable, the spuds, poppyseed rolls. I remember these suppers most for their constraint and subdued hue, the charged atmosphere of secrets on the verge of exposure. The culinary point, it seemed, was to moderate secular excitement (presents!) and channel it as much as possible into a religious countdown.

First, the hours between supper and Mass, all of us quietly restless, then church—for me, always a bit of a spiritual intrusion, snapping the spell of private emotions. I suffocated from the sardine closeness of parishioners, biding my time until, in an icebox station wagon, we would cruise back home to the gifts waiting to be opened. And, once they were opened, the way was made clear for my grandmother's legacy, perhaps coarse fare to some but in my heart and to my appetite an exquisite con-tribution: the obscene pot of kielbasa steaming on the stove, the slick pale links streaming rich juice when stabbed with a fork. In the oven would be a ham, and in a second pot the eggs my father boiled with onion skins to color them a lovely bronze. This prosaic family rite, its earthy peasant flavors and thatched-cottage aromas, was, for me—I know now, since the presents have been forgotten—Christmas's most poignant seduction, a gastronomic return to all that had been left behind or lost in the family's long journey.

Inevitably, my adult life proved poor soil for my ethnic roots, that sausage-and-rye heritage overtaken by a more generic, slightly Waspy norm mirrored by the lives around me. And so a few years ago, spending

the holidays with a Bahamian friend in Freeport, I was delighted to discover that his breed, much like my own but with a piquant tropic style,
valued the culinary expression of an intriguing past. My friend was one
of the youngest generation of an old and wealthy Caribbean family
spread across the basin from Trinidad to Florida. The Antoni house was
packed with extended clan for the ten days of Christmas, and there was a
grandmother in residence, nearly a century old and as good a matriarchal
prototype for *One Hundred Years of Solitude* as you're likely to find. No
bigger than a stork, she never shut up but spun endless stories about the
history of the family, chirping the tales in patois, her dark eyes sparkling,
a bald flirt, as if she had remained in her soul as voluptuous as was her
granddaughter.

In the days of her childhood, in winter, Dutch sailing ships would
bring enormous Edam cheeses to barter with the islanders of the
Netherlands Antilles, who, in turn, would trade along coastal Venezuela,
where her father owned a ranch. The fourteen-and a-half-pound Edams
would last all year, and the following December the waxed rounds would
be scooped-out shells, as bright-red as a Christmas-tree ornament. The
household cooks would stuff the empty globes with a cooked ragout (a
mixture of diced sirloin, sausage and shrimp, with a body of chopped
mushrooms, onion, green pepper, olives, raisins, capers, chilies, tomatoes, and eggs) and then slowly bake them. This dish, called *keshi yena*, is
traditional in Curaçao, where it originated, and for the Antoni family, it
was the jewel of their Christmas Eve table.

How natural this delicacy seemed on a warm Christmas Eve. The
inner crust of matured cheese informed the ragout with its oils, adding a
slight tang to each ingredient, and I thought as I ate it that *keshi yena*
was the perfect complement to an island sensibility, the metaphor for the
tropic ethos that a holiday should not be passed in sober reflection but
in luxurious celebration. And between recollections of a hot world filled
with magically real doings, Grandmother Antoni forked down whatever
landed on her plate, knitting together the generations of her bloodline
with both menu and memory.

How precious to our tribal palate and the nourishment of self-identity was my own grandmother's kielbasa, her *keshi yena*, each bite savory with the contradictory spices of disappearance and renewal.

LITHUANIAN KIELBASA

To 5 pounds coarsely ground pork butts add 1 heaping teaspoon pulverized whole mustard seeds, 1 heaping teaspoon whole allspice and ½ teaspoon whole black peppercorns. Add ½ large onion and 1 large clove garlic, finely minced; ¼ cup salt; and ½ cup water. Mix thoroughly, and stuff into casings (available at most meat markets). Poach or boil for 20 minutes.

MAKES 6 TO 8 SERVINGS.

KESHI YENA

Cut a round slice from top of a 4-pound Edam, and hollow out cheese with a knife and spoon, leaving a shell about a half-inch thick. Reserve scooped-out cheese. Soak shell and lid in cold water for about an hour, then drain and dry.

To make ragout: In a frying pan or casserole, melt 1 tablespoon butter; add the same amount of vegetable oil. Dice and brown ½ pound sirloin. Remove sirloin from pan, and brown ½ pound hot Italian sausage, with casings removed. Put sausage aside, and let cool. Discard drippings. In same pan, saute until tender 1 medium onion, finely chopped; 1 green pepper, finely chopped; ½ cup chopped mushrooms; and 2 cloves garlic, pressed. Stir in 1 can tomatoes, drained and chopped; ¼ cup raisins; 2 tablespoons capers; ¼ cup chopped black olives; and 2 teaspoons chopped fresh chilies. Cook until most of liquid has evaporated. Add sirloin; sausage; 2 hard-boiled eggs, chopped; 2 tablespoons bread-crumbs; and 1 tablespoon flour. Stir until well mixed. Turn off heat, and stir in ½ pound raw shrimp, peeled, deveined and sliced in halves. Season with salt and pepper.

Cube one quarter of reserved Edam, and add to ragout. Fill Edam shell with mixture, replace lid, and secure with toothpicks. Place shell in a round baking dish, and bake in a cool oven (150 to 200 degrees) for 1 to 1 ½ hours.

MAKES 6 TO 8 SERVINGS.

LOVE AT FIRST BITE

Before I met Miss F., I used to think of bleak, icy February as the devil's own month, but falling in love with her altered that perception forever. February became our anniversary month—this particular February marking our fourteenth year together. Not a shabby record for a relationship that is mutually self-invented, which is to say common-law. The arrangement suits the two of us just fine, thanks, though upon occasion Miss F., whose materialistic needs are modest, will become wistful about one aspect of weddings: the ritual whereby everybody you know and even selected strangers are stuck giving you presents. In this regard she has nothing to be ashamed of, judging by the behavior of her cutthroat peers, and it is incumbent upon me to take up the gift-giving slack.

I had been absent from my domestic life, gone some few but faraway and lonely months, teaching at a midwestern university. Now, I was coming home to Miss F., after promising her that on the first day she had me back I would cook the most romantically glorious supper I could devise. The week before I repatriated myself, I visited a jewelry store in the Kansas city that had adopted me for a semester. I knew exactly what I wanted: a diamond ring. In our many years together I had given Miss F.

plenty of rings and such, but never a diamond. We couldn't afford a proper one, so why bother?

"I don't like diamonds anyway," she would occasionally state in a brave voice. "They're so ordinary," she'd say and sigh. Now, however, my paycheck was adequate to skim off the price.

"When's the wedding?" the sales clerk asked as I inspected a tray of gold-set solitaires. "My dear fellow, I don't want to marry the girl," I replied, rubbing my unshaved cheek, "I only want to squander a sufficient amount of money on her, for the usual reasons." I found the right stone and setting I was looking for, bought the ring, drove back to my apartment, and phoned Miss F.

"Miss F.," I said, "I just procured for you a big, fat, expensive present. Don't ask me what it is."

"What is it?" she begged.

"Now, now," I clucked. A man is out of his mind if he gives the love of his life a really good present without using it to extort some small pleasure in return. I told her I would give her the aforementioned item during the promised dinner, but she would have to reciprocate in some manner.

"You have something in mind, I take it," she said warily.

"As a matter of fact, I do," I said. "I want you to have a surprise for me, and it must be a surprise that's concealed in such a way that I can't possibly know what it is until you undress."

"Well, all right," she agreed, "but tell me—"

"I'll say no more," I said. "I'll see you next week."

I knew Miss F. would work hard on her assignment. In vain, she petitioned her girlfriends at school. Sexy lingerie, they advised. Miss F. shook her head. It's not that he wouldn't like that, she told her friends, but it wouldn't really be a surprise, and he'd be disappointed. Inspired by revelations concerning George Schultz, Miss F. considered the notion of an elegant and elegantly placed tattoo, but an aspiring lawyer with just such a tattoo warned against it. An image began to form in Miss F.'s mind. She queried one of her male colleagues for his opinion.

"How long have you been with this guy?" the colleague, a married man, asked in his best courtroom manner.

"Fourteen years," answered Miss F. correctly.

"Forget it," he said. "That's too long. You can't surprise him. It's impossible." Miss F. confided in him, telling the fellow what she thought might get the job done. His jaw dropped. He stared at her. He turned and walked away, speechless.

My first full day back home was a Friday. A friend we hadn't seen in years flew into town on business and we met him at a *tapas* restaurant for a leisurely lunch. As a result, I got a late start shopping for the night's heralded meal. The menu I had settled on was culturally illogical but not without its own gastronomic sense: lobster-and-asparagus sushi, leek bisque, tarragon duck with mushrooms and crushed pumpkin seeds, and the real clincher, visually—a raspberry charlotte. And of course Miss F.'s favorite food, champagne.

As much as I love to shop for food, this day I was defeated by the ambition of my menu. Some scoundrel had gone before me, pillaging the town's stock of live lobsters. Store A sent me to Store B, where I was waved on to Store C, each fishmonger reporting that the lobster glutton had been there already and laid waste to the inventory. It was the same story, butcher-wise, with ducks; the same story, produce-wise, with raspberries; and the same story, bakery-wise, with the ladyfingers required for the raspberry charlotte. I persevered, however, haunted by the mystery of this alter ego forever one step ahead of me, and I was dying to know what sort of great surprise his dining companion had in store to reward his foresight in having gotten there first. Well after dark I found my way back home, far too exhausted to establish myself in the kitchen. Miss F. consoled me, and we went out to eat.

Saturday was different. I entered the kitchen in the late afternoon, mentally and physically fit. By eight in the evening, the right music rippled from the stereo, the dining-room table blazed with candles, the sushi cooled in the refrigerator, the leek bisque simmered on the stove and the duck on its platter, the raspberry charlotte sat on the back porch chilling in the February air. The diamond ring was centered on the table inside its velvet box, and the kitchen was a magnificent mess. I popped the cork on the champagne, yodeling for Miss F., who had wisely isolated herself in the bedroom. She appeared—staggering—gorgeous, wearing a high-necked, long-sleeved, low-waisted, full-skirted, publicly disruptive black dress with equally incitive high heels. With her hazelly eyes flashing mischief, she kissed me.

"Gosh," I said. "Wooeee." I could have said much more, but I knew Miss F. preferred understated dignity to slobbering proclamations.

"Look at you," she said. "You not only shaved, you put on a tie."

"Heh-heh-heh." I can be shrewd upon occasion. When you rarely wear a tie, the presence of one around your neck is akin to a major social accomplishment, with all the impact of a promotion. This is a trick that won't work if you wear a tie every day. I poured champagne. We drank. We sat. We stuffed ourselves with sushi. Rice tumbled off our chins. Our sinuses dilated from the potent horseradish in the sauce. We licked our fingers. The music whispered perfect, perfect, over and over. I ladled the bisque into shallow enamel bowls. Miss F. discoursed about God knows what, and I felt tears in my eyes. She displayed enormous self-restraint by keeping her eyes off the little velvet box. I brought out the duck on its platter.

"I don't know what's gotten into you," Miss F. said, "but I just can't imagine living without it."

At the appropriate moment I stumbled to the kitchen, shook the charlotte out of its souffle dish and brought it in. "You son-of-a-bitch," Miss F. gasped, aptly, because the charlotte was truly a wonder—I couldn't quite believe it myself. After we both had had seconds, after the champagne was gone, after the smoldering thematic tension had been pushed into the red zone, I told her to go right ahead, and slumped in my chair when I saw the ring on her finger. I want my surprise, I croaked, and my dear Miss F. rose to her high-heeled feet. The shoes alone had the romantic capacity to make me bark. She crossed her arms over her waist, bent to take the hem of her long skirt into her hands, straightened up. Off came the whole shebang, pure Miss F. except for—.

All I can say is that Miss F. knows the way to this boy's heart is through a damn good boffo laugh. You can have your bawdy panties and lacy bras, you can have your indelible tattoos. This was the sort of side splitting surprise that would keep me home for years, indentured in the kitchen. Sorry, gentlemen, no unmerited thrills here. It was my dinner, my present—and my surprise. Surely there are merchants selling diamonds, ducks and raspberries, wherever it is you live.

LEEK BISQUE

2 large leeks

2 tablespoons butter

¼ cup fresh chopped parsley

1 carrot, peeled and chopped

1 clove garlic, pressed

1 teaspoon fresh marjoram leaves (or ¼ teaspoon dried marjoram)

½ teaspoon grated lemon peel

White pepper to taste

1 cup chicken broth

2 tablespoons flour

3 to 4 cups milk (depending on desired consistency)

Toasted almond slivers

Trim base and top two inches off leeks. Peel and discard papery outer leaves; rinse and slice leeks into thin strips. Melt butter in a deep saucepan. Add all ingredients except flour, milk and almonds. Bring to a boil; reduce heat and simmer for 15 minutes. Stir in flour. Transfer mixture to food processor and blend until creamy. Return to pan, add milk and heat until steaming, stirring often. Sprinkle individual servings with almond slivers.

MAKES 4 SERVINGS.

TARRAGON DUCK WITH MUSHROOMS AND CRUSHED PUMPKIN SEEDS

1 5-pound duck

*3 stems plus 1 teaspoon fresh chopped tarragon leaves
(or ½ teaspoon dried tarragon, divided)*

Salt and pepper to taste

1 ½ tablespoons butter

⅓ cup Calvados

1 cup dry white wine

12 washed whole button mushrooms

5 tablespoons whipping cream

¼ cup roasted pumpkin seeds, crushed

Place tarragon stems (or ¼ teaspoon dried tarragon) into cavity of duck; sprinkle cavity with salt and pepper. In a deep skillet over medium heat, melt butter. Brown duck and skim off grease. Pour Calvados over duck and flambé just as it begins to boil. Let flames die out, then cover pan and simmer for 45 minutes. Stir liquid occasionally; add a spoonful or two of water if needed. Remove cooked duck and keep warm in heated oven (at 200 degrees). Skim grease off liquid in pan, return to heat and add white wine. Reduce volume by half by boiling rapidly on high heat, uncovered. Add mushrooms; stir in whipping cream and tarragon leaves (or ¼ teaspoon dried tarragon). Boil sauce for 2 minutes, stirring constantly with a wooden spoon. Remove from heat. Trim legs off duck, carve breast and arrange on serving platter. Spoon a small amount of sauce, garnish with mushrooms. Sprinkle pumpkin seeds (available in health-food stores) over duck. Serve with diamond ring.

MAKES 2 SERVINGS.

RASPBERRY CHARLOTTE

1 cup milk

3 tablespoons sugar

½ teaspoon vanilla extract

Pinch salt

3 egg yolks, beaten smooth

1 envelope unflavored gelatin

⅓ cup water

Butter

15 ladyfingers

1 cup whipping cream

1 pint raspberries

In a medium-size saucepan, heat milk, sugar, vanilla, and salt to boiling point. Remove from burner and beat in egg yolks. Return to heat and stir constantly, until mixture starts to thicken; don't allow to boil. Remove from heat. Thoroughly dissolve gelatin in water, then stir into hot milk-egg mixture. Cool until mixture begins to thicken (refrigerate if necessary). Lightly butter sides (but not bottom) of a 12-inch charlotte or soufflé mold. Arrange ladyfingers vertically along sides of mold, pressing gently to make them stay. Sprinkle sugar in bottom of mold to make unmolding easier. Beat cream in an ice-cold bowl until stiff peaks form. Beat milk-egg mixture vigorously if it has gelled. Carefully fold whipped cream into milk-egg mixture with a rubber spatula until well blended. Pour a third of mixture into mold, add a layer of raspberries (reserve about a dozen or so berries for garnish); layer another third of mixture, then raspberries and, finally, mixture to fill. Cover and refrigerate overnight. To serve, dip bottom of mold in warm water for a couple of seconds, then invert over a serving plate. Garnish with reserved berries. Serve with berry purée (recipe follows).

MAKES 6 TO 8 SERVINGS.

BERRY PURÉE

2 pints raspberries

½ cup sugar

Juice of 1 lemon

Purée berries in a food processor with sugar and lemon juice. Serve with charlotte.

PÂTÉ ANIMAL

I hope you don't think less of me to learn that lately I have spent more than a single idle minute musing about pâté, when perhaps you would have me more fruitfully occupied, doing something truly pointless like, say, playing golf. For instance, where in the devil did pâté come from? Who were the imaginative but maybe toothless oddballs who invented its soft forms? Is it not sold anywhere in the capitals of states like Florida and Missouri? And why do I now experience a craving for pâté while for most of my life I would spit it out into a napkin when, after several cocktails, I had put it in my mouth, mistaking it for some substance I might actually enjoy? Difficult though it may be to sort pâté fact from fiction, I should think it's worth it to get to the bottom of these and all gastronomic riddles.

First, the persistent problem of terminology. You may have noticed that the French have their own, deliberately troublesome words for things, phrases that are excessively confusing and illogical and which we—being born on the more lucid, pragmatic side of the Atlantic— would be better off to just ignore, as we are now right to finally ignore split infinitives. Here's an example of what I mean. When the French say pâté, they are, one would like to presume, making precise reference to mashed or hacked-up meats, fish, vegetables, or fruit, tamped down and baked within a pastry shell, then served hot or cold. However, to trick English speakers, they also say pâté when they actually mean *pâté en terrine*: minced meat, game, or fish packed into a steep-sided dish (a terrine) lined with bacon and then cooked, but always served cold, in or out of the dish. You see? The French have a capricious habit of saying simply *terrine* to describe *pâté en terrine*, which is what we Americans commonly insist upon meaning when we say pâté. Understand? No? Well, listen, the French have muddled the issue further with their *pâté en croûte*, which again employs the traditional ingredients, but is cooked in a mold in a pastry crust mercilessly called *pâté à pâté*, and also served cold. Finally, there is *pâté pantin*, the same thing as above but shaped by hand into a loaf, like bread, rather than stuffed into a mold. The French are unforgivably playful this way, and I have it from a reliable source that this lexical hooliganism—particularly the unnecessary if not incestuous relationship between pâté and terrine—was a typical Gallic prank, in this case instigated by de Tocqueville, who delighted in visiting the New World and establishing himself in New York's more ostentatious restaurants of the time, pathetic reproductions of their Parisian models, whereupon he would have a good laugh with the waiters as they overheard the native diners trying to comprehend the menu, ordering a goat melted down into a pie when what they really thought they asked for was pot roast.

I don't know how the French came to have dibs on pâté anyway, since it was the Romans of Empire fame who came up with the idea for this particular method of constituting food. Be it *pie, pasty,* or *patty,* all cousins of pâté, the etymology of pâté is rooted in the Latin word, *pasta.* If you didn't know and never guessed, *pasta* means something made of or with paste (which has everything to do with my original aversion to pâté, but I'll get to that in a minute). We should pay no attention to the fact that, at the time, the Romans were energetically refining techniques for turning Christians into pastes very similar to the ones being developed by their master chefs. And we should dismiss entirely as apocryphal the gastronomic legend of Junius, the short-order cook at the Colosseum canteen, of whom Juvenal was said to have remarked, "His pies are the final measure of glory or defeat; whether you go into them, or they into you."

We know for certain though that the promiscuous Roman gourmets had "a distressing vulgar streak," according to Reay Tannahill in her gastronomic epic, *Food in History*, and that the first *pâté en terrine* seems to have been commissioned by the emperor Vitellius, a "noted glutton." It was prepared with "pike liver, pheasant brains, peacock brains, flamingo tongues, and lamprey roe." All of these ingredients seem a bit flamboyant to me, best suited for the sacrificial buffets of witches, but I believe I could today digest the recipe's liver, brains, and roe with only a perfunctory queasiness, whereas I would feel compelled to draw both a culinary and ecological line at flamingo tongues. A good gastronomic rule of thumb here: never eat an endangered species, or a species you've only seen at the zoo, even if it's only the tongue. Never mind that though pork provided the bulk in most imperial Roman pâtés, spiced and marinated birds' tongues were a prime and favored ingredient, a gastronomic condition that resulted in another great invention of Western Civilization—whistling while you work, practiced by enslaved tongue-pluckers to entertain one another, since the Rome of antiquity was plagued by a notorious shortage of songbirds.

The French, equally fond of extravagance at any cost, sought to preserve this exotic tradition of birds-tongue pâtés, but grew lazy and careless in its craft, until eventually the pâté makers merely diced up the whole damn bird—whether lark, thrush, blackbird, woodcock, or partridge—and crammed it into a pastry. Still, if we must cast blame, let's blame the Brits for the utter degeneration of the classical bird *pâtés*, a gastronomic event infamously recorded in a popular nursery rhyme. From an imperial gourmand's point of view, those four-and-twenty blackbirds were the culmination of a depressing trend, for by the Middle Ages, aviocide fell in disrepute among chefs—why spend a week catching and carving a flock of pheasants, when one fat sheep's tongue would do? The ultimate corruption of pâté, however, took twenty centuries, so that the merchants in the Tallahassees and Jefferson Citys of America will claim that they do in fact sell pâté in the country's most ubiquitous and popular version: Spam.

Potted, patted, or pasted, one of the more uplifting aspects of pâtés is that throughout the ages they have been customarily dedicated and named for famous people. Besides the requisite *pâtés à la reine*, for which each chef of the day was given the culinary opportunity to ingratiate himself to king or queen, we have had a parade of pâtés honoring important historical figures, from the well-known *pâté à la mazarine* (named for Cardinal Mazarin, though there remains a question as to whether this guy himself was really famous or not), to such Americana notables memorialized in the manner of *pâté à l'Elvis*—puréed ham hocks bound with hominy and pig's-feet jelly, molded in the form of a Les Paul guitar—and such postmodern innovations as *pâté au Letterman*—leftover all-the-way pizza, marinated in Rolling Rock, smushed into a ceramic coffee mug terrine, rebaked and served cold. Indeed, if you've already seen to it that a star's been named for someone you cherish or admire, you might next try having that name forever affixed to a pâté. I tried this cute gift idea already with Miss F., however, and she refused the honor, claiming that she wouldn't be able to forget the earlier conceptual problem I associated with pâtés. I would hesitate to speak about this problem, but I've asked around and discovered that my former dread of pâté was, at one time or another, shared universally by my friends. Unlike the gourmets of old, I have never been willing to put just anything into my mouth. First, what I was about to eat had to look and feel like food. Mostly, my prejudice focused on texture, not source, although with meats and fowl, reprehensible texture seems married to unacceptable source. Being carnivorous is one thing, but I am loath to play the vulture, so I refuse to eat the organs of animals, whether calf's liver, sheep's kidney, pork brains, chicken gizzards, beef hearts, or etcetera. It doesn't impress me in the least that an appreciation of the singular flavors of these viscera expresses one's gastronomic sophistication. Offal is more appropriately consumed on roadsides by scavengers, rather than tablesides by gentlemen and ladies in evening dress. The taste for such things is, I think, a vestige of the Roman "vulgar streak," and even allowing that this is not so, even if kidneys weren't tart and whiffy with animal urine, livers not ripe with bile, hearts not overrich from their lifelong soak of blood, I could not eat these things because of their pasty or gummy textures, the way they squished in my mouth, which, frankly—and I wish there was a more delicate way to say this—was the feel of something we try to avoid stepping in in a barnyard.

In a lounge or at a wedding, a mound of chicken-liver pâté, looking for the world as if it had been prepared by a cow, would make me shudder, and I would be in awe of the decadence of those who could spread such muck on toast rounds and nibble happily on the combination. How, I wondered, did these otherwise respectable people cultivate an appetite for the heady taste and texture of decay? I had eaten raw turtle eggs, iguana, rattlesnake, so I didn't think my problem with pâté was, at its core, a question of manliness, but at a party we attended early in our relationship, Miss F. returned from the sideboard array of appetizers licking a cracker smudged with goose pâté.

"That's unspeakably gross," I said, and announced I wouldn't kiss her until she washed her mouth out with Listerine. She laughed at my hysteria and asked if I wanted a bite.

"No, never." I told her what I thought pâté looked and tasted like.

"That's ridiculous, not to mention childish," Miss F. clucked. "It tastes delicious, you *wuss*, and what does it matter what a good pâté looks like? You don't not eat hot dogs, do you, because of their phallic resemblance? Or sausage? You don't not eat hot cereal because it looks like elephant snot, do you? It seems to me," she chided, "that when it comes to eating the finer thing, you're still six years old."

She pried open my mouth and jammed the pâtéd cracker into my maw. It took me a while to bite down, but when I did, I felt the strangest desire for the best wine I could get my hands on, something elegant in taste to compliment the unique pungency of the pâté. I can't explain what happened to my phobia about texture, except to say it went the way of all adolescent hesitations, became a wry smile on the face of adulthood.

Whatever my past misguided feelings were about pâté, these days when I go to someone's house to watch a ballgame, or for a dinner party, or just to schmooze around, I would much prefer to be presented with a weird terrine, than be bored by the usual gratings—snacks, Brie, veggies, cold cuts. Something to keep in mind when the holidays approach, and you find the likes of me showing up at the door, sniffing about for something good to eat.

HERB PÂTÉ

Unless you live in a Very Big City, you're probably not eating it unless you're eating it out of a can (by the way, the best canned pâtés are made by folks in Richmond, Michigan, and stamped with the accurate slogan, "One of the 'Good Little Cans' that go all over the world!"). Given the indifference to most provincial markets, I started making my own, working on the principle that fresh is better than imported anyway.

6 slices bacon

1 pound pork shoulder

4 pounds veal

4 eggs, 3 of them hardboiled

1 large onion

3 cloves garlic

2 cups fresh spinach, chopped

2 tablespoons each of fresh basil and rosemary leaves, minced

1 tablespoon fresh thyme, minced

2 teaspoons fennel seeds

1 teaspoon each salt and pepper

1 tablespoon unsalted butter

3 tablespoons brandy

Using a meat grinder or food processor, purée or grind the meats. Sauté chopped onion and minced garlic in butter. Add the spinach, cook for several minutes, then transfer mixture to a large bowl. Stir in the meats, brandy, one uncooked egg, salt, pepper, herbs, and fennel seeds. Preheat oven to 350 degrees. In a 6-cup loaf pan or mold, arrange the strips of bacon along the bottom and sides, letting the ends hang over the edges. Add half the pâté mixture, arrange the shelled, hard-boiled eggs in a line down the center of the pan, add the remaining mixture and fold bacon slices over the top. Cover with foil and place in a baking dish filled with hot water to the midpoint of the loaf pan or pâté mold. Heat on top of the stove until the water simmers, then put in oven and bake for 1½ hours. Remove and cool, uncovered, for an hour. Replace the foil, place evenly distributed weights on top of the pâté (3 canned goods will do just fine as weights) and refrigerate overnight. To serve, remove pâté from pan and trim excess fat.

Also, experiment with different herbs in the recipe, depending on what's in season.

(Recipe adapted from *Cook's Freestyle Cuisine*.)

WANTON SOUP

Whenever I fall in love, I begin with potatoes.
—NORA EPHRON, FROM *HEARTBURN*

I'm at the back of a walk-up railroad flat, in a rather downscale kitchen. Gravel-voiced blues sift from an old box radio on the counter. There are a cracked linoleum floor, a Formica table, two dinette chairs, a bottle of dago red. The light's not soft, just weird, a strange luminous haze that I assume is Spanish fly flurrying down, left over, like ozone in the atmosphere, from the stormy fantasies of a million lovelorn boys, each crying out in the night to Eros the immortal words of those bards of modern romance, 2 Live Crew: *"Me so horny"*!

A woman occupies one of the chairs. Not just any woman, but a voluptuous, sloe-eyed goddess, the handmaiden of lust. She seems to sprawl in her chair in a sort of narcotic fog (if there's a fog of war, there must also be a fog of love). Her dishevelment seems to have an internal source, a secret engine. She's not falling apart, she's undergoing a metamorphosis. Unbrushed to wanton perfection is her auburn hair. Her lips are painted crimson, and she wears a necklace of fat pearls at her throat, where the skin appears flushed with preprandial heat. Her blouse is loosely buttoned, her cleavage a bit frightening, deep, no place for babies. And, sweet Yasu, she has a tongue that can tie a knot in the stem of a cherry.

Her chair is pulled close to the table so that you know she feels its hard edge as a bar of pressure across her abdomen, and you can't see, unless you stand back, how her knees have angled apart or how high her silky red skirt has hiked up her electric thighs, revealing the tops of her stockings, the flowered clasps of a garter belt, and beyond, farther up in the tendinous confluence of flesh, a glimpse of the Lithuanian national flag, triangled, obscured in a blur of steam. I have come to understand that her underthings are meant to be a forecast of the evening's bill of fare. Good Lord, I say to myself, taking the empty chair, I wonder what she has in mind.

"I have something special," she says, "just for you." As you might imagine, she's breathing heavily and I'm holding my breath. Her hands snake under the table; I can't tell you where they've gone exactly or why she throws her head back and makes little yelps of pleasure. All I know is that I've been invited for dinner and I am a hungry, hungry man. I clear my throat and dare to ask what's cooking. Last time around it was reindeer filet in currant jelly; the time before, braised turbot with vermouth.

She moans with a slight tone of frustration and straightens up, takes a second to refocus her inchoate eyes. I don't know how it got there—this is a surprise—but suddenly she's holding a potato, and the thing is smoldering as though it's about to blow up.

My disappointment is, I'm afraid, apparent. A woman who believes in the amorous properties of potatoes shouldn't be difficult to please, but frankly I don't recall any mention of starchy foods in the *Kama Sutra*. Common sense tells me that not many of us, male or female, tend to be sexually aroused by spuds. They champion neither evocative shape nor aesthetic lure, have a taste only a bad poet would bother to describe, are conceived in subterranean ignorance of passion, quickly mature to frumpy ordinariness, and connote the long pedestrian haul of love rather than the wild lather of its overture. What pitiful son-of-a-bitch has ever looked upon a lump of mashed potatoes, then raised a wolfish gaze to the coquette responsible for the lump, put two and two together and concluded, *"Good Lord, I must have my way with her! I must!"*? (Carl Bernstein, that's who, which makes you think even a yam would set this guy's pants afire.)

On second thought, however, I decide better a potato than an apple. Given their track record in the history of lovemaking, apples are not to be trusted. Our sexual past thunders with the consequences of their blinding aphrodisiac effect. They cost us Paradise and provoked the Trojan War. Plus there's that film clip of Marilyn Monroe rolling an apple around her bosom, wearing a pair of big, dorky white cotton panties that make her look absolutely nunnish. Apples are a sexual jinx, an emblem of entrapment, and when I say that women who have served me a prim and matriarchal apple pie as a means of encouraging my affection have invariably chilled my hormones, I swear I am serious. Miss F.'s apple cobbler has my blessing but not my appetite: she must eat it alone, or with more patriotic men than I. If pie is to be employed in my seduction, I much prefer a dark, oozy slice of blackberry, a more savory inspiration, and if the topping is a ballistic spurt of whipped but unsweetened cream, I won't complain.

But I might as well come right out and say it: Is this slippery business of aphrodisiacs a joke or not? I don't understand them or their vanities, although I admit to an appreciation of the bawdy, pampering decadence they engender, the gastro-sexual trail that leads to those shimmering, phosphorescent erotic dinners choreographed by soon-to-be lovers. I understand what an excellent bottle of red wine or dry champagne means to Miss F. (quote: "I love it and I'll drink it and then I'll do anything"), but what giveth with Oriental men, with their shark fins and ambergris, monkey parts, and obscene powders of rhino horn? Isn't sushi sexy enough? Where did they get this Neolithic sense of sexual prowess? What failings are they trying to compensate for? Are Eastern orgasms so elusive as to require such voodoo and coercion?

Or is stamina—rather, the lack thereof—a universal problem that I've so far been spared? (Brag, brag, brag.) Even my pal Scott confesses that on his honeymoon he invested heavily in buffalo steak, as if rich and wild meat were an erection's insurance policy. Forever, it seems, that's what men have thought. When virility was the question, game was the answer, consumed in a ritual of mock cannibalism, in which power is gained not from devouring an enemy but from eating what is most admired, transferring its desirable traits to ourselves. Pheasants and pigeons, for instance, have been prized by self-styled Casanovas because these birds court with such robust determination. Likewise sea turtles—and, by extension, their eggs—for when turtles mate they remain joined up for hours, days. You'll also find offal on the libertine's grocery list, and though I can see the savage logic for feasting on *animelles* (testicles of ram, lamb, and bull), I regard the reputed stimulating nature of sweetbreads, brains, kidneys, and *amourettes* (the spinal marrow of calves and sheep) most appropriate for the palate of a necrophiliac.

On the other side of the equation, if the point is to get those girlies poised to abandon themselves to passion, the accepted gastronomic tactic is glandular inflammation, spicing them up to a level of high squirm. Thank you, Marco Polo, for carrying home these deceptive agents of lust—pepper, pimento, cinnamon, nutmeg, chives, saffron, vanilla, and ginger—and immersing them in the lives of housewives. It makes you wonder about Betty Crocker. *Really* nice girls stay away from sugar and spice.

As you can see, there's a problem with our received knowledge of aphrodisiacs, a popular but deluded mythology at times so simplified as to constitute culinary smut. The most stereotypically perceived feature of an aphrodisiac, its anatomical shape, is also the most primitive, which as a metaphor does indeed raise eyebrows but in practice gets to be a bit heavy-handed. If giving a child a toy car foreshadows his future ownership of the real thing, so it must follow that the more lewdly shaped shellfish and vegetables operate on the same premise. (What women must think in supermarkets: "Mr. Zucchini is so big!")

Yet if shape were innately potent, and not merely unsubtle, lovers everywhere would insist on hot dogs nestled in the warm, yeasty folds of buns, though they'd likely end up in the ballpark, not the bedroom, regressing to a state of prepubescence. When what's on the table seems too graphic or deliberate, shamelessly contrived to harden your Johnson, then the art is lost and the pornography of food is all too obvious, clinical and, finally, boring. The hope of love is to discover the right catalysts that help us reveal ourselves to one another—tender revelation, not lurid exposure—and the gastronomic role in this complex affair is a paradox of intimacy, suggesting sensual associations and unexpected wonders that illuminate, even as we bare ourselves, a delicious sense of mystery. Call it passion, whatever, it can't be sated, it

can't be overfed, it can only be starved out to forage in the solitude of obsession. That's when you find yourself tearing the horn from the head of a rhinoceros.

Back in the goddess's funky kitchen, I'm still waiting for the air to crackle with erotic tension, but I'm fast losing confidence in the goddess's skill. If she's trying to appeal to my Baltic heritage, I'd prefer that she ply me with vodka. Maybe my most ancient ancestors were round-bellied, weighty-jowled studs in the notoriously horny Clan of the Latke, and the goddess wants to connect me with my primal self. But it's not working: I'm registering no measurable dilation of faraway capillaries, no vascular glow; I hear no wolves begin to howl from the hilltops of lust. "Goddess," I confess, "you've stumped me with your spud." Sighing, she stretches languorously to give me the modest tuber. Her voice is like a hand on my crotch. "Remember that girl," she asks, "long ago? When every secret taste and smell drove you crazy?"

That still happens, I confide, but I don't know what girl she's talking about. I think the goddess is kidding (but she's not) when she next commands, rather vulgarly, I think, "Scratch and sniff," unleashing a lurid set of magazine images on my imagination. She gashes the skin of the potato with a harlot's fingernail and bids me to lower my proboscis. So I humor her and take a cautious whiff, with little faith in Nora Ephron or in the promiscuity of the lowly *pomme de terre*, but I lift my head in awe, blinking, having inhaled a memory that penetrates far back into the erotic residues of experience. I feel my face reddening, for the goddess is an absolute mistress of the arcana of sensuality, and under her gastronomic manipulation, I eventually get the message that our libido has a menu of its own. Years ago, and embarrassingly callow, I knew a virginal beauty who granted me full olfactory rights to her body. Her skin, I soon discovered, emanated an essence that made a terrific impression on me, a fragrance not especially fecund but fresh and loamy, and when I caught scent of it, I was so mystified I stopped in the middle of this ecstatic reconnaissance to declare "Hey, you smell like potatoes!"—candor, as it so often does, winning out over romance. These ghosts of taste and smell and touch, how good they are to have nearby.

One thing about the goddess, I can't fool around with her. I have to eat what she fixes and get out of there, back to Miss F. As I recall George Bush once saying, "I'm going home to Barbara with my morale sky-high." On my way, I can't resist the impulse to pick up a ten-pound bag of Idaho Desirees. What can I tell you? I have friends in Miami who think cornflakes are an aphrodisiac. And meat loaf. And bok choy.

POTATO-AND-LEEK PANCAKES

8 medium Idaho potatoes

2 leeks

2 eggs, beaten

¼ cup unbleached flour

¼ teaspoon baking powder

Salt and coarsely ground pepper, to taste

½ cup vegetable or olive oil

1 pint sour cream

Salmon roe

"Gastronomy," said M. F. K. Fisher, "is and always has been connected with its sister art of love," so in that spirit let us rehabilitate the potato and show, finally, it too as being capable of evoking lust. Peel potatoes, pat dry and using either a hand grater or a food processor, grate coarsely. Allow to drain on paper towels, transfer to a mixing bowl and set aside.

Clean and grate leeks and stir into potatoes. Add eggs, flour, baking powder, salt and pepper and mix thoroughly. Heat oil in a large skillet over medium-high heat and try small pancakes until golden brown on both sides, pressing each side with spatula. Drain on brown paper bags and serve on a warm dish, arranged around a center of sour cream topped with the pretty, orange pearls of roe.

SERVES 6 TO 8.

THE COOK, HIS
BRIEFS . . .

The dinner party, if we are to believe the embittered reports of essayist Phillip Lopate, is a smug, mind-numbing, and, worst of all, suburban form of entertainment, and dinner-party chatter is the communicative equivalent of wandering through shopping malls, trying to build a consensus for our trivial purchases.

Fiddlesticks, Mr. Lopate. I beg to differ with this self-described ingrate, who has scarfed many a freeloader's meal and then retired from the table to chronicle the bloodless morons he encountered there. No matter, we diners shall do ourselves and the world of gastronomic fellowship a service by ignoring the less noble aspects of Mr. Lopate's disposition, and instead join in one well-fed voice to sing the timeless glories of the one domestic institution that clearly articulates our superiority over the beasts of the world: the civil ability of our species to come together at the trough and feed our faces without shoving or doing grave injury to one another. I for one offer the evidence of a dinner that Miss F. and I attended in recent years, a lovely event that I think representative of the general lot we drag ourselves to.

The dinner was hosted by Ms. J., a thirtyish and devoutly aerobic blonde who had made a respectable name for herself as an anthropologist specializing in the mythological origins of pre-Columbian oratory: essentially, Mayan rap songs. Ms. J., or rather, Professor Ms. J.—or really *Mrs.* Professor Ms. J., in light of her husband George's wishes, which she invariably found amusing—had called the dinner in honor of her esteemed colleague, Dr. Blake C. Black. Dr. Black had returned the week before from a twelve-month meander through the Indonesian bush, collecting field data on the prenuptial agreements among tribes that only a year earlier had been considered Stone Age, but now, thanks to the discovery of oil on their ancestral lands, were able to include such catalogue-ordered marvels as Nintendo and Fredricks of Hollywood lingerie in the dowries of their comely daughters. Black, we had been told, would treat us to countless fascinating anecdotes of dating in the aboriginal jungles. As for George, like myself he was a trained observer of life, and he recorded it dutifully, though as a poet; and although I didn't hold that against him, his wife did. George was also a gourmet cook, limited however to one dish, buckshot-riddled wild turkey, which often as not he would find roosting in his backyard. This particular night in question though, our guest of honor had requisitioned the kitchen to whip up something special.

This was in Charlottesville, Virginia, where Miss F. and I resided at the time. Contrary to media depictions, we found the inhabitants of the town and surrounding countryside congenial, not at all packed with as many bigots, megalomaniacal scholars, slumming movie stars and make-believe gentry as we had been led to believe. They welcomed us with open arms, in fact, once Miss F. let it slip that her grandfather six or seven times removed had been captain of the Mayflower. Moreover, I'm comfortable saying that our gathering provided an accurate slice of the acceptable community, with nary a dusky face or whiff of white trash in sight, for such peoples were strangely considered to be French in Charlottesville, and these were the days when Francophilia was in decline and the Italian movement held in ever higher regard. Needless to say, in a society sensitive to the geopolitical flux, a guest list can be a devilish challenge.

Also in attendance, Miss F. and I soon discovered, as Mrs. Professor Ms. J took our coats and threw them on the floor for Old Balls, the family terrier, to curl up on—this was of course to be a casual evening—was

THE COOK, HIS BRIEFS... 93

the Prez, a distinguished administrator and champion of bureaucrats, rumored to be in line for the stewardship of Dartmouth College, once the fix was in. If you've kept count so far, you know that the Prez made six of us, the recommended number for a perfect dinner party, but my own arithmetic for ciphering social success is more compatible with the formula employed by Ms. J.: Double the ideal number of guests, plus or minus one; in case your original set somehow fails you, you are backed up by a second, plus an odd man out to assist you in the kitchen, knocking down tequila shooters.

Numbers seven and eight were the Old Admiral and his consort, the widow Terbill. Nine and ten were a charming, deliberately bald and cross-dressed younger couple, the Heatherton-Peets, recent graduates who were fully engaged as art consultants to the booted and horsed crowd, exploring avant ways to squander old money. Our eleventh was Cookie, a pixieish travel agent responsible for the anthropology department's overseas bookings.

We joined our fellow guests in the parlor and found them enjoying a log fire blazing upon the hearth while George served aperitivos or hot toddies to all but Black, who preferred sipping a type of *grappa* flavored with the grasses removed from the stomach of the Indonesian mountain hare. Apparently, Professor Black still felt himself divided between two worlds, for his feet were bare and impressively dirty, and he wore a luminous saffron sarong around his waist. Yet above this, he wore his tweed jacket with elbow patches and his oxford shirt and bowtie, and one of the lenses of his hornrimmed eyeglasses was cracked straight down the middle.

J. asked if we were interested in hearing the latest Toltec harvest song she had browbeaten out of an ancient chief in Chiapas. "It's about the corn god, Mixtitpultahuaoc," she elaborated as she squatted on her heels, her knees spread apart and her arms above her head. "Listen to the grinding beauty of the diphthongs." She began an eerie chanting, clearly a spiritual *tour de force*, though as the verses gnashed on, it seemed more like an epic than a mere song.

"God, I hate this," announced George about halfway through, and left the room, presumably to set the table. The Old Admiral, though, was enthralled by J.'s performance, as though he were being channelled back into a realm of forgotten mysteries, but I realized that from where he sat he was taking advantage of the fine view he had, straight up Ms. J.'s tartan skirt. "Splendid, sing it again," he crowed, obviously stirred, when she had finished, but George summoned us to the dining room and we went to take our seats. I don't mean to sound as if I'm patting my relationship with Miss F. on the back, but we both make an effort to resist the real temptation to serve our infrequent battles as the evening's entree, since to do so would transform our dining companions into gluttons, one way or the other. Still, in the presence of thoughtful and compassionate guests, a little airing out of the laundry sometimes sets the stage for insights that could not otherwise be achieved. Such was the case when our hostess proclaimed gratuitously at the outset of the meal that she wasn't concerned about her husband having an affair, because he was exceedingly boring and passive, lacked libidinal imagination, and had been genetically denied the complexity it takes to have a secret life. Ambushed by this harangue, the guests, much more perplexed and victimized than the victim himself, became politely infatuated with their salads—except for the Old Admiral.

"A secret life, is it?" he said, stormy-voiced, delivering the fierce scowl that had been a seafaring asset in days past, when he captained a scallop trawler on the coast into bankruptcy. "Why, not a man or woman here would know a secret life if it crawled out and bit 'em, and furthermore, it's my opinion that what's wrong with this once-great country is no one has a secret life anymore, especially our delightful hostess"—here he raised his tumbler of whiskey to salute Mrs. Professor Ms. J., never one to lose her composure as she saluted back with her goblet of Barolo—"who's made no secret of her exploits of a blue nature with them savages down South."

"A curious word, this word 'savage,'" remarked our guest of honor, who withdrew into a meditative pose.

"Curious, my ass," thundered the Old Admiral.

"One of my stated goals is to develop a federally assisted grant program for savages," confided the Prez, suddenly frowning as he saw he had forked a grubworm out from among his greens. Grubs, Professor

Black quickly interjected, were common to the diet of the Inchiladee tribes of the northern Bartok range, who were the inspiration for the night's fare. These particular grubs were not top-drawer, but good enough to preempt only the most sophisticated criticism, and as I mentioned, it was a casual evening, with no place for complaints. The Heatherton-Peets were quite happy with their own grubs, and made clever earrings out of the leftovers.

One might judge that the Old Admiral, given his brusque manner and full glass of whiskey, was an intemperate soul, but nothing could be further from the truth. Indeed, he was disgusted by drunkards, ostracized them along with the very best of contemporary role models, and kept his own intake to a moderate navy pint a day, much reduced from his youth, when drinking was an upright profession. What he abhorred though was the invention of the designated driver, which the widow Terbill had seized upon, and in light of the six-pack of tall boys she customarily used to lighten her days, her own abstinence on these occasions was commendable.

"Honey, just sit back and enjoy yourself," she said, patting the Old Admiral's hoary paw. She smiled conspiratorially up and down the table. "I'm the designated driver," she stage-whispered, and patted his hand again.

"Oh, Christ Almighty!" the Old Admiral lamented. "Who here would guess this blind old bat is able to drive a bargain, let alone sit at the helm of my Chevrolet. She has chained herself to the wheel and I can't get rid of her. Why, the very first time I gave her the keys, she flew past three stop signs like a getaway moll, and when I discerned she would run a fourth, I advised against it, seeing how the crossroad was thick with traffic, but she forged ahead, paying me no mind, listing her petty concerns regarding the estate of her long-lost husband, may he rest in peace, until I judged it was prudent to slide over and wrest the wheel from her hand."

"It was my bosom he sought to control," sniffed the widow Terbill, "only that."

"Well, sir," the Old Admiral went on, "she wouldn't give up the wheel or let off the gas, and the result was we plowed into the sign, knocking it under the carriage of the vehicle and out of sight, so that she didn't believe it had ever existed, and without hesitation or thought accused me of sexual assault, being a modern woman. I can think of no worse fate for a man who values his safety and reputation, than to have a driver designated upon him when he's capable of his own affairs. *Now,* I've eaten my share of cockroaches that have fallen into the galley soup, but I'm not going to eat these damned savage worms. What's the next course? Is there nothing more to eat!"

Several more bottles of Barolo were uncorked and poured. Black excused himself, went to the kitchen and, after ten minutes of awful racket—shouting and grumbling and begging of mercy, with the good professor seeming to wrestle with spirits of a questionable nature—returned to the table with individual terra-cotta cups of pepper pot, garnished with sauteed tuber and chickens' feet. Very tasty. George raised a hen's foot and studied it as if it were a rare jewel. "When I was a boy," he said, ignoring J.'s yawn, "we used to call these 'scratches.' Mama would deep-fry them, in goober oil, I believe." Heatherton-P. sucked the gravy from hers and hooked it on one of her earlobes, alongside a grub. I noticed that Miss F. had licked the corner of her linen napkin and was trying to scrub a birthmark, which she had mistaken for sauce in the candlelight, off the cheek of the Prez.

Cookie, who so far had proceeded with sheepish caution, cleared her throat and showed us her hunger to participate in the free marketplace of ideas and discourse. "I was just wondering," she ventured innocently, "I mean, the places y'all go to, like the Third World? Most of our clients at the agency just want to go to Disney World or Paris, you know, and it's your job and all, but why do you do it?"

"I'll tell you why they do it," the Old Admiral broke in. "Because the heart of darkness has contaminated their souls. They do it to eat shit and bark at the moon. Am I right, sir?" he queried Professor Black.

The professor nodded his head thoughtfully. "I believe you're onto something deep, Admiral. We are all primitives underneath our socialized exteriors."

"Nonsense," growled the Old Admiral. "Liberal decay. Don't include me in your savage wonderland. Being stuck with the French is bad enough."

Everyone in town knew that the admiral was always ready for political argument, and if nobody started one he would do it himself. Likewise, it was the Prez's nature to mediate animosities, which he would do automatically, with or without an actual dispute. "Tell us, Professor," he said, employing the strategy of digression, "what are your natives like? Give us a glimpse of their amorous rituals. Are the maidens deflowered at a tender age?"

"Yes," encouraged J. "Tell us what the connection is between the genitals and the soul."

Professor Black shrugged. "Love is love" was all he'd say.

"What he means," interpreted the admiral, "is that even in the jungle it costs an arm and a leg." He once more inquired if he could anticipate more food, or would the widow Terbill have to swing by the all-night Hardees on the way home. The professor rose from the table, bowed, and retired to the kitchen to conclude preparation of the main course. After a moment's breathholding, Cookie said, "I'll just go see if there's anything I can help with," and followed after him, thus missing out on the Old Admiral's eloquent hour-long diatribe against the modern democratic tendency to coddle invalids, which set Miss F. off on a round of quadriplegic jokes while George maundered to himself about the love that was the prime ingredient in his mother's cuisine, and the Heatherton-Peets handrolled fat cigars out of an exotic blend and began to rock and sway in a manner that suggested religious contemplation.

By this time I was famished myself. "I'll just go see if they need an extra hand," I said. As I walked back through the house, I could hear music, faint at first but growing louder, music like waves of broken glass crashing into beehives, and the atmosphere became increasingly hazy and replete with delicious aroma. Finally, on the threshold of the kitchen, I pushed open the door and was greeted by a fragrant billow of smoke that momentarily obscured my vision. The heat of the room was oppressive, but I stepped inside and made out a wheelbarrow that had been placed in the middle of the floor and turned into a coal brazier. From the beamed ceiling, on hooks that once held Ms. J.'s Boston ferns, two chains descended to support an iron spit, on which was impaled a wonderful suckling pig, its belly stuffed with squash blossoms and litchi nuts—I soon learned—its juice dripping onto the coals with a constant crackle and hiss.

It was a marvelous sight and an unexpected one, but not so unexpected as the sight of Professor Black and Cookie, veiled by smoky mists but clearly stripped down to the basics—he in tattered Jockey shorts, she in ghost-white bra and panties—locked in sensuous embrace. Like Babette and her feast, the professor had transformed dinner into a kind of love, an affair that made no distinction between bodily and spiritual appetites. And when the rest of the tribe joined us one by one in the kitchen, wondering what in the hell could possibly be going on, we achieved that sublime, transcendent harmony that is the goal of all dinner parties; we recreated the family and captured its transient bliss—the Old Admiral shivering with joy because he loved a pig pick more than life itself—and the Christians among us could only wish that the less socially advanced, like that unlucky man Lopate and of course the French, were there to enjoy the professor's gastronomic vision of the universe, so sacred, so lip-smacking and profane.

Heatherton wore the snout home. Peet, the ears.

ROAST SUCKLING PIG

⅓ cup garlic, sliced thin

1 20-pound suckling pig, cleaned for cooking

3 sprigs fresh rosemary

3 sprigs fresh thyme

3 sprigs fresh sage (forget the sage if not fresh)

½ cup salt

¼ cup freshly ground black pepper

4 tablespoons cayenne pepper

1 cup olive oil

Preheat oven to 325 degrees. Slide the garlic slices up under the skin of the pig's legs. Mince the fresh herbs, combine with half the salt, black pepper and cayenne pepper, and coat the inside cavity of the pig with this mixture. Sprinkle the remainder of the seasonings over the pig. Tuck the front feet backward, the back feet forward, and tie in place with string, wrapping from the underside of the pig and knotting on the top-side. Tack the ears back with 2 small skewers; truss the body and neck cavities with 2 skewers and string. Place the pig on its side on a roasting rack, then set rack in a large roasting pan. Coat upper side of pig with half the olive oil and place in oven. After 30 minutes, remove pig from oven, flip it over, coat with olive oil and return to oven. Baste after 15 minutes, then flip and baste every 20 minutes for the next 2 hours. Next set pig upright on the rack and allow to roast for three more hours (total cooking time: 5 to 6 hours, or 15 minutes per pound). Remove pig from oven, take out skewers and string, set on a large platter and garnish with whatever pretty things strike your fancy. My favorite garnish is pomegranate seeds and white grapes, adding the appropriate effect of pearls before swine, which might be especially apropos if it turns out your guests can't behave themselves.

SERVES AN ARMY—10 OR MORE.

HOW GREEN WAS
MY GULLET

Years ago, before I met her, Miss F. had a romance with the vegetarian way of life. She was out to pasture, so to speak, for about three years, not including a minor flirtation with the meatless habit during high-school days, when she was briefly infatuated with a fellow named Barry. Barry, a nascent star of the counterculture, was a fruitarian. He would eat nothing but fruit with a water content of 80 percent or more. Guavas and oranges, okay. Bananas and apples, no. You would not be incorrect to associate such a regimen with toothless monkeys.

Miss F. really only fell headlong into the vegetarian mode, however, with her first true amour. His name was Cosmo. Miss F. is frank about her motivations: she abstained from meat simply because she started living with Cosmo, and Cosmo thought the carnivorous path unworthy, splashed as it was with blood from the barnyard. Fair enough. Needless to say, he considered humble beans and brown rice to be the gastronomic pillars of the moral high ground. Since Miss F. always liked veggies, her tagalong conversion was no big deal. She even read Adele Davis and took the cause to heart—spoke openly of her admiration for tubers, bulbs, leaves, and pulses; championed nutritional standards; quietly venerated cheeses; was in every way gastronomically chaste. In her kitchen, one text, *The Vegetarian Epicure*, had the force of gospel.

As it turned out, Cosmo, despite his pious rhetoric, was no less a team player than the accommodating Miss F. He had switched culinary allegiance himself because the supervisor at the store where he worked was a no-meat guy—actually, another crackpot fruitarian. One night the boss came to dinner. Miss F. served a delicate split-pea soup, which the boss narrowed his eyes at and declined to eat. Instead, he proselytized about the greater benefits, spiritual and physical, of his own melon-ball doctrine. Throughout the lecture, he stuffed his face with an entire bowl of decorative marzipan fruits that Miss F.'s mother had sent her from Belgium. Miss F. took a closer look at the role model Cosmo had attached himself to. How his skin was soured with blackheads, how his gaunt cheeks and muddy eyes resembled those of a catacomb attendant in the Middle Ages. Later, Miss F. meditated on these contradictions while studying her own increasingly wan complexion in the bathroom mirror.

Months passed and Miss F. found herself at the doctor's for a checkup. The doctor diagnosed her as severely anemic and prescribed desiccated liver pills, which contained enough iron in a daily dose to turn her into an I-beam. She left his office and made a beeline for Safeway, where she purchased two pounds of the antidote in its nonpharmaceutical form. Cosmo arrived home that evening to find her cooking it with onions. After throwing up, he tossed out the desecrated pan. Few relationships survive the low point of one partner vomiting at the sight of what the other partner eats. Miss F. moved to her parents' house in Belgium and rediscovered sirloin—rare, please. When I introduced myself to her the following year, she was apple-cheeked and shamelessly omnivorous, thank God, though not yet comfortable as a patron of oyster bars, where life on the half shell made her squeamish. Still, she told me that as a small child she had, in the spirit of gastronomic investigation, eaten earthworms. I considered this encouraging news.

As for me, I admit my salivary glands become mildly stimulated whenever I visit children's petting zoos. "Oh my, look how fat that goose is," Miss F. might say in all innocence, and I will stare at the bird like a fox. That's good food, I hear myself thinking. If I went over and wrung that goose's neck, plucked its feathers, built a fire and roasted and ate the creature, everyone would think I was a savage and parents would sue me for the emotional trauma I visited upon their kids. But if I went to the supermarket, bought a goose butchered by an invisible hand, prepared it nicely and served it up at a dinner party, everyone would say "How grand!" Well, so what if the laws of nature make Oliver North look like a sensitivity trainer, or if there's more mercy shown in a gang war than on the treacherous links of the food chain? The goose is a goner, one way or the other, and no one has to eat what he or she doesn't want to, given a choice, including George Bush. I'd trust a broccoli-loving president no more than one who exists on ham sandwiches, given that the traditionally vegetarian cultures of the world are just as violent and crazed as the flesh-eating ones.

Sometimes, licking my fingers in the hickory-smoke-filled chapels of the South, I have had the revelation that Adam and Eve bailed out of Paradise because they heard there was a terrific barbecue joint down the road. "Wouldn't this pretty apple be just the thing," Eve asked in persuading her mate, "in the mouth of a suckling pig?" And so what if, in the mythological scheme of things, you're a rabbit or a goat or a horse and I'm a vulture or a shark or a dog or a Bengal tiger? I'm not going to eat *you*, after all, am I? Unless it's by karmic accident. Let's just not find ourselves together, stranded in the Andes.

The truth is, for a flesh-, fowl-, and fish-eating brute like myself, vegetarianism is one of life's great mysteries, its practitioners as baffling to me as celibate marriage counselors. I know that no matter how hard I search for it, the soul of a chicken will always elude me. Yet beyond my inability to understand anybody's aversion to Buffalo wings or moo shu pork, I have no grudge with the vegetarian ideologies. This is not a macho-versus-sissy issue, and meat eaters need no elaborate apologia. History has seen to that.

The idea that you are what you eat is as old as humankind itself, and we have been, for the most part, as wild as our diets. Half a million years ago, there was nothing on the menu but "real food"—70 percent venison; 30 percent otter, boar, wild sheep, buffalo, rhino, or tiger. Brussels sprouts were out; devouring a nagging mother-in-law was in. Health food was anything you could digest that didn't kill you first.

Meat ruled the world until about 12,000 years ago when Neolithic women invented farming, which was their way of tricking Neolithic men into staying at home and inventing animal husbandry. We call this immobilization the birth of civilization. The agricultural revolution stabilized humanity's food supply, allowing Neolithic teenagers to invent the population explosion—3 million world inhabitants in 10,000 B.C. swelled to 100 million by 3000 B.C. You can imagine the housing shortage. Cities had to be invented and, once they were it was only a matter of time before some home boy discovered urban decadence. Of course, then it was imperative that somebody else discover moral reformation. By 1800 B.C. the distinction between right and wrong had become a growth industry. Holy men started test-driving the great modern religions, delivered from the mountaintop assembly lines with weird dietary taboos. And all this because women figured out how to cultivate grain and bake flatbread.

The Hebrews and the Hindus both divided the edible universe into clean and unclean. Animals had souls, but you could eat various species if you followed the rules. The nomadic herdsmen of the Near East and the Middle East were so offended by how ill-equipped the pig was for grazing that they became devout pork haters forever. The Greeks had Pythagoras, the Romans had Ovid, both of whom preached abstention from the flesh of beasts, but they were ridiculed for their sentimentality toward animals. Their humanity and compassion, however, echoed forward into the tenets of Christianity, when blood sacrifices evolved into the symbolic liturgical offerings of bread and wine and meat was forbidden on fast days, of which, by the sixth century, there were 200.

In the end, I suppose, the meat/no-meat controversy is a relative affair. Italians think nothing of eating a horse, nor will many traditional

Chinese turn a nose up at a dish of plump puppy, yet even veal-hungry Americans regard the consumption of a horse as barbaric. Well-bred Victorian ladies visited the slaughterhouse to chug a glass of fresh beef blood, thought to be a preventative against tuberculosis. One hundred years later, the majority of us are conscientious objectors to the ugliness of the abattoir. I'll eat a hamburger, we say, but I don't want to have any-thing to do with butchering a cow—a rejection which, to my way of thinking, is a serious breach of contract between humanity and the ani-mals that provide for us.

My final word on all of this, though, is that I am guided by a mother-ly suspicion in my feelings about vegetarians. Ellen Goodman probably won't believe it, but the mothering part of me (not a soft heart, but a strong stomach) worries that vegetarians are table-side masochists (just as they are concerned that we meat eaters are closet sadists); that they have imposed a feeble diet of fodder and rabbit chow upon themselves to atone for unnamed sins; that they are in fact suffering, at least from epi-curean monotony; that they might not survive a harsh winter; that at any minute they may collapse from undernourishment and only an immediate transfusion of chicken broth will put them back on their pale feet. To be honest, I regret the diminishment of my domestic powers when confronted by a vegetarian: I'm disappointed that I can't wave a leg of lamb in their faces and make their mouths water. Waving an egg-plant makes me feel restrained, ungenerous, guilty. "Is that all you're giv-ing me?" I expect them to howl.

We mother types aren't kidding about this. Ten years ago, my literary agent's mother offered me a $200 reward if I could get her daughter Gail to stop eating mush and start eating meat loaf. I have yet to collect on that, but since then, my agent has married a pastrami lover and given birth to an octopus-eating son. Come on, Gail, close your eyes and open your mouth and eat this one little sardine. It will make us all feel better. Mama loves you, baby.

•   •   •

My blood lust is too aflame at the moment to volunteer a meatless recipe. Vegetarians, meet me halfway. You bring the greens, I'll bring the beef, and we'll have ourselves a refreshingly carnivorous midsummer salad.

PRIX DE FRANCE STEAK SALAD

1 pound flank steak

6 tablespoons olive oil

2 tablespoons fresh lemon juice

1 pound mushrooms, sliced

4 teaspoons wine vinegar

1 clove garlic, minced

1 tablespoon fresh parsley, minced

½ teaspoon each of chervil, basil, and thyme

¼ teaspoon dry mustard

Salt and pepper to taste

1 cup red onion, sliced

1 head red leaf or romaine lettuce

2 pints cherry tomatoes

Grill or broil flank steak, allow to cool, then cut into 2-inch julienne strips. Heat 3 tablespoons oil in skillet, add lemon juice, and sauté mushrooms. Set aside to cool. In a bowl, whisk together remaining olive oil, vinegar, garlic, herbs, mustard, salt, and pepper. Add steak, mushrooms and sliced onion, toss, and let mixture marinate for an hour.

Arrange a bed of lettuce on a large platter and top with steak-mushroom-onion vinaigrette. Sprinkle with parsley. Garnish with cherry tomatoes.

SERVES 4 TO 6.

For those vegetarians who can't bring themselves to eat steak, this one's for you:

FRITTATA ALLA ANYTHING-AT-ALL

½ stick butter (4 or 5 tablespoons)

1 green pepper, coarsely chopped

3 tablespoons chopped fresh parsley

2 tablespoons minced shallots (or scallions or chives) and/or herbs

1 to 2 cups vegetables (zucchini, eggplant or potatoes), sliced or cubed and quickly steamed

6 to 8 eggs

1 cup heavy cream

4 to 6 tablespoons grated Parmesan

Salt and freshly ground pepper to taste

Brown butter in a casserole dish in a hot (450 degrees) oven. Add green pepper, parsley, shallots, and herbs (if you like) and mix well. Reduce oven heat to about 350 degrees and let mixture get partly cooked. Add cooked vegetables, mix well and let butter reach bubbling point. Stir (do not beat) eggs gently with cream, Parmesan, and salt and pepper, and pour into casserole. Turn off oven, return casserole to it, and bake the mixture slowly in the heat, taking care that it does not bubble. Draw the edges of the mixture toward the center once or twice with a fork. Serve as soon as fairly firm in center, otherwise it will be overdone by the time it reaches the table. For a more pungent frittata, use olive oil rather than butter and use additional herbs and ingredients according to personal taste—garlic, anchovies, that sort of thing.

SERVES 3 TO 4.

(ADAPTED FROM M. F. K. FISHER'S
AN ALPHABET FOR GOURMETS.)

BEHIND THE GREEN DOOR

"Don't touch me," Miss F. commands, shooing me off with a dime-store fan, as though I were a greasy bottle fly. Mercy, it's August. Her lust for the crisp and fresh and cool is not to be trifled with, and I don't fit the bill. Wishing to wrap Her Sultriness Miss F. in an embrace, I am pre-empted by the fact that I slog through these dog days with a personal body climate that reproduces the conditions found in the mouths of camels. "You remind me of the Dead Sea," says Miss F., standing aside so I wouldn't splatter her as I pass. I muddy everything with this downpour of sweat I generate. I soaked loan papers at the bank, signing on for central air. I am a natural phenomenon, my own thermal hot spring.

"Touching you in August," Miss F. explains, "is like having someone spit warm motor oil all over you while you're running a high fever." I am told to take cold showers and to generally stay away.

Hey, it's northern Florida, not to panic. Down here, in August, we're under the impression that our brains are slowly being poached inside our skulls. It's worse than Communism, so it's hard to blame Miss F. for her aloofness. "If you were a garden-fresh spinach salad," she says, lifting her hair suggestively with her fingers, "then you could just about have your way with me."

It's August, sure, and we all have to compete with the vegetable world on the field of sensual pleasure. I know what Miss F.'s talking about: the genteel and orderly gardens we cultivated in the bracing days of spring, on our hands and knees like supplicants courting the earth, have become organic engines of mass seduction. It's me out there in the dirt, pimping for her, but having my way with a second planting of snow peas, too, in August's explosive boom of ripening. The zucchini are in, God bless 'em, with an X rating: monstrous and engorged. Yo, those tomatoes! Hubba, hubba! How to react decently to the libidinal swell and fold of the bell peppers, the red ones like the tongues of harlots? Everything's coming in all at once, bulging firm flesh, leaking juice.

"What were you doing in the garden before?" Miss F. wonders, seeing what an oozy mess I am. "Oh, you know," I answer evasively. "Same old

stuff." I maintain only a thin illusion that I am engaged in an exercise of self-sufficiency. It's simply August, the season of promiscuity in the garden. I cull a peck of magnificent cucumbers and bring them to Miss F. "Wow," she says, wide-eyed, blushing, dropping her fan. "What are we going to do with all these? Get the salt and pepper, quick."

Regarding the physical rewards of the garden, I have this to say: we are a horny pair, Miss F. and I, slaves to our gastronomic hormones.

Don't presume, however, that this passion of which I speak can be graphed in a straight ascendant line through the growing season, start to end. In a way, it's a fool's campaign to sow a garden, and we gardeners earn twice over whatever nutritional gold and culinary ecstasy we reap. By August it seems I've been bent double forever, involved in fastidious foreplay with the soil so that my beauties might be voluptuous some day past the solstice. Or might not. There were times I dearly wanted to settle down with a predictable can of corn or some chaste store-bought broccoli to lead a steady and quiet life without fear of frost or storm, to make my peace with pests and renounce my prurient appetite for the virginal home-grown, untainted by the hands of strangers. Why it is, I don't know, but the real rites of spring for me are dishonest. Each March, when the dogwoods begin to blossom, Miss F. will inquire if I'm putting in a garden this year. I'll tell her I'm not, the answer is unconditionally no. I have more important things to do; my spine won't survive the journey; I haven't the heart for another season's warfare with rabbits and aphids; I'm still pissed about the horses that invaded one of my gardens back in Missouri, trampling what they didn't eat. My fingernails are still diseased from the garden I innocently attempted to plant on a toxic-waste site in Iowa. It makes more economic sense, I say, to buy from the market, since by the time I add together the cost of tools, seeds, manures, stakes, chicken wire, water and hose, Ben Gay and Off, etc., and factor in all the many hours I will labor like a coolie at, say, even half the minimum wage, each carrot I will manage to bring into the world will ring out at about twelve bucks, so I'd rather "donate" my efforts to fishing, which is a little less cost-effective, with each bluefish caught running about $34, but a hell of a lot more fun. "Nope, no garden this year," I tell her. "I've wised up. Gardens are for the deliberately unemployed; therapy for the mentally ill at ease. Better to be patriotic and leave it in the hands of Big Business."

"Fine with me," says Miss F., grinning. "You'll probably be easier to live with this summer."

"Yeah, well . . ." Always, right at this moment, is when I remember that for two decades, American agriculture has applied its genius to the development of the world's worst tomato, meeting with great success. "Maybe I'll just set out a couple of tomato plants," I say, "so we don't feel utterly impoverished at the table four months down the road."

"It's up to you," says Miss F., who has her own yard routine, refining a system for torturing flowers.

"I don't really want to," I confess, "but it's probably a good idea."

Next day, I mark off a piece of turf about the size of a welcome mat; fetch the shovel and pick, rake and hoe. I turn sod, smash clods, go buy a bag of dusty old cow shit, massage it into the soil, make mounds, go buy seedlings, since I haven't germinated my own already, as I once did, being gung ho. I plant, water, wash off, inspect my manly blisters.

Next morning, I'm outside with the teapot, watering again. It's pathetic. I can't believe my lack of ambition, my shortsightedness. Miss F. comes moseying around on the pretense of admiring my handiwork. "Hmm," she remarks casually, "no green beans this year? I suppose that's a relief." We still have jarsful of the beans we canned in Missouri in '85.

I look over at her and get the picture; she's fooling nobody. I can see it's a huge mistake, a betrayal of the South, not to have one or two measly pole-bean plants. I drive to the hardware store for a packet of Kentucky Wonder seeds. There's, like, this serpent's voice in my head. *Red-leaf lettuce*, it hisses, and I give in to it. I go home, dig two more mat-size plots, hoe circumspect parallel rows, line out the seeds and press them into the fragrant ground. But when I'm finished, the seed packets are still half full. What a shameful waste, I rightfully say. This won't do, not with folks hungry in Africa. It is incumbent upon me to prepare more ground, but the blisters on my right palm have broken, which is nature's way of letting me know it's time to rent a Rototiller. I go get a tiller, fire her up and—Jesus, this always happens!—I have some sort of weird on-my-feet-and-moving blackout, because when I run out of gas I'm shocked to discover I've inadvertently plowed the entire backyard. "I figured," Miss F. says when she arrives home and sees what I've done. "You can't restrain yourself. Cooking or gardening, you go too far."

I toe a clod and speak in my own defense. "Those watermelons and cantaloupes are greedy, you know. They want a lot of space."

"You're planting melons?" Miss F. says, surprised. She knows I resent these fruits, since I've not been able to encourage a first-class crop of them. Softball-size dwarfs instead are my destiny.

"Actually, it's the pumpkins that really grab up the room."

"Pumpkins!"

"Well, you know, Halloween and all. Pumpkin pie."

"You hate pumpkin pie," Miss F. recalls.

"True, but I sorta like Halloween."

You know the rest of this story. I've got it all out there, everything: carrots, sweet peas, snow peas, spinach, collards, cabbage, and three types of lettuce, planted at two-week intervals. Green onions and red onions, garlic, Brussels sprouts and green beans, potatoes, and what looks to be a quarter acre of white corn, eggplant and green peppers and banana peppers and jalapenos and chilies, three kinds of squash and, of course, radishes and some mutant novelty vegetables. There's also fennel this year, and Miss F.'s herbs.

I just don't know how this happened, and by May, I'm pretty fed up with it all.

Who would disagree: Gardening is a pain, however sublime, in the ass. Until around payday, that is—July and August. And this is how it is in August. There's the heat, right? And I'm a sweathog, and Miss F. won't touch me. You know all this already. But with the lawn fresh-mowed this morning, there's that sweet, sweet perfume of summertime goodness hanging in the twilight air. The humidity has retreated from Instant Death to the balmy lower reaches of Itch Rash. This late in the season the lettuce has turned tragic, so I've spent the late afternoon readying the ground to plant a second crop—tomorrow—for the fall, but tonight I've hauled the plastic-and-aluminum chaise longue out into my garden, and you can bet I'm lounging on it, in my Jockey shorts, and somewhere there's an open bottle of ice-cold beer. I've got the hose running, looped over the back of the chair so its miraculous stream bells out over my head, onto my arms and chest, cascading down on all the vegetable babies I have gathered to my bosom. Back in the pines, the lightning bugs have something going on. On one side of me, the corn towers like a muster of palace guards. Behind me there's a chicken-wire screen holding a tapestry of leaves and pendulous cukes, and to my other side, like robed attendants, are my tepees of pole beans. There's noise like primitive song coming from the darkened perimeter of the yard, that dusky hum of life that can get so amazingly loud. This is my throne room, and I know it. I'm the Honorable Mr. Too Hot to Touch, some damn northern Florida fertility god, or just Adam on a fine summer's night. I've hoarded all my treasures and am redolent with them.

The back door to the house cracks open, and Miss F. pokes her head out through a bar of light. "What are you making for dinner tonight?" she hollers.

"Dinner's in progress!" I crow back, saluting with the chewed end of a crookneck squash. There's corn pulp delicious in my mustache. "Better come get it while it's cool and fresh."

This is how I lure Miss F. come August. She moves across the ground, in a halter top and shorts, stepping barefoot down the rows to me, looking, I'd say, very Eveish. I've got to tell her this: we need field hands or next year I'm taking up a sport. Something that requires summer travel to chilly, barren venues. Spelunking.

But I've got her to come this far, this close, and who knows what might happen next. I hand her a tomato. *Paradise Lost* is okay with me.

GARDEN SALSA

5 to 6 large, ripe tomatoes
1 large red onion, chopped
2 cloves garlic, minced
2 bird peppers or 1 jalapeno, seeded and minced
½ cup chopped bell pepper
½ cup chopped cucumber
¼ cup chopped fresh cilantro
¼ cup chopped fresh parsley
1 teaspoon Worcestershire sauce
1 tablespoon red-wine vinegar
Salt

Slice tomatoes and chop into bits. Mix all ingredients in large bowl. Chill and serve with tortilla chips, or ladle over burritos, grilled fish, steak, etc. Be sure to keep refrigerated when not using. Lasts about a week before turning soggy and losing its terrific freshness.

MAKES 6 SERVINGS.

BRUSCHETTA WITH TOMATOES

12 pieces Italian bread, each sliced 1 inch thick
⅓ cup olive oil
2 cloves garlic, cut in half

2 to 3 large, ripe tomatoes, chopped

⅓ cup chopped fresh basil leaves

Salt and pepper

Toast bread for 6 minutes each side in an oven set at 400 degrees. Warm olive oil over very low heat for 3 minutes. Remove bread from oven, rub top side of each slice with garlic clove. Mix together tomatoes, basil, salt, and pepper. Spoon onto bread, drip a little warm oil over each slice and serve.

MAKES 12 SERVINGS.

SAUTÉED ZUCCHINI WITH BASIL AND PECORINO ROMANO CHEESE

This recipe comes from *Cucina Rustica*, by Viana La Place and Evan Kleiman.

2 pounds small, fresh zucchini

6 tablespoons olive oil

2 cloves garlic, minced

3 tablespoons grated Pecorino Romano cheese

Salt and pepper

¼ cup chopped fresh basil leaves

Wash zucchini, trim ends and slice ¼ inch thick. Heat olive oil in a large pan, add zucchini and toss until tender. Add garlic and cook 1 minute more. Remove pan from heat, add cheese, salt and pepper, toss and sprinkle basil over top.

SERVES 6.

GRILLED VEGETABLES

Wash vegetables (leeks, green onions, radicchio, bell peppers, red onions, artichokes, fennel, etc.), halve and quarter into 1-inch-thick sections, brush with olive oil and grill until tender. Season with salt, pepper, a dash of balsamic vinegar, and sprinkle with fresh garden herbs, or serve with lemon wedges.

TWO PARTS BITE,
ONE PART WIT

For essayist and anti-gastronome Phillip Lopate, friendship is a long conversation, which seems nearly right to me: in the ballpark though slightly free-floating and disembodied, like angels winging through pure discourse. I'd at least like to imagine those angels with bottles of beer in their hands and mustard stains on their gowns from wolfing down an occasional celestial Coney Islander. After all, Louis Malle's paean to pals was called *My Dinner with André*, not *My Long Conversation with André*. A friend is hardly a friend if you can't eat together and otherwise imbibe in spirits. In fact, I'll dare to say that what sex is to lovers, food is to friends, and any recipe for friendship ends up watery without a soup stock that nourishes the body and inspires or at least gratifies the palate, the better to release the intellect and encourage the soul. Or to be less noble and more in tune with the dynamic of my own friendships, to provide sensible interruptions between arguments: "Shut up, Bob," says Miss F., "and taste the linguini."

And so, the revised metaphor: Friendship is a long meal with plenty of gab (contentious or earnest, the flavor doesn't matter) served by a chef who takes pride in mischief, sympathy, and surprise. We refuse the right to seat bores and bastards. Also any bourgeois shithead who pretends he or she is the guardian of high culture. Finally, no innocents allowed—except as ornaments to be dashed, upon the conclusion of the evening, into the fireplace, to a chorus of *olés*. That is, unless they've paid their dues to friendship by joining in the fray, risking the barbed words or poignant disappointments that true friendship seems unable, constitutionally, to avoid. But I suppose there is a hidden grace in that. I would never speak to my enemies, either in confidence or in anger, the way I speak to my friends.

I'd rather bond with cement than with most males, who seem only to pump hormones helplessly into the air and piss on the furniture. Or else they're so sensitive even tofu makes them feel a bit uncomfortable and brutish. Still, my avatar of friendship is Captain Tay, a salty, opinionated, but tender fellow. We've been most unlikely friends for, Lord, almost two decades, which is also the difference in our ages. Food brought us together and, during the wilder, rougher, more volatile moments of our friendship, which are frequent, food keeps us together: a fresh start on a new day, a common denominator broadcasting our affection for each other when, in the course of vigorously exercising the scope of our friendship, the relationship begins to look like an unnatural pairing— dogs and cats, Israelis and Arabs, Kevin Costner and Madonna.

Captain Tay's a Texan and like every Texan I know, a softhearted son-of-a-bitch. He prefers to make his fashion statements with camouflage and tattoos, and he'll say something like "Let's turn Iraq into a parking lot" just to rile me up, even though I know he spent time in one of Batista's jails for running guns to Castro's revolutionaries in 1959. What he remembers of the experience is right in character: "The black beans and rice they gave us," he says, "were so fucking good. And the coffee. And they made this delicious bread with shortening. Man, oh man."

Captain Tay is on guard against the stupidities and cruel petty acts that darken the everyday world; he always wants to give me a gun to protect myself and Miss F. from God-knows-what horror, but what he gives me most is food and forthrightness and medicinal doses of hell, which are complementary ingredients in any friendship worth cultivating. I met him on a small island in South America, where he and his extraordinary wife, Linda, were treasure hunters, honest, and operating a primitive, two-table island-style gourmet restaurant. The Captain could render a red snapper into an elegant pleasure, and being far from civilization, without benefit of reliable electricity, I appreciated that. I think Captain Tay's first words to me were, "You're not traveling with any anchovy paste in your luggage, are you? No? What a pity."

Because the food was good, it segued into conversation. Because the conversation was good, it led to storytelling and lies, and because the stories were good and the lies were even better, we quickly established the habit of endless all-night arguments, irrigated by rum and cooled by tropic breezes. I stayed on the island for a year to argue with Tay and Linda. We mashed through everything: cooking, literature, sailing, culture and counterculture, politics, aesthetics, music, the death of Europe, the rebirth of Europe, corruption and failure and happiness. We'd argue about arguing, and when we got tired of arguing in English we'd argue in Spanish, pausing only to raid the kerosene refrigerator or to open a tin of potted corned beef. We were unfit for the rational, reasoning world, and lucky.

Unfortunately, Tay and I have in common our big mouths and a volcanic style of presenting our deliberately contrary opinions. Since we'd met, we've adventured together, sailed one or two of the seven seas, been lost together in the heart of darkness, relaxed like shipwrecked kings in the glorious balmy light of the islands, bunked together, cooked together, crawled home together and mourned together, and all of those days have been overwashed with a high flood tide of yakking—gentle and loving, sarcastic and sharp-witted or, just as readily, when it seemed inevitable, confrontational and bitter. Sometimes he'll banish me with curses, sometimes I'll leave in a huff, hurtling insults. Sometimes he'll haul out his guns and flourish them to mock my pacifism; I'll accuse him of being a lush, a ne'er-do-well, a soul brother to every deluded mercenary scraping through the bush. Then we'll settle down or pass out or simply grow weary of the sudden and inexplicable hostility of our candor.

No matter how savage the night, though, in the mornings we don't even bother being contrite anymore. Captain Tay, red-eyed, will say, with the plain goodwill that keeps the world and all friendships together, "What can I fix you to eat, honey?" and there we are again, united in fellowship against all the deaths and betrayals and disappointments that haunt a life, fortifying ourselves to carry on in the best humor we can manage. The food doesn't repair so much as remind us we've done all the preliminary work and don't have to dodge or dick around. We're friends. We have a rapport. It's not so easy to establish a rapport in these politically-correct days, except with Communists and Republicans. We're friends; whatever we do, it's not a waste of time.

More than three centuries ago, the English poet Ben Jonson, while inviting, in verse, a friend to supper, suggested that no matter how much they stuffed themselves and indulged in wine during the course of the evening, they should nevertheless part as innocently as they met—without guilt.

"No simple word" Jonson wrote, foreseeing just such a friend and dining companion as me, *"That shall be utter'd at our mirthful boord, Shall make us sad next morning: or affright The libertie, that wee'll enjoy to night."*

To all my friends whom I have made sad or inhibited the liberty of their affections or generally appalled, injured, or treated like the scoundrels they might for a moment have been, let me extend Captain Tay's invitation as if it were my own: "What can I fix you to eat, honey?"

WEST INDIAN PEPPER POT

1 4- to 5-pound boiling chicken, cut into individual pieces
1 pound oxtail, jointed
1 fresh pig's trotter or 2 fresh or smoked ham hocks
1 pound pork loin, cut into 1-inch cubes
1 pound lean beef, cut into cubes
½ pound salted beef (optional), cut into bite-sized pieces
Several cups cold water
⅔ cup cassareep (see recipe below)
1 large onion, halved and sliced
2 fresh hot chili peppers
4 cloves
1 cinnamon stick (2 to 3 inches)
1 tablespoon brown sugar
½ tablespoon dried thyme
1 tablespoon malt vinegar
Salt and pepper

Pepper pot, originally an Amerindian dish, is one of those legendary, almost mythological, stews—the gastronomic embodiment of tribe. Because cassareep is such a splendid preservative, pepper pots have a communal timelessness about them. In the folklore of Guyana, the pepper pots they ate were handed down through the centuries, from generation to generation, replenished with fresh cassareep and whatever provisions a friend happens to bring by. After a while, the taste of a good pepper pot is the taste of generosity and fellowship, a culinary testament to the collective goodwill.

Combine meat in a large kettle or pan; add cold water to cover by about an inch. Bring to a boil, skimming off the foam. Reduce heat and simmer for one hour. With a large spoon, skim as much fat from the surface as you can. Add cassareep, onion, chilies, cloves, cinnamon, brown sugar, and thyme. Simmer for 2 hours more, stirring occasionally, until meat is tender and the liquid is a thick gravy. Remove pepper, cinnamon and cloves. Stir in vinegar, and fine-tune with salt and pepper. Serve over white rice.

MAKES 6 TO 8 SERVINGS.

CASSAREEP

Cassareep, an ancient Amerindian flavoring agent, sauce thickener, and preservative, is made out of the juice extracted from raw cassava root (also called yucca or manioc).

2 medium-sized sweet cassava roots (about 4 pounds),
peeled and cut into chunks

1 cup water

By hand or in a food processor, finely grate the cassava into a bowl, add water and mix well. Strain the mixture through cheesecloth or a sieve, saving the juice and discarding the pulp. Put the liquid into a saucepan and bring to a boil, stirring constantly. Reduce heat and simmer until the cassareep is smooth and thick. Store in refrigerator until ready for use.

SEMI-TOUGH TO SWALLOW

There's some terrible, timeless dynamic at play between food and sport; specifically, between eating and spectating. You've noticed it, right, that you're no more likely to find a recipe in the sports pages than you would be to find a copy of *Paradise Lost* in Mike Tyson's carry-on luggage. It does indeed make the stomach turn to imagine the unshaved fan chirping *affaires gastronomiques* at the breakfast table: "Why, look. The editors of this bunkum sheet have seen fit to publish a truly marvelous recipe for Candied Sour Ass, right here under this week's list of drug suspensions. What say we whip it up come Super Bowl Sunday?" Uh-huh, sure. Probably the only thing this guy's going to be eating on the day of the Big Event is the money he bet on Denver.

But let's face it, sports fans, particularly football fans, eat like swine at the trough, though it's a well-known fact that the porcine palate is more discriminating. Should my pal Scott show up on a Saturday afternoon to watch the Michigan-Iowa game with the guys, and should Scott be toting a five-pound cellophane bag of petrified squirrel turds and a six-pack of the cheapest beer this side of Baltimore, it's not like anybody is going to reprimand Scott for his negligible generosity. No one's going to say, "Hey, man, we're not going to eat this shit or drink this swill." On the contrary. Before Iowa throws another interception, the shit and the swill will have vanished down our gullets. It makes for a universe in harmony when your beloved team of heroes is just as awful as the food.

As gastronomic head coach here, I'd like to start by blaming the Spartans (of Greece, not Michigan State). The Spartan motto was, "We ain't pussy," which I suppose is a good enough motto for a bunch of guys making historyproof headlines with their athletic prowess. The Spartans were also the talk of the Mediterranean for their notoriously vile cuisine, as evidenced by this anecdote from Cicero:

> Once, when the tyrant Dionysus was dining with them he remarked that he did not care for that famous black broth (made from pork stock, vinegar and salt) that was their principal dish. "No wonder you don't," said the cook, "because you haven't got the seasoning."
>
> "What's that?" asked Dionysus.
>
> "Hard hunting, sweating, a sprint down to the river Eurotas, hunger, thirst. Those are the things Spartans employ to season their banquets."
>
> Cicero thought the Spartan point of view regarding appetite was extraordinarily hip and noted approvingly that the same lesson can be learned from animals. "They are satisfied with any food you fling at them, provided their instincts don't reject it; and then they don't bother to look any further."

To my knowledge, no group of eaters in the developed nations more resembles Spartans and starving dogs than fans of the gridiron. All week the fans have hunted hard on Wall Street and Main Street. They have sweated getting taxed and getting laid. They have sprinted to the dry cleaners and the twenty-four-hour cash machine. And they have carpooled with Hunger and Thirst, those inarticulate nags who are not very good at telling us what we want, and so we are consoled on weekends and Monday nights with a hogshead of party mix and an unlimited pissy river of desperate beer. Ticket holders start in the parking lot and, like rats, chew their way into the stadium, belching and farting tailgate cuisine. For home viewers, it's a shameless buffet of mossy Doritos, unmentionable bean dip and death-row chili, guacamole in various stages of decomposition, and unearthly cheese spreads manufactured by the same chemical companies that produce joint compound. All the updated ingredients of that timeless black broth, seasoned by life as we are confused by it today.

During the Cleveland game a couple of weeks ago, I told my pal Scott the story of the tyrant and the Spartans. We were at his house, watching the contest on his wide-screen, the audio patched into his stereo speakers so the room would vibrate when the crowd roared. We were sitting on the floor, since Scott's is the austere domicile of the genuine baseball

lover/scholar, a breed of ascetics for whom furniture is superfluous. Baseball nuts are also known to cultivate hunger to sharpen their brains, so that the esoterica might flow unimpeded. But it was now football season, baseball fans were feeding again, and Scott grumbled into his bin of corn doodles as he listened to my account of Cicero's tale.

"What's that noise you're making?" I asked him. More indigestive seizures? "You're a brave and reckless man," I said, "to entrust the life of your stomach to the doodle industry."

He lifted his head from his munchings, cast a look my way, as if I had committed a grave impertinence, and motioned for me to pass him another tin can of vintage Goat Bladder Ale. I watched as he popped the tab, washing his mouth free of obstruction before he spoke.

"Indigestion is an unmanly affectation," Scott burped. "I don't understand its current popularity. As for your innuendo regarding alleged gastronomic misdemeanors of the sporting life, it is slanderous and spurious, actually a goddamned lie, likely invented by Californians and unwittingly repeated by yourself.

"First, the Spartans need a good press agent. They can be as badass at the table as they want, but they need to clean up their image. For starters, I would advise that they ditch their old motto and adopt the slogan used with great success by Yankee Stadium throughout the years: 'A dog and some brews chase away the blues.'

"What's really out of bounds, though," Scott continued, his passionate gestures raining doodle bits on the floor, "is this insinuation that we fans of the pigskin are indifferent to the nature of the comestibles we employ to insulate us against the brutal to and fro of the game. That is vicious untruth. The nature of the garbage is an essential complement to the spirit of the game. Golf enthusiasts, for instance, are inspired by the traditional downscale rations of unemployed construction workers on welfare: miniature poptop cans of beanie weenies; plastic-wrapped microwave sandwiches; eggs in brine and all manner of pickled meat products. These refreshments are absolutely deadening, which is why they find favor with those who play golf, a sport with all the attraction of slowly inhaling an odorless poison gas.

"Now, as to football, I will concede that to the sincere fan, the quality of the eats is of no importance whatsoever; taste and nutritional value even less so. What gets us fired up instead is texture; we are fucking geniuses of texture. Anything that crunches is pure manna to our souls. We are the connoisseurs of snap, crackle, and titillating pop. For the purists, walnuts in shell do nicely. For the plebs, any sort of chip, pretzel or cracker. Frozen yogurts and dips and such are really only good for smashing down on with your fist. The point is, for the football aesthete, the food must provide a visceral connection between your gut and the action on the screen. Dislocated shoulders, broken fingers, sprung knees—these are what the fans bite down into, devouring the very essence of the game. Crack open that second crate of doodles, would you? And throw another case of Goat Bladder on ice. Third quarter's about to begin."

I thought I might respond by reminding Scott that around the globe, soccer fans, seemingly with less resources and an equal amount of head bashing, are eating great stuff, but he cut me off, doing the thing refs do with their arms to signal an incomplete.

"I don't want to hear any complaints, you tyrant," he said. "If you can't bear up to the chow, there are plenty of other sports you can attach yourself to. I recommend polo, fox hunting, or horseshoes. Or tennis, if you want to regress to quiche. But if you're a football fan, and your ingesta ain't brittle as bones, I'm telling you, Jack, you're not doing justice to the game."

The clock started running again. Scott sank back into the severe concentration he lends to the sport, crunching the knuckles of his enemies between Spartanlike molars. He has hunted hard for this pleasure, but as for myself, I'm counting the days until basketball season, when the menu chez Scott teems blood-red with borscht and a ruthless Celtic stew.

Next time you invite the guys over to curse their favorite team, forget Scott and stick with Dionysus. At least accord your pals the respect that Italian futbol fans display for the sportsman's palate. Here are three panini recipes, plus offerings from New Orleans (the Saints) and New York (the Giants, not the Jets—Jets fans feed themselves on despair).

CARPACCIO BAGUETTE

1 baguette or similar type of bread

8–10 paper-thin slices beef (eye of round or tenderloin)

1 bunch arugula, stems removed, leaves cut into strips (mustard greens, turnip greens or spinach are acceptable substitutes though a bit more crude)

¼ cup Parmesan cheese

2 lemons

1 clove garlic, peeled

½ cup extra-virgin olive oil

½ cup mushrooms, raw and sliced

Rub a medium-sized bowl with the garlic. Add olive oil and juice from lemons. Whip with a fork for 2 to 3 minutes. Add salt and pepper to taste, then marinate the raw slices of beef in this mixture for at least 15 minutes. Any butcher, even in a supermarket, will be happy to slice the meat for you if you ask. With a potato peeler, shave curls of Parmesan cheese (grating the cheese won't do). Slit the bread lengthwise and layer with meat. Top with Parmesan, sliced mushrooms and shredded arugula. Sprinkle on a little of the marinade and fold bread shut. Slice into 3-inch sections and serve.

SERVES 2.

TAGLIATA BAGUETTE

Same as above, except instead of marinating the slices of beef, sauté them quickly (only a few seconds!) in olive oil, put the sandwich together as explained above, then squeeze lemon juice over the arugula.

SERVES 2.

FOCACCIA WITH PROSCIUTTO
AND MOZZARELLA

1 8-ounce focaccia (Italian flat bread)

¼ pound prosciutto, sliced thin (preferably Parma)

8 ounces mozzarella

¼ cup extra-virgin olive oil

1 sprig fresh rosemary

10-12 leaves fresh basil

1 large vine-ripened tomato (if you can't find a good tomato, forget it)

Green peppercorn mustard (optional)

Sprinkle rosemary on focaccia and bake in preheated oven at 400 degrees for 6 to 8 minutes, until golden brown. Slice bread open. Drizzle olive oil on the top half. On the bottom half, spread peppercorn mustard, layer with prosciutto, mozzarella, tomato, and basil leaves. Close up the sandwich and cut into manageable portions.

SERVES 2.

OYSTER POOR BOY

2 poor boy (submarine) rolls

8 ounces shucked oysters

½ cup flour

¼ cup olive oil

¼ cup mayonnaise

1 tablespoon black caviar

½ lemon

Louisiana hot sauce (optional)

Heat oil in skillet, dust oysters with flour and fry, adding pepper (but no salt) to taste. Slit bread rolls, mix mayo and caviar together and spread on bread. Squeeze lemon juice onto the oysters; splash on hot sauce if you want. If you want something green on this, go for something thick and slightly bitter: romaine lettuce, spinach, endive, arugula or shredded mustard greens.

SMOKED-FISH BAGEL

6 bagels

1 cup smoked fish (whitefish, lake trout, mullet, etc.)

8 ounces cream cheese

¼ cup each fresh dill, fresh chives, red onion

½ lemon

Dash of Worcestershire sauce

Mix ingredients together to form a spread, either in a food processor, a blender, or in a bowl, by whisking. Slice and toast bagels, spackle with the spread, then sprint back to the game. Your team needs you.

ADDICTED TO LUNCH

"To eat eighteen of anything," reports my friend Scott, "is very satisfying," and those of us who are never satisfied with *anything* can only
hope that this is true, if only for the rewards we can imagine for ourselves if we were ever to overcome our dread of toxins and body image
and sheer, unadulterated, unleashed normalcy, a condition that's about
as modern as clipper ships. Given the quiet authority of Scott's girth,
and the vast experiential resources he brings to the field of addictive
behavior, I would not care to dispute his claim, but I would also hesitate
to assign the guy to the troughs of gluttony, which is where I suspect
some geniuses of human nature think he belongs.

"Something about packing them in is wonderful," testifies Scott,
and, hearing his lucid tone, seeing the serene light in his eyes, measuring
that manly waistline, you know it's true. Eighteen of those little ham-
burgers sold six to a box at your more disreputable grease retailers. Or
nine cannelloni, three by three by three. Or, given the serendipity of certain street corners in Philadelphia, where Scott resides, a brace of
twelve-inch cheese steaks will satiate his being with positive thoughts
and spiritual calm, the gastrointestinal equivalent of white noise.

Perhaps some of you are thinking *swine,* unless some of you happen to be highly trained apologists wondering if you might be able to send Scott a bill for your compassionate advice, in which case you're probably thinking *eating disorder.*

Whither healthy deviance in America today? "Like, everything's bad," another friend of mine lamented. "Suddenly, every flake of neurosis has its dire pathology, every weird compulsion its fiendish implications. Suddenly, everything's an obsession and must be treated, because everything's treatable these days: shopping, jogging, sleeping, working, being nice. Sex. I know of a woman who found herself a boyfriend named Fred and proceeded to engage in those activities that lovers find most engaging, and now, at her urging, both she and Fred are receiving counseling for being sexaholics. "I don't get it," said the guy who told me this story. "I thought the point of having an affair *was* sex."

"If I would have known how trendy this addiction thing was going to be," my friend Scott admits (a bit wistfully, I might add), "I'd still be getting fucked up on the hour." Not many years ago, Scott was indeed wrapped up in a few of the more commonplace curses, so terribly fond of pot, potato chips, and cable TV that he was in danger of becoming the world's biggest barnacle. Finally, he shuttled himself off to Narcotics Anonymous, where he was given a twelve-step bone of self-control to chew on:

1. We admitted we were powerless over our addiction and that our lives had become unmanageable.
2. We came to believe that a Power greater than ourselves could restore our sanity.
3. God, etc. . . .

The trouble with Scott is, he's always been sane, which I would readily classify as the biggest obstacle he faces in today's environment. He digested two of the sessions and called it quits, on Narcotics Anonymous, on pot and booze, on getting fat and fatter but not, I was relieved to hear, on the joys of eating, no matter that his feeding pattern sometimes finds its precedent in what is primitive and wild. Gorging, binging, sort of a male version of bulimia, without forfeiting the sublime bloat for the harping insecurity of the mirror. Most of us have been there, on Scott's couch, moaning as a prelude to snoring, our gravity doubled, having shamelessly stuffed ourselves—and happy for it—to the gills.

As I mentioned before, Scott is sane, and frequently rational, and he has discipline, and though he's overweight, he's not much overweight these days, and he works out (not much but enough to make a difference), and he has some very sound principles (like never declare bankruptcy without first spending a week in Paris to mull it over), and he also has wholesome and inspiring role models. Such as Larry Bird, who during a two-and-a-half week layoff from the Celtics because of a back injury snarfed down ten gallons of ice cream and seven wedding cakes. "Why wedding cakes?" asked a journalist. "'Cause you knew they was gonna be good," said Bird. "I mean, who would screw up a weddin' cake?"

Hey, I don't see a problem here. These are normal, regular guys. If Scott wakes up in the middle of the night, he fixes himself a timid bowl of Cheerios and milk, or peels a carrot, and then paddles back to bed, comforted. It's not as if he's getting up and cramming down eighteen packages of coconut-sprinkled pink Sno Balls or seven mashed-potato-and-marshmallow sandwiches. Nor is it like the woman whom M. F. K. Fisher once saw eat seven dozen snails and seven dozen oysters at one sitting. "She turned a purplish red," wrote Fisher. "I have often wondered about her." Unless you told me that this woman got up from the table and played an hour of full-court basketball, I'd have to wonder about her too. Even so, I'm in awe of her appetite, the voracious lust she had tried so earnestly to channel into respectable activity, and would recommend only that she knock two or three dozen—snails or oysters, it's of no importance which—off the order, to avoid the unpleasant and unbecoming color change she seems to have experienced.

"I'm really sick of these people who won't eat things," said the guy who told me about the sexaholics, and I confess that that's what I'm really sick of, too. With foodaphobics, normalcy—an open-minded, tolerant, curiosity-driven and all-embracing life—is thrown on the defensive, then goes absolutely under siege when set up against the tyranny of Genuinely Fucked-up Persons in the Process of Recovery.

> GUEST: Excuse me, I'm on a diet, please don't eat in front of me.
> HOST: But this is my house.
> GUEST: You're revolting me.
> HOST: Are you sure you should be dieting? You can't weigh more than eighty-five pounds, dressed.
> GUEST (shrieking): Eighty-three, you prick!

It's surely no surprise to the French or the Italians that sex and food—one notes with a shudder the troublesome connection—might legitimately be regarded as addictions, yet whatever the Continental sensibility finds appealing about such bondage, its Yankee counterpart perceives as appalling. Which means, I think, that American culture, when we export it, should be shipped out with a warning label attached: "CAUTION: PRODUCT MAY INFLATE AND DISTORT USER'S EXPECTATIONS ABOUT HUMAN NATURE."

An image comes to mind, one that I choose to let stand for the gastronomic standard we keep, Miss F. and I, in the house that we share. Last Thanksgiving, we smoked a turkey, as we traditionally do, and it is my custom to boil down the giblets and neck, then use the broth for gravy. Miss F. came into the kitchen, spied the giblets cooling on the cutting board, sliced off a piece of the heart and popped it into her mouth, not an uncommon thing to do for a girl raised in the Shendandoah Valley.

"Good Lord," remarked one of our guests, aghast. His roots were Bostonian. "I've never seen anyone eat turkey heart before!"

The eclecticism of Miss F.'s appetite has always impressed me. It's not the only reason I adore her, but it makes the shortlist.

Sushi, you might say, is the mood ring of foods, perfectly adaptable to whatever phase of eating disorder or neurotic feeding habit you happen to be indulging at the moment. However weird your gastronomic criteria may be, sushi is flexible enough to satisfy a plaid spectrum of obsessions. Sliced sushi rolls, for instance, meet Scott's eighteen-of-anything rule. Or, anorexics can pick away at a single slice long enough to whine about how stuffed they feel. Sashimi (sliced raw fish) will placate the palate of those who crave unorthodox sensations; *kampyo* rolls (dried gourd strips) will surely pacify the bloodless appetite of animal-rights counterterrorists. Stylists will be held spellbound by sushi's color and form, and by the same token, the more infantile eater will find plenty here to play with. Losers will appreciate it as the cuisine of the folks who blew WWII; winners, as the fuel of the fellows who are dominating the global economy. Just the thing for diners who find the exotic compelling, and since sushi's been around for so long by now, as have the Japanese, just the thing for a new age oh-so-American multicultural snack. And, finally, for those of us who snap awake with a postmidnight desire for a bizarre or masochistic bite (to eat) to allay those terrible anxieties about the Democratic contender or the war on drugs or which is less safe—sex or Geraldo—that persist in fouling our sweet dreams, leftover sushi with its bits of conger eel or gizzard shad, cuttlefish tentacles or delightfully dismaying sea-urchin roe will snap you right back out of your woes and again to bed, safe and secure in the knowledge that should your nightmares return, they'll have been amply fed. Should you have one of those rare, utterly seamless and neurosis-free personalities to which sushi does not apply, I recommend a savory tonic I noticed recently on a Tokyo menu: double-boiled turtle-and-hormone soup. If you're willing to eat that, might I humbly suggest that you've been kidding yourself for too long?

Most food co-ops and Oriental-food shops sell short-grain sushi rice, packages of four-by-seven-inch *nori*-seaweed sheets, *wasabi* powder (which must be mixed with water to make a pale-green paste), and bamboo rolling mats, which you'll need to hand-roll the sushi into tubes.

LOBSTER-AND-ASPARAGUS SUSHI ROLLS

2 cups sushi rice

2 ½ cups water

½ pound fresh, young asparagus stalks

2 1-1 ½-pound lobsters

3 ½ tablespoons rice or cider vinegar

1 teaspoon sugar

1 ½ teaspoons salt

4 sheets nori seaweed

Wasabi (powdered Japanese horseradish)

Soy sauce

In a large saucepan, clean and soak rice in water for about 30 minutes, then drain, cover and cook, using fresh tap water, over medium heat. When water boils, raise heat to high for 1 minute. Turn heat to low for 5 minutes, then reduce to the lowest possible heat for 10 minutes longer. Turn off heat and let rice stand for another 10 minutes, then remove lid and let rice cool.

Trim and wash asparagus, steam lightly in a skillet, steamer or saucepan, and set aside. Steam lobsters in a large pot, remove tails, and extract cooked meat from shells. (Save claws to arrange on the sides of the serving tray.) Slice tail meat lengthwise into ½-inch strips; set aside. In a small glass mixing bowl, combine vinegar with sugar and salt. Put rice in a large, nonmetallic mixing bowl; sprinkle on vinegar mixture, stir with a wooden spoon, then cover bowl with a damp cloth.

Add water to the bowl you used to make the vinegar mixture—you'll be dipping your hands into this to prevent the rice from sticking to your fingers. Place a sheet of nori seaweed, shiny side down, on a bamboo mat. Spread rice about ¼-inch thick over nori sheet, leaving about a ½-

inch at the top and bottom of the sheet uncovered. Flatten the rice with the back of a wooden spoon (dip it in water if rice sticks to it). Place 2 asparagus stalks and line of lobster strips atop rice in center of sheet, running from the left edge to the right edge of the seaweed. Wet your finger, run it along the top edge of the seaweed (to help glue the roll together). Lift end of bamboo mat closest to you and roll seaweed tightly into a tube, as you would a cigar. Open bamboo mat, remove roll, press end tight with your fingers to pack in any loose grains. Cut roll in half, then slice each half into 3 or 4 wheels. Repeat with remaining ingredients. After you've learned to roll sushi with deftness and confidence, use whatever ingredients your sick, sick heart desires in place of the lobster and asparagus. My favorites are raw tuna and Spanish mackerel. You might prefer prawns or abalone. Or *daikon* radish and cucumbers. Or wieners and cheese, which I swear is a recipe offered in the *Quick and Easy Sushi Cook Book*. With a theme like this one, you couldn't ask for a better recipe.

To eat sushi, mix a little paste of wasabi and water with a little soy sauce and dip the sushi in it.

SERVES 4.

GROUSE, GROUSE, GROUSE

In 1989, at the end of the summer, Miss F. and I flouted common sense by moving from Florida to Italy by way of Montana.

Our beloved Tyrone had died, and we were delivering our new Irish setter pup, Issabel, to our friends' ranch, deep in the federal wilderness of the Northwest, where she would presumably prosper in dog paradise until we returned in a year from overseas. North of Libby, Montana, we turned off the state road—the power lines and the phone lines ended—and drove thirty-five rugged miles on a one-lane loggers' track toward the valley where Rick and Miss E. resided. Every mile or so, white-tailed deer pranced across the road. Miss F., having too much imagination for her own good, refused my suggestion to peer over the steep edge of the shoulderless byway to where, far below, a moose sucked on marsh weeds. Two weeks earlier, Rick had called Florida to report he had seen a grizzly bear, and now, as the wild and daunting vista unfolded, I had one bad thought on my mind: Once we dropped Issabel at the ranch, we would never see her again, because some fierce beast was bound to devour her. Maybe Rick's bear, maybe a wolf or a mountain lion. Hell, I thought, maybe the untamed folks up here in the high country themselves, since they were known for exercising their right to bear arms and for eating anything they surprised roaming the forest. Life consumed life. Period. That's where we were taking Issabel, back into an almost lost world, where truths were bald and instincts—man's included—were ancient. We crept around a blind curve, trying to avoid being obliterated by renegade logging trucks, when Miss F. squawked and threw up her hands. Two flying butterballs, sluggish and heavy as water balloons, catapulted out of the underbrush into the side of our pickup.

"Were those chickens?!" wondered Miss F., a little disbelieving.

They were grouse, and we were both reminded of the time we lived in Iowa, with kamikaze pheasants careening out of the corn stubble dead-on into our car. If you're not thinking "Lordy, free food!" you come to resent this birdbrain behavior rather quickly, this crossing of paths that were never meant to cross.

At the ranch, Rick and Miss E. displayed the laconic passion of seasoned naturalists; they wanted to know what sort of critters we'd spotted on our way in. I told them about the grouse, and Rick, his eyes brightening, glanced expectantly toward the truck.

"You stopped and got them, didn't you?"

"Naw," I said, shrugging. I had no experience thinking that way. None. In fact, once, in the islands, on the way to a party with a West Indian friend, we ran over a manicou—an opossum. My friend pulled over, put the road kill in the trunk and, at our destination, built a fire in the driveway, tossed the opossum in the flames, drank a beer while the hide carbonized to a black crust, raked it from the coals, peeled off the char and ate the fucker, licking the bones. "Have some," he encouraged me. "It's good meat, mahn."

"You're a savage," I said. "You'd eat your own mother. You'd eat a dog."

"Dog ain't so bad, ya know," he teased, laughing at my squeamishness.

Back in Montana, Rick shook his head and looked at me as if I were a bit queer. "Man," he said, "that grouse, that's good meat."

Rick and Miss E. are not shy about serendipitous windfalls of good meat. That's the way they are, no apologies. Rick's pa, a Texas oilman, made sure his son received an education in self-reliance as it is understood in the roadless out-of-doors. Miss E. was similarly well equipped for the wild side, preferring as a companion a .357 magnum handgun, a gift from her mom in Mississippi.

I, on the other hand, was born into a wussy family, nary a hunter among our tribe. Except for pond fish and Annapolis blue crabs, what didn't come from the supermarket didn't exist. Like most ten-year-old boys, I had a BB gun, which I employed in the persecution of songbirds. When one of my older brothers joined the NRA, I enlisted too, but after earning about five inches' worth of marksman's bars, nothing in the world bored me more than firing a .22 at a circle on a piece of paper. Not until my first year in college, on my roommate's family's farm in Missouri, did I seize the opportunity to assassinate something with a bullet. I picked off a squirrel in an oak tree, tore away half of a cardinal's head, then contemplated the limp dead things at my feet and said, simply, *I'm not doing this any more.* I was more relieved than remorseful, having finally fractured the mystique of death, which, after self-defense, is the true attraction of guns.

I regarded this as a fairly normal rite of passage for a teenaged boy, sort of like condemning yourself to hell for all eternity by telling lies in the confessional. I didn't quite feel I had learned a lesson: no mentor was at my side, teaching me to respect the animal kingdom by propelling lead into a select few of its subjects. What happened was more or less juvenile delinquency: I had felt the mindless compulsion, I acted on it, that was that, and I imagined I was finished with it because I had also slain whatever pathetic small blood lust was there, trying to define itself within my character. Or so I imagined. So we all imagine.

We were still in Montana when grouse season opened, as did deer season for bow hunters. Rick and I took Issabel for a romp on the mountainside; he stowed his shotgun and bow in the truck, and we set out for an area that had been logged maybe twenty years back. Issabel ran far ahead of us, carefree, rising in and out of sight like a dolphin in the waves. Then she would brake, riveted by a seriousness, a spell of concentration that was as magnificent as it was amusing. Birds! her body whispered, this most exquisite tension of muscle and nerve. The closer we came, the more her restraint faltered, and at last she would lose control, rocketing into the scrub to be dazzled by the elusive muffled rhythm of wing beats.

Rick was almost impressed. He and Miss E. owned two Mississippi hounds, as obedient and hard-nosed as marines. Issabel was sweet, stubborn and a bit goofy. How much and how often she and Rick would contradict each other in the months ahead was anybody's guess.

"Look at that," Rick marveled, watching the pup turn to stone. "You train her for the field?"

"I didn't," I said. I trained her only to be kissy-face, to bring joy to our lives, to come or stop or sit without endless shouting.

"She's a natural-born hunter."

"Seems to be," I agreed. Issabel sprang into a clump of huckleberry bushes and launched another covey of grouse. Rick fired twice, missing. The thought that I could do better never crossed my mind—there was no way in creation I could have—but I asked if I could hold the gun for a while, and that was okay with him.

Having the shotgun in hand, hefting its weight, made me magically more alert; otherwise, I felt no different, experienced no power thrill, no transformation into the great white hunter because, frankly, I had already decided I wanted to eat a grouse. After walking the forest with Issabel for two weeks, I was ready, my spirit was ready. Understand that if I could have clubbed a grouse with a stick or conked one with Rick's slingshot or strangled one (or hit one with a car), that would have been fine, too. The gun wasn't the point—the point was the decision to kill and eat. My days of moronic adolescence were long past. I had awakened into a role more threatening to the animal world: I was a cook with a lethal curiosity, intent on expanding my culinary universe, willing to sidestep the middlemen and venture to the source.

Well, why not? Eighty million buffalo had been slaughtered not for their food value but so that the American continent could be converted into wheat fields and pastureland. If there is no more authentic wilderness or wildlife left in America, it is because we've domesticated the land to grow tomatoes, corn, beans, rice; to graze cattle and sheep; to build chicken coops. Every salad we stab our fork into carries an enormous environmental pricetag—the vast herds of antelope, the wolf packs, tens of thousands of bears, not to mention the Native Americans, the forests, the aquifers, the rivers, all the lost species. What happened to the wilderness, to nature? Easy answer. We cleared it, plowed it, planted it, packaged it. And then we ate it. All of us.

Having industrialized the production of food, having regulated and sanitized the fundamentals of survival, we the people of the twentieth century have made hunting an anachronism, a nostalgic fantasy, an ultra-macho indulgence and, worse—for its hypocrisy—a cruelty. When Miss F. and I finally found our way to Rome, I was reminded, perusing Italian menus, that both high and low cuisines always welcome the gastronomic expression of wildness. Venerate it, in fact, as a luxury, one regarded identically from two opposed points of view. The aristocrat's roebuck, the peasant's hare—symbols of extravagance and crudity, yes, but also vital points of contact with nature's ever-more-circumscribed bounty. Without these points, the natural world's remaining essence becomes that-which-is-forgotten. Our most damning crime against nature is not progress but disassociation.

Over and over, the polemic looped through my mind on my walks in the Montana mountains with Issabel. I was neither royalty nor rustic, but I had resolved to eat wild game, and therefore I had soberly resolved to kill what was precious and free, as long as it was legal to do so and the animals were plentiful—a meaningless term, I know, except to fish-and-game authorities. I would not kill a moose any more than I would shoot a bald eagle, and I would never hunt what is most like us: that is, anything that kills. The killers—mountain lions, bobcats, bears, wolves, coyotes, etcetera—are taboo. They wanted what we wanted: meat, good meat. Birds I wanted: grouse, ducks, pheasants. Maybe an elk or a deer. Maybe.

We walked down the slope of the mountain, Rick and I and the dog, a perfect sky above us, as if we were descending from the sun, an appropriately hubristic conceit for hunters. Soon enough, Issabel flushed another pair of grouse. I raised the gun, held my breath, aimed, and led one of the birds in its low glide through the pines, my index finger taut against the trigger. These were the barbaric thoughts that boiled in my mind: Split the breasts, grill with applewood, smother in a Calvados sauce, garnish with Rainier cherries.

Issabel flushed three birds, four birds, five, each flight described by the barrel of my shotgun. They were such bottom-heavy fliers, I could have hit them with a rock. I could sense Rick standing a respectful distance behind me, anticipating the report. But I never pulled the trigger, never took a shot. After half an hour, I handed the shotgun back to Rick, unable to explain myself. Maybe I didn't want to miss. Maybe I didn't want to do the dirty work.

Rick's luck was better. We took two birds home to Miss E., who added two more from the refrigerator and baked them stuffed with apple slices, basted with white wine. It's impossible to tell you how delicious they were, the meat tangy from the grouse diet of larch needles, just as it's impossible to tell you why I never squeezed the trigger.

Only this: I am going to try again this fall, out in the woods with Rick, because I have feasted on grouse and deer and elk at his table, and they did not come wrapped from the supermarket.

Miss F. sends me off with rules of her own: Don't shoot the dog, and don't shoot Rick. In that order.

There's a culinary paradox we budding neo-primitives like to sharpen our teeth on around the campfire, and it is this: To serve wild meat properly requires a cook's most elegant and refined skills. Try, for instance, the following recipe for Pheasant Nelson, which I cooked last spring in Washington, the place once billed as the Evergreen State but that is now promoting itself as, get this, the Gourmet State, since the logging industry has more or less toppled the old image. You'd think Seattle was Siena these days, as measured by espresso bars. And superlative cooking.

PHEASANT NELSON

2 carrots, finely chopped

2 stalks celery, finely chopped

1 large onion, finely chopped

½ cup asparagus tips, finely chopped

2 cloves garlic, minced

¼ cup prosciutto, cut into short, thin strips

1 bay leaf, crushed

Sprig of thyme

8 tablespoons butter

4 breasts of pheasant

Salt and pepper to taste

4 tablespoons flour

6 tablespoons chicken stock

1 ¼ cups white wine

Bouquet garni

1 cup each chanterelles and artichoke hearts

1 cup cream

¼ cup Calvados

To enhance the flavor of the game, prepare a *mirepoix* by sautéeing carrots, celery, onion, asparagus tips, garlic, prosciutto, bay leaf, and thyme together in 4 tablespoons of the butter for 20 minutes or until tender. Dust each pheasant breast with salt, pepper, and 1 tablespoon of the flour. Over moderate heat, fry breasts in mirepoix until golden. Allow mirepoix to brown and even burn. Add breasts, chicken stock, white wine, and bouquet garni to a second saucepan. Cover and cook for 20 minutes over low heat. Remove pheasant and drain liquid by half. In a skillet, sauté chanterelles and artichoke hearts. In the first saucepan, remove all but 4 tablespoons of the mirepoix, then deglaze pan with cream. Add remaining 4 tablespoons butter and allow to boil for 1 minute. Add liquid from second saucepan and Calvados. Add pheasant breasts, chanterelles, and artichokes, then allow sauce to bubble for a few seconds and serve.

SERVES 4.

PART TWO

REMEMBRANCE OF
THINGS PASTA

As devout pasta worshippers, Miss F. and I anticipated, upon relocating ourselves to Italy, being awestruck by the sublime and mystical rewards of direct contact with the sacred source. I remember how fervently we intoned our prayers; in flight across the Atlantic, we chanted "Yum yum yum" (*"gnyum gnyum gnyum"* in Italian) with our heads bowed. Deliver me unto divine taste, I beseeched the Lord. Miss F., already a novitiate in the sect of *alla carbonara*, was, I thought, likely headed for sainthood in the days ahead. As for me, I would crawl to Naples on bleeding knees for its macaroni *all' arrabbiata.* I would pound my breast in ecstasy upon being seated in the most hallowed Florentine trattorias. To the god Tagliatelle would I sacrifice wild boars in Tuscany. In Venice I would weep tears of joy over the precious mystery of the cappelletti. I would prostrate myself in Sicily before the altar of Neptune, offering mussels and clams to sprinkle like rose petals into the fusilli.

And so we proceeded, like any Christian pilgrims to St. Peter's, in blind faith and with bottomless stomachs, eating our way through the Italian landscape, singing hosannas week after week, until our uncloistered innocence began to resound with the insistent and demanding tones of the fanatic. I was not at peace unless I communed with the god-head. It happened all too rarely: Once in Vicenza, served a tagliolini anointed with shredded duck's breast and fragrant crumbs of goose liver; once in the Aeolian Islands, during a very intense meditation involving rigatoni, fresh sardines, tomatoes, and capers. In Orvieto, I was blessed by a most transcendent vision of purity thanks to a single half-moon raviolo of biblical proportions, its "lily-white candor" (a Norman Douglas phrase honoring the apotheosis of pasta) bearing the scarlet stigmata of its superb beet and leek stuffing. And only once more, viscer-ally, I witnessed a halo above Miss F.'s reverent brow as she sat in a Florentine cellar and slowly consumed, strand by strand, a dish of fet-tucini inlaid with tender ivory shavings of truffles.

Alas, as sometimes happens on earnest quests of murky spiritual nature, disillusionment set in. Whereas once I made the sign of the cross to protect myself from an Italian dining companion who expressed dis-content at the fare in a popular eatery in Trastevere, now I sniffed cyni-cally at the steaming bowls placed before me. "For Christ's sake," I would curse, "these Roman devils oversalt *everything*." Or, "I find this pesto to be a severe penance."

Indeed, I was in a state of crisis, and all the signs pointed to an incipi-ent agnosticism. To atone for my dogmatic errors, I retreated to a study of pasta scripture and discovered the existence of an unpleasant sobriquet for those who behaved as I had those first gluttonous months, an appropriate eighteenth-century slur that fit me like a pair of pointy Neapolitan pimp shoes. I was, like Yankee Doodle, a "macaroni," the nickname given to the fops of grand-tour days, those punk aristocrats dispatched to Rome with their tutors to make crayon drawings of ruins and statuary, fill their heads with the stuff that ensures triumph at Trivial Pursuit, adopt something called "Italian" man-ners, which involved a great deal of clutching and arm waving, and, final-ly, to write squishy sonnets in praise of pasta. A macaroni, therefore, was the product of mixing classicism and timeless yuppie pretense, thus giving cul-ture a bad name.

The Italians themselves had never, until recently, regarded the noodle as an upscale food, and considered it especially ill-suited for conversion into iambic pentameter. As was intended by the gods on high, pasta, like Christianity before Lenin, though nevertheless a virtuous dish, was meant to serve as an opiate for the masses.

Across the early history of pasta, an apocryphal veil has been drawn. One cult canonized Marco Polo, suggesting that he returned from the Orient with his saddlebags bulging with linguine, thus "discovering" pasta, but in fact it seems the sensuous Etruscans were boiling their dough some two millennia beforehand. At the very least, the first-century cookbook writer Apicius championed lasagna before he ceremoniously killed himself, fearing he had not the resources to maintain his swank standard of living once his bank account dwindled below a solid ton of gold bullion. Centuries of furtive noodle-slurping darkness followed the decline of the Roman Empire, but by the twelfth century enough light shined through on mankind's filthy kitchens for all to realize it was time to enact some sort of quality-control legislation for pasta making. For

both the Sistine Chapel and ravioli we have the Renaissance to thank, yet until the advent of modern times, pasta was universally a coarse, rough and rustic food.

Came the nineteenth century, and the great Neapolitan pasta engineers delivered the noodle into the industrial revolution, with their fantastical machines: presses, extruders, rollers, dies, and cutters. Spaghetti factories proliferated and the iconography of semolina flour exploded—into fishes, stars, snakes, gears, crucifixes, teardrops, playing-card symbols, hats, hoses, O-rings, buttons, bows, mushrooms, scallop shells, telephones, paddles, orange slices, and wheels. By the end of the century, more than 600 shapes had been mass-produced; after the first World War, only about fifty remained, and these survive even today.

The truth is, humble pasta was never ordained to wear the purple robes of *haute cuisine* and it's perhaps the mark of infidelity to treat it otherwise. Still, pasta, like church on TV, has become Big Business and Big Noise, inviting an inevitable schism between simplicity and luxury.

Indeed, I stumbled across mounting evidence that there was a cabal of cooks loose in the land who were without scruples, beguiling those who arrived on ponies, with feathers in their caps. The previous night Miss F. and I had dined with an all-American boyish and eager type from Minneapolis. He repeatedly elbowed me at the table and giggled as he forked rigatoni, bathed in a baffling orange rind and sweet cream sauce, into his mouth, declaring his love for it because it tasted just like Fruit Loops. Several weeks earlier, I had ordered farfalla (butterflies) with octopus and crab meat at a renowned restaurant in Syracuse, only to be served the blasphemous "sea legs" in lieu of the cherished crustacean. And oh, here and there, what desecration to watch a dish of penne shoved proudly into a microwave. Heresy! As for the countless *arrabbiata* sauces I had indulged, they never ever seemed really *angry*, which is what *arrabbiata* means and how it should taste. Instead, they seemed, sadly, only slightly miffed.

This I surmised, is what happens when orthodox practice slamdances with the likes of American Express and package tours. The religion of the people had been grievously abused. Godless, reeling with guilt, I entered a phase of abstention, fasting on prosciutto and olives and rather lusty bottles of Chianti, praying for deliverance, a lost lamb, an idolater, my dreams chilled by a Fellini snowfall of novelty noodles.

But stay, Faith. The ending to this trial glows with enlightenment. It came to pass that an angel was sent unto me, bearing an invitation to dine at the apartment of an expatriate American writer whose Italian husband had recently been appointed ambassador to an Arab nation. Miss F. and I were seated at a table among members of the Italian diplomatic corps, the Italian press, and their wives. Our hostess employed a Sri Lankan cook, and we were treated to heavenly bowls of curried chicken, rice noodles garnished with green onion and cilantro, eggplant sauteed with tomatoes and fennel. The Italians helped themselves to seconds and thirds, which emboldened me, and finally I summoned the nerve to ask these robust appetites for the keys to their kingdom.

"Can you tell me the name of a good restaurant in Rome?"

A vigorous debate ensued in husky Roman dialect. Heads shook skeptically, mouths frowned. The wife of the journalist asked for clarification. "What region" (or did she say, *religion!*) "interests you? Tuscan. Venetian, Genovese, Sicilian . . . ?"

"Let's start with Roman," I said.

The debate flared up again but only momentarily. "Uh unh," she translated. "Roman food is impossible. We are glad Americans love Italy, but you are so starry-eyed, the restaurants could serve you mud, and you'd think it was marvelous." Her countrymen bounced their heads up and down in agreement. "You have this myth that you can't get a bad meal at a restaurant in Italy, and when you do, you are so crestfallen, you are so hurt, you take it so personally."

"Well, then," I pleaded, "just tell me where I can get the best bowl of pasta to be had."

The debate did not resume; there seemed to be a consensus on the point. The woman turned back to me, smiling with the serenity of Eve in her gardening days. "The answer is," she replied self-assuredly, pointing to herself and the other wives, "my house . . . or her house . . . or her house."

"The mammas!" I said, kicking myself for being such a fool. The mammas have kept the faith, the mammas are home cooking up miracles, renourishing the vital tenets of Italian food: Venerate the hearth. Gather the flock. Make it beautiful. Amen. Back in the kitchen, again I am Lazarus, reborn.

The poignant simplicity of this dish has the supernatural power to lure forth eloquence from the mouths of mute men, to make tone-deaf babes sing like Ella Fitzgerald.

FETTUCINI WITH GORGONZOLA AND BROCCOLI

2 cups broccoli flowerets

8 ounces Gorgonzola cheese

½ cup mascapone cheese

Ample fettucini noodles for four (about 3 to 4 ounces per person)

⅔ cup plain yogurt

Boil the broccoli until tender, then drain. Cut the Gorgonzola into small pieces. In a saucepan, melt the Gorgonzola and mascapone together at low heat, stirring frequently. Fill a large pot with plenty of water and bring to a rapid boil. (The more water the better, to cook pasta perfectly.) For each pound of pasta, add a tablespoon of oil and a little salt to the pot. Throw in the pasta, bring back to a boil, and cook *al dente*—the best way to test for doneness is to fish a piece from the water and bite into it. (Fresh pastas take a mere two to three minutes of boiling to reach perfection, considerably less than dried pastas.) Keep testing it every minute or so to prevent it from becoming overcooked and pasty. Meanwhile, add the broccoli and yogurt to the cheese sauce and heat for a few minutes more. Drain the pasta in a colander, shaking to remove most but not all of the water so it doesn't stick together. Pour into a warm serving dish and toss with a few spoonfuls of the sauce. Serve onto plates, ladling the remaining sauce over the individual portions.

SERVES 4.

This is Miss F.'s serve-it-to-me-every day recipe:

THE CULT OF CARBONARA

⅓ cup butter
½ cup freshly grated Parmesan cheese
2 eggs
¼ cup cream or half and half
6 slices of bacon
½ cup frozen or fresh peas
2 teaspoons chopped fresh chives
1 pound spaghetti

Soften or melt the butter, mix with the cheese. Mix in the eggs and cream. Fry bacon until crisp, drain off oil, break into small bits, add to the above mixture, and cook gently, constantly stirring, until eggs begin to thicken. Stir in slightly warmed peas and chives. Pour sauce over freshly drained spaghetti, toss, and serve immediately.

SERVES 4.

(For a variation, substitute flakes of prosciutto for the bacon, and artichoke hearts for the peas.)

THE BIG OVER EASY

I take it as an unwritten law of the universe that we Americans love breakfast, and try to excel at it. Here in Rome, our friend Ross, a devout early riser, can be found at 7 every weekday morning at the Bar Giancolo, elbowing the Italian workforce at the counter. An Italian breakfast is strictly snack culture—cappucino, cornetto, spremuta of orange or apple juice. A panino of prosciutto, for those of hoggish nature. The style is to take these standing up while being jostled, and then to beat it. Ross, being a patriot, reveres breakfast; his 7 A.M. rite at the Bar G is like a religious instinct, beyond his control, yet I know he returns to his architect's studio with his breakfast prayers only partly answered. Last month, after he took an eight-day sojourn home to New York, I asked him how the trip went. "It was great," Ross confessed exuberantly. "I ate breakfast." Not one, but three, his first afternoon in the city, and at least two a day throughout the visit, luxuriating in a marathon of eggs and hash browns, the sausages and pancakes and muffins of his favorite morningside hangouts.

I can't tell you how much I envied him, not having had a decent breakfast myself in months. It's not just Rome that's holding me back, or the *petit déjeuner* of the continent. The problem is, my own breakfast-taking mode is handicapped by a constitutional flaw.

Wherever I happen to be living, most mornings I fall out clumsily—and always, it seems, prematurely—from the democratic ranks of sleep, discharged back to my own personality, which takes more than a minute to find. I lay tangled in bed, marvelling at the perverse fragility of my condition, and wonder: am I a cruel person or a sweet one? a laborer or an idler? a misanthrope or a fun guy to have around? Like a hellish multiple-choice exam, you can never be sure that the correct answer isn't All of the Above. Miss F., who is vigorous and alert and prompt upon rising, perhaps sees me as a sluggard, hiding under the covers with my head entombed in pillows, but the messy truth is that I awake not knowing myself, let alone my desires or aspirations, as if sleep were a robber and not a restorer. In many ways, this slow morning grope for identity is the hardest work of the day. Coffee, brought bedside by Miss F., helps to shape the self-perceptions, but not always. Sometimes its message, lit up on the empty screen of consciousness, is much too simple—*Coffee is good*. Sometimes, it's the more complex revelation—*Coffee is hot and good*. The dog helps too, encouraged by Miss F. to leap on my chest and dig me out of the sheets, thus illuminating my brain with more important information—*Bob likes dogs*—and its tricky converse, *Dogs like Bob*. I suppose a shower would expedite the process of relocating my intelligence, but showers scare me in the morning. I bathe at night, before retiring, and take it on faith that I haven't gotten dirty while asleep. No, cold showers in the morning are an assault I couldn't survive, and warm showers only prolong the drowse.

Eventually, though, I find myself turning to what I hope will be the ideal remedy at such a difficult time, the teachings of the gastronomic buddha, who enlightens us to the transcendental clarity of the breakfast state of mind. Wake with images of what you wish to eat, says this buddha, and you will spring from bed a complete person—Warrior Priest, Servant of Light—arriving at the breakfast table with a profound appreciation for your place in the cosmos, seeing in every goo-goo-eyed pair of fried eggs the happy face of God, his link-sausage mouth bowed upward in a greasy smile.

Wish it were that easy. There are some mornings when I even despair of knowing my nationality, and so commit the serious un-American act of having no breakfast at all. Inevitably, whenever this happens, I think back to the Soviet bureaucrat I met one snowy morning in 1971 on the Moscow subway. His early-morning-shitty-day good cheer haunts me still. He declared to me—I forget why, probably because he was feeling lightheaded and therefore brotherly—that he began each day with a cigarette and a bottle of beer. I was impressed by the sound of masculine satisfaction in his voice. No breakfast of champions for this guy, no wimpy croissant—he fueled up for a day of irony and existentialism. No pampering moms or aproned wives need apply. When I'm wrestling with my own breakfast state of mind, I regard this fellow's leathery regimen, or the late Anwar Sadat's ascetic cup of morning tea spiced with lemon and honey, as the very mountaintop of self-knowledge.

And the absolute pit of spartan abnegation, a severe squint at a loveless world.

Failing to target what I need to lure me out of the sack and into my life, I'm reassured by the fact that breakfast itself is a culinary late-riser, not having appeared on history's menu until recently, and we gastronomes are still trying to figure it out. The ancient peoples of the Mediterranean would snatch a handful of olives and flatbread on their way out the door in the morning, or stop in at the local gruel shop for a quick mug of watery barley. Long before sunrise, the Aztecs were up and about their business, pausing only at 10 A.M. for their first meal of the day, a sustaining bowl of maize porridge. From the Renaissance until the beginning of the nineteenth century, folks grazed on cold meats and patés and cheese, eaten before dawn or earlier, and for millennia—except in the Far East, where tea was cultivated—humanity's paltry breakfasts were washed down with wine or ale, since water was often unsafe, and milk was a problematic commodity. Coffee was popularized by Muslim dervishes in the thirteenth century, who found caffeine to be a great aid to whirling, but it took another three or four centuries for the Europeans to sober up and adopt the habits of the well-brewed bean.

Breakfast as we know it today had its genesis during the French

Revolution, when mealtimes themselves underwent their own *perestroika*. Instead of two meals a day, now there was a third for entrepreneurial early birds—a meal, say historians, that evolved as a recognition of the existence of the bourgeoisie. The Golden Age of Breakfast, though, came and went in the nineteenth century. Nowadays, we gringos adore our breakfast, in spite of the fact it's often our most conservative meal of the day, as staid as flannel pajamas, and usually not worth the breath it takes to repeat its elementary recipes. But during the last century, the traditional American breakfast was a grand, and possibly indigestive, affair. Ladies and gents sat down to a spread of littleneck clams, mushroom omelettes, grilled plover, filets mignons and/or robins on toast. A typical middle-class Yankee breakfast in 1863 seems to contemporary appetites a bit daunting: the partakers thereof kept the robins on toast from the previous menu, substituted oysters for clams, preferred wild pigeon to plover, scrambled their eggs, and bolstered the selection with fresh spring shad, pigs' feet and buckets of black tea.

The English Victorians were equally gluttonous upon waking, entering into a prolonged meal of ham, galantine, omelettes, ox tongue, kedaeree (rice, flaked fish and chopped egg), roast partridge, then fruit, honey and biscuits, washed down with tea. Here was a perfect menu, not for breaking the fast of the night, but for taming the night's lingering residue of lust. I suppose, given the mix of prudish wife and virile husband, a terrific breakfast is inescapable.

Lovemaking, however, wasn't responsible for the demise of breakfast's heyday, but rather the insipid cornflake and a wave of "moral vegetarianism." Toward the end of the century, Dr. John H. Kellogg invented "hygienic comestibles"—the first peanut butter, a cereal that became known as Granola, and wheat and corn flakes—for the hypochondriacal patients who visited his health clinic. Kellogg's fast-talking brother, Will, changed the course of marketing history with these invalid foods, proving that consumers were suckers for a brand name. A Mr. Borden, a Mr. Swift, and a Mr. Armour took note, as did a Mr. Lipton in England.

Unlike Miss F. or our friend Julie, I'd stay in bed forever if all I had to look forward to was Dr. Kellogg's mushy, gushy, milky, flaky, fruity idea of a wake-up call. For three months now, Miss F. has been breakfasting on lumps of hot oatmeal, like grey primordial ooze rising from milk shallows. Whereas she experiences upliftment in her gummy spoonsful of porridge, I feel punished by this wholesome paste. Julie, on the other hand, seeks out a bowl of hot cereal because its warmth and squishy textures are an extension of the womblike comforts of her bed, which she abandons ever so reluctantly. Perhaps I too am clinging to fetal pleasures when I get going with biscuits and gravy or cream chipped beef on toast. But there are as many quirks and angles to waking as there are to breakfasting. Usually, what I don't want is to have the dreamy child in me consoled by cereals and juices. I want to be startled in the morning, even shocked; I want to be born on hard pavement; I want to be bruised by ethnicity; I want to hoard my sensual pleasures and eat them too.

Does this make sense? Of course not, but so go the idiosyncratic moods of breakfast. I'll take Lancashire's grilled blood sausages. I'll take the Caribbean's mashed sardines and saltfish cakes, Japan's pickled vegetables and seaweeds. Ditto Mexico's *huevos rancheros* or my grandmother's sunrise plates of steaming spaghetti. And—ah!—to come awake to a bagel smeared with cream cheese, layered with flabby lox, mounded with slices of red onions. Give me fruits that have no name and emanate weird fragrance. Give me something volcanic, and something arctic, and on bad, bad mornings, give me the gentleness of soft-boiled eggs and cocoa.

This is how my mind wanders and falters and tries to patch the world together in the morning hours, and still I lay shipwrecked on my mattress, undecided. It's no good to dwell on those splendid days, early in our relationship, when Miss F. had the time and inclination to serve me breakfast in bed: eggs over easy, fried plantain, a purple hemisphere of guava. Now she's out the door before I know it, and the truth is, neither of us can cope with fixing a proper breakfast except on weekends. It's then she'll sprawl late in bed herself, feeding on the morning paper, and I'll command the kitchen, fixing the Stars and Stripes of breakfast. Coffee and a bloody mary for me; orange juice and champagne for her. Eggs a hundred ways, hash browns jeweled with exotica, fresh spicy sausage, a line or two of bacon. . .

And here's the end of my morning ruminations, that 8 o'clock search for identity, that striving for the breakfast state of mind. By now it's 9 o'clock and I know who I am. I'm a guy late for work. And I know what it is I want to eat. Lunch.

DUCK HASH

3 medium size potatoes

1 cup chopped onion

4 eggs

1 teaspoon chopped rosemary

2 tablespoons olive oil

Shredded duck meat, picked off the carcass of last night's feast

This breakfast recipe, inspired by the food writer John Thorne, takes a familiar morning staple and transforms it into something just the right, lusty side of decadent. Leave the skins on the potatoes. Wash them, and dice, the smaller the better. Heat the oil in a frying pan, add the rosemary, then add the potatoes and cook until they start to turn brown and crispy. Then add the shredded duck, and the chopped onion. Stir frequently, and cook until the onions turn transparent. Lower heat, break the eggs on top of the hash, cover the pan, and cook a few minutes until the egg whites are firm, but don't let the yolks get too hard. Salt and pepper to taste.

SERVES 2.

EGGS CLARE

½ pound sea trout filet per person
2 eggs per person
2 English muffins per person
1 cup hollandaise sauce
Sprinkle of caviar
1 tablespoon olive oil

Clare is a beautiful woman in Cedar Key, Florida. Her family used to own and operate the only first-rate restaurant in town, until a hurricane of one sort or another came along. Don't ask. I would kill right now for one of Clare's breakfasts. The trick, of course, to perfect Eggs Clare is the freshness of the trout. I suggest going down to Cedar Key and catching it yourself. Dust the filets in flour, and fry lightly two or three minutes in olive oil. Remove from pan, drain on a paper towel, and put aside on a hot plate. Poach the eggs, toast the muffins, put the trout on the muffins, put the eggs on the trout, put the hollandaise on the eggs and sprinkle with caviar. Simple, eh? Why don't you do this every day. Now, take plates in hand, go on get back in bed. Someone's waiting.

I'M DREAMING OF
A BLIGHT ON
CHRISTMAS

I know it's probably wrong of me to feel this way, but when the Seussian Grinch stole Christmas, it made me very happy—and very disappointed when he gave it back. Keep it, I said, who needs it? Tie it up in a burlap bag, close your ears to its pathetic mewing and toss it into the river. It's a fourth-rate feast day anyway, lagging in liturgical importance behind Easter, Pentecost, and (my own favorite) Epiphany. Nobody even bothered to notice Christmas until the Middle Ages anyway, when it is widely assumed the European grain supplies became contaminated with hallucinogenic molds, causing the Germans to suddenly decorate and worship cute little trees, the Franciscans to go screwy gluing together scale models of the Bethlehem Maternity Ward and, strangest of all, the stuffy English to defy their fundamental nature by singing carols and exchanging gifts. It's all too weird to be explained even by the concept of God or of miracles, and I think New Englanders were entirely right to suppress the holiday well into the nineteenth century.

In fact, what is this business about Christmas being a holiday for kids? Who fucked that up? The correct holiday for giving anything besides a spanking to children is December sixth, the feast day of Saint Nicholas, to my mind a much more appropriate date for gratuitously showering tykes with toys, since they'd still be in school and too preoccupied to break them. Getting their toys on December sixth would relieve the kids of the stress of getting them on Christmas, thus freeing up the children to behave properly, as Jesus Christ himself would have wanted them to, on his birthday.

No, there's no doubt in my mind kids would prefer to get their presents on Saint Nicholas's Day, once they understood the totally awesome fact that this dude is the patron saint of children because he restored the life of three rad skateboarders after the local butcher flipped out, chopped up the three boys with a cleaver and pickled them in a barrel of salt as a warning to all skateboarders everywhere to stay off his sidewalk. And, listen, this next documented fact is very important: The above event did not take place at the North Pole; Saint Nick never had anything to do with the North Pole, he hated the place, he was a fun-in-the-sun guy and lived on the coast of Turkey (which explains why we eat what we do on Christmas). If it weren't for New Yorkers in the nineteenth century, who were too dumb to pronounce the Dutch *Sint Nikolaas* correctly, but instead could only say Santa Claus, and who changed the saint's career from savior of children to enslaver of dwarfs and reindeer, and then idiotically confused Nick's birthday with J.C.'s; if it weren't for all these deliberate New Yorker attempts to steal Christmas for Macy's, then kids wouldn't be forced to celebrate the wrong guy on the wrong day, and we'd all head for the beaches in Florida come December and liberate them from the senior citizens, who for obvious reasons were in on the original Santa Claus misinformation conspiracy. (Saint Nick, a.k.a. Santa Claus, is also the patron saint of pawnbrokers and whores, but we won't go into that.)

Now, you may well ask, why am I being so humbuggish as to explode all our dear and cherished Christmas myths and pull down the pants of our lovely traditions? The answer is because Christmas as we know it is really our own invention; we have made it what we wanted it to be: the annual target date for interpersonal crisis and domestic misery; a hideous mutant beast, with the golden head of a canary dragging a miles-long scorpion's tail of shopping days behind it. It's the holiday of airport congestion on earth, good will toward credit limits. Perhaps the greatest argument for Islam is that its adherents have absolutely no Christmastime tradition whatsoever and are in fact anti-Christmas and therefore at liberty to enjoy or ignore the month of December as they please, which is a position I increasingly envy.

I know almost for certain that Miss F. is not deeply devoted to cruelty but only maintains a casual, if not completely guileless, interest in the art. Still, what was I to think, short of suicide, when Her Brightside Miss F. recently proposed yet another year's plans for the holidays, the 1990 version of sugarplummed fantasy, hoping for the best, an admirable but foolish thing to do, rather than the worst, which we had come to learn the hard way to expect.

First, she suggested, we would motor north to her ancestral grounds, the icy mountains of Virginia, where Miss. F.'s parents had deliberately finished an addition to their colonial farmhouse and were poised to receive the entire clan, who were now under subtle obligation to show up to justify the expense of expanding the house.

Miss F. expressed what I took to be a wholly unwarranted optimism regarding the forthcoming festivity. The first Christmas I had spent with her parents, which was also the first time I had met them, they hid the booze from me, gave Miss F. and myself a room with a double bed and then disapproved of our sleeping together, and delayed retiring for the evening until I did, fearing I would toss a cigarette on the sofa and burn the house down. The second Christmas I found myself among her tribe, I was exiled to the attic with my dog, which was being abused by Miss F.'s father's dog, a situation which caused Miss F.'s daddy and myself to trade threats as we readied ourselves to be seated for Christmas Eve dinner.

Wait, I urged Miss F., let's discuss this, let's reassess our commitment to Christmas, let's figure out a strategy to close the gap between the received wisdom of the holiday—we'll have a wonderful time—and the reality of Christmas as it played out through the Eighties. After all, I reminded her, no matter how well we planned for it, no matter how hard we worked, having a nice Christmas had turned out to be one of the most difficult and dispiriting challenges of our life together.

"But it might be nice this time, it might work out all right," she said with a sigh, tempering my tone of doom with memories of all the great Christmases she had as a child, the most memorable being when her dog Tippy went up in flames, having fallen asleep too close to the log fire Santa Claus had left in the fireplace.

"It was remarkable," Miss F. reminisced fondly. "Poor Tippy didn't even smolder. One minute he was fine, the next there he was, a fireball."

"My God," I commiserated, "what did you do?"

"Well, naturally, we screamed and cried and tried to keep him away from the presents," said Miss F.

"You can't have a Christmas like that anymore," I said, sharing her nostalgia for the days of innocence. "We're going to have to rethink this thing, come up with some new traditions. This year, let's fly off to a non-Christian country instead, preferably one without children or shopping malls or Bing Crosby, just the two of us, and keep out of sight until the season passes over and it's safe to come home."

But that isn't what Miss F. had in mind at all. If one or both of us survived part one of her plan, then part two would take us to the suburbs of Washington, D.C., where we would pay a visit to my own parents, who had shrunk themselves into a one room apartment in a retirement home for military dictators. The children, however, were under no obligation to come home, not just because home had a SOLD sign in the front yard but because for the past decade we have regarded one another with all the benevolence and trust of the Arab League. The last time we even tried to negotiate trying to try to get together, the stock market dropped 300 points, and if we ever have a reunion, Don King will be the one to promote it.

Which is to say, my family, and Miss F.'s family, are very much like your own tribe of well-intentioned, good-hearted relatives, give or take a few scars. And I have to admit that, given the supporting evidence, the onus of dysfunctional Christmases might be improperly and, upon occasion, unfairly assigned to the family nuclear, since Miss F. and I have done a good job of mutilating the holiday by our own selves, left to our own devices, without interference from those we love. The first Christmas she and I spent together under the auspices of a balanced bank account, she was 100 percent sure I would give her the only thing in the world she longed for—a raku kiln—and was not what deserves to be called appreciative when I gave her a pair of skis instead, and took her to Colorado, where she expressed her disappointment by being hospitalized for "trauma from flying through the air." Then, two Christmases ago, we destroyed the holiday forever by getting ourselves snowed in under life-threatening conditions in an isolated cabin in the Uinta Mountains of Utah. We made it out alive, but our poor old dog, Tyrone, didn't—it was a Christmas we can only remember for the merciless way it went about crushing our hearts. Only avalanche victims have ever had a whiter Christmas.

Last Christmas started out all right, but then each one never fails to begin that way, so sweetly promising. We were in Rome, living at the American Academy, whose only clear institutional goal is to make life ruinous for the couples it houses. But with the advent of the Christmas season, Miss F.'s spirits perked up, from fatal depression to crazed cheerfulness, and she happily cruised the holiday stalls circling the Piazza Navonne, buying bits of Christmas candy and clever wooden toys for the bambinos of our friends, soaking up the pagan euphoria with which Latins approach the feast day of the Nativity. She festooned our cell door at the Academy with a garland of cut-out Santa Clauses, helped decorate the salon with pine boughs, made tree ornaments with pasta. With a group from the Academy, she went off to Naples and returned cheery, her pockets full of tiny glow-in-the-dark Baby Jesuses and stickpin putti and miniature creche animals that, being recklessly willing to get into the Christmas spirit, she considered made her trip worthwhile.

But of course she couldn't leave well enough alone and decided that we would host a Christmas-day dinner at a friend's house. We would invite all the singles left behind at the Academy for the holidays, and I'd cook a traditional all-American feast for them—turkey, oyster stuffing, peas and pearl onions in cream sauce, mashed potatoes, et cetera—and we'd all have a terrific time.

All I can or will say about last Christmas is, the dinner inspired in the community of the noble Academy those special holiday attributes of confusion, betrayal, rejection, and massive guilt. For even thousands of miles away from the homefront, Christmas is Christmas, and should be treated with the respect Texans like to show to rattlesnakes.

Peace on earth, good will toward men, keep your back covered, and know where the exits are at all times.

GRILLED TURKEY WITH OYSTER STUFFING

1 12-pound turkey, preferably fresh
Grand Marnier (optional)
1 clove garlic, peeled and halved
Salt and pepper to taste

Remove giblets and neck from turkey. Rub inside of cavity with Grand Marnier if desired, and stuff with oyster stuffing. Rub outside of turkey with garlic clove, salt and pepper the skin, then place turkey in a roasting pan and cover it, with a lid or tinfoil. Roast turkey for only half of the recommended cooking time—in this case, for two hours in an oven pre-heated to 325 degrees. Don't baste it, don't look at it, don't touch it for two hours. About a half hour before it's time to remove turkey from the oven, soak 3 or 4 handfuls of wood chips (mesquite, hickory or apple work well) in a pot of water, and light about 5 pounds of charcoal in your grill.

Remove turkey from oven, allow to cool about 15 minutes. Drain wood chips and put about half over hot coals in grill. Remove turkey from roasting pan and place on a square of tinfoil, about 4 to 5 sheets thick. Place on grill and cover. If your grill doesn't have a lid big enough to fit over the turkey, make a perforated tinfoil tent, properly vented, that will fit over it. Keep the coals medium hot, adding extra wood chips and coals as needed to keep a steady stream of smoke coming out of grill vents. Grill turkey for remaining cooking time—2 more hours for a 12-pound bird—or until done. Either the implanted timer will pop up or the legs of the turkey will wobble freely when you tug them. I guarantee this will be the juiciest, most flavorful turkey you'll ever eat.

SERVES 9 TO 12.

OYSTER STUFFING

½ cup olive oil or 1 stick butter

1 medium-sized onion, chopped

8 ounces mushrooms, sliced

3 or 4 scallions, sliced

½ cup celery, chopped

¼ cup parsley, chopped

2 cloves garlic, minced

1 bay leaf

¼ teaspoon thyme or sprig of fresh thyme

½ teaspoon sage

¼ teaspoon mace

*1 teaspoon each of salt and freshly ground black pepper
(or more, to taste)*

1 quart oysters and their liquor

3 loaves stale white bread

Heat oil (or melt butter) in a saucepan and sauté onion, scallions, celery, parsley, and garlic until onions are transparent. Add bay leaf, thyme, sage, mace, salt and pepper. Simmer for 20 minutes. Chop oysters coarsely, put them in a pan with their juice and cook over low flame until firm, then add to sautéed vegetables and spices. Tear the stale bread into small pieces. In a large bowl, mix bread, vegetables and oysters. Remove bay leaf and discard. Stuff turkey three quarters full.

Merry Christmas. Leave your weapons at the door.

AFTER MIDNIGHT

Christmas, the consensus goes, is for children—that is, what's left of it after God and the retailers take their cut. It's a holiday, we might agree, most delighted in by new and not-yet-dysfunctional families, thirtyish parents with toddlers fluttering about the domestic premises like *putti*, a day with a penetrating spirit, capable of reviving—in jolts and bursts and moans—that cigar-smoking, belching, unshaved, overweight, bediapered child who lies passed out on your heart's sofa, deep within your worldly self.

New Year's Eve, on the other hand, is an essentially grown-up affair, which, in these puritanical, postyuppie, pre-Geritol, politically correct days, is defined as a morally tenuous, sinfully late, but nevertheless circumspect night passed in the company of one's mature associates, irrigated by a pitiful brace of diet beers or a naughty flute of champagne, the entire phenomenon overseen not by a compassionate Lord, but by his servitors on earth: the Holy Order of the Designated Driver. So be it. Whoopee. Pass the carrot sticks.

But as I recall, it wasn't always this way, not so long ago back in the Vice Age, when freedoms and values ran amok, before we felt compelled to sanitize a night like New Year's Eve with neo-Victorian seriousness and sobriety, before we began to murder holidays and innocent appreciation, not in cold blood, but in hot campaigning, as if such special days and nights have no cumulative meaning, no style or presence of their own, but now require a contradictory juggernaut of marketing and moralizing to get them off the ground.

During the Clarence Thomas hearings, right-wing columnist Cal Thomas wrote that America "is a country drowning in sex and perversion," and cited the permissiveness of the past three decades as the source of this cultural rot. Maybe so. Still, when it comes to such facile linkage, to implying a syllogistic relationship between sex and perversion, nobody does it better in the western world than an American. A sweet tooth, the logic unfolds, leads to eventual obesity; sexual attraction spirals into the inevitable expression of lust. But there's a muddling here between erotic tension and unwholesome desires that I can't abide, and it's this Calvinist sensibility that I find apropos when I think about what New Year's Eve was and is, and could or should be.

My first quasi-adult impression of New Year's Eve has stuck with me and, through the sexual murk of the ensuing years, has remained a problematic standard of measurement—but a standard I'd rather cherish and expand upon than abandon. New Year's Eve, I thought early on in my career as a boy, was not just another occasion for collective intemperance, since those occasions, at least to a high schooler, seemed common enough. More than any of the other 364 midnights that clicked us forward into our futures, New Year's Eve struck me as a wonderfully concentrated, tightly framed and, yes, titillating countdown to potent contact—physical and emotional, evanescent, yet forever memorable—with my dreams, with my hormone-induced fantasies, with the mystique of womanhood. Specifically, with members of the opposite sex who wouldn't be caught dead in my arms any other time, under any other circumstance, celebrating any other moment less sublime than my irreversible disappearance from their sight.

At the twelfth stroke, the illusion manufactured by one unlikely embrace—Whoa, this is going to be some year, lad!—was the immediate, visceral source, the sensual headwaters, of the New Year's promise of luck. At least that's what I felt when, as a freshman attending my first unchaperoned New Year's Eve party, I had the great fortune to, number one, still be upright and on my feet at the appointed hour and, number two, to be in deliciously close proximity to the neighborhood goddess, a girl named Katie, a gorgeous sophomore who was terrifyingly endowed with breasts so astronomically sized that I had nicknamed them, in the privacy of my own mind, Katie's Colliders. They were of such unfathomable proportion that I could think only of them, then and now, as an abstraction, innately off limits, untouchable; I was fascinated by them in the same way I was fascinated by, say, sharks, or the Civil War: something to be studied and marveled over, but never approached. Like quantum physics, they were a complete body of knowledge in which my quest for understanding would be limited to only the most academic musings, seeing as how Katie was beautiful, older, and popular, and that I was busily preoccupied, helping to invent the personality type that, a decade later, would be unveiled as the Nerd.

But then, of course, the clock's hands read a magical twelve and Katie was smitten with democratic goodwill. After thrusting herself (clockwise) against boys A, B, C, and D, she found herself facing me and, bless her, she didn't falter or hesitate. Happy New Year's, she said breathlessly, whoever you are, knocking the metaphorical wind out of me with her Colliders and electrocuting me with a kiss. Up to that point, I had invested all my holiday stock in Halloween, but after winning three seconds of Katie's attention in the New Year's Eve instant-squeeze lottery, I never tricked-or-treated again.

I should point out that no sexual license was applied for or issued; nor is it untoward, I think, that an extreme and sweaty form of nostalgia might arise from such a moment, enriched by all the other suddenly amenable flesh and spirit I was able to wrap myself around, ever so briefly, transcendently, throughout the New Year's Eves of high school and college, until the great good luck I had persistently anticipated landed me in the long arms of one Miss F. at a somewhat tempestuous New Year's Eve party at a Ramada Inn in Jefferson City, Missouri—a most severe venue for fortune to finally shine down upon me. It was a particularly literal evening, I confess, since out went the old (girlfriend) and in came the new. If there's a lesson here, perhaps it is that spontaneity, however it applies to yearning and desire, is not necessarily risky business, but rather the agent of timely endings and harmonious beginnings.

Yeah, boy—the indelible thrill, the exquisite communication of a warm, spontaneous and not altogether expected embrace conveyed the true meaning of the final day of the year being relegated to the books. Yet, somewhere along the increasingly straight line of the Eighties, New Year's Eve began to grate on me. In fact, as a category of celebration, holidays began to terrify me in general. New Year's Eve, the night when our appetite for luck—in life, in love, in endless possibilities—should register at its most ravenous pitch, began to seem contrived, and nothing starves luck faster than contrivance. It was as if everybody Miss F. and I hooked up with after twilight on December 31 had planned in advance to be bores, to spend the evening clock-watching or aspiring to long-awaited bowel movements. Hosts exerted strict control over the liquor, or drank it all themselves and became ugly and fiendish. Food seemed to be catered by people most familiar with the eating habits of finches. Once-lively women, refreshingly bawdy and open-minded in the not distant past, now presented themselves as brittle dowagers. As the decade cranked on, I came to believe that traffic court held more appeal than the anesthetic atmosphere of New Year's Eve, and I was especially depressed by the evolution in the interplay between the sexes. Best I could tell, everybody had, in growing up, grown afraid of one another, afraid their actions would be misconstrued, afraid of spontaneity and alienated from all but the most token images and symbols and gestures of luck, which were entities that now seemed superfluous in the adult world, or simply synonyms for the uncontrollable—and therefore bad.

I want to state that Miss F. made absolutely no contribution to this sad neutering of New Year's Eve. To the best of my knowledge, she has never begrudged me my benevolent curiosity toward babes; in fact, she felt exactly as I did, that the holiday had become an outrageously safe affair, and when we lived in Cape Hatteras, she and her pal Miss Vickie rebelled against its fashionable staidness by each chugging a couple of bottles of champagne and drawling sweetly to each other in a foreign language—Mandarin, I think—thus reinventing a sacred tradition, a crushing New Year's Day hangover. And Miss F. has been gracious about my most intimate metaphor for luck—the allure of a lovely woman—since she herself represents its perfect embodiment.

All of this to say that both of us were fed up with the minimalist trend of New Year's Eve, had eschewed its ubiquitous parties, which had become as festive as a meeting of the Senate Ethics Committee, and had hunkered down, considering an early retirement from the anything-can-happen posture that once had made New Year's Eve joyous, so that we expected very little from the evening. It was then that we found ourselves in Sicily with another couple, Rosso the architect and the glamourpuss, Nina.

We were in the uppermost town on the slopes of Mt. Etna, before the lava fields spread like geologic plague up to the snowy cone of the volcano. As twilight fell and the streets emptied, we went in search of a restaurant. Easy enough, it might seem, but we soon discovered that the majority of them were closed. Finally, we happened upon a dimly lighted trattoria, with a lone diner hovering greedily over a table heaped with antipasti. The proprietor/chef/waiter gave us our choice of empty tables but warned us that we would have to finish eating by ten, since he would be closing then. Well, all right, we would spend the first half of the evening enjoying good food, wine, and fellowship, a bubbling stream of gentle wit, a bit of cross-flirting between couples, and call it a night. Nothing at all wrong with that.

But old habits certainly do die hard, no matter how much you've wearied of them, and, as we took our well-fed selves back out into the chill and vigor of the dark streets, I noticed that a single bar remained open across the way and begged my companions to join me for a brandy and whatever good cheer we might find inside. Once again, we were the only customers, except for a woman buying a boxed cake, and the bartender let us know that he would soon be locking up, too. The Sicilians, I figured, had a greater fear or loathing of New Year's Eve than I did. The prospects were unpromising, but I resigned myself to their messages: We would return to our weird, echoing, sanatorium-like hotel and, without further ado, go to bed.

Then into the empty bar came Fabio, a Sicilian version of Tom Cruise. He ordered a drink, something complicated to make and pinkish, which tweaked my curiosity, and so I started a conversation. When I asked Fabio about the Sicilians' apparent dread of New Year's Eve, he reported that, on the contrary, his people were absolutely devoted to the holiday, and invited us to come along with him to a small party being hosted by his aunt and uncle at their restaurant further up the mountain, for family and select friends. Well, sure, why not, okay, we said, and off we went into the night, winding our way up through the lava fields.

What we found up there, I have to say, rehabilitated my faith in New Year's Eve. First, there was the spontaneity of the invitation itself. Second, there was the restaurant, gloriously resurrected from Etna's last eruption, which had made the structure flower with flames. Third, there was the armed, uniformed cop posted on the restaurant's veranda, who, within an hour, would be letting Rosso and me fire his pistol in the direction of the dawn of 1990. Fourth, there was the earthy familiarity of the aunt and uncle, who ensured, with hugs and a flow of booze, that we were made to feel at home. Fifth, there were the wild-goose cheer and uninhibited humanity of Fabio's family and the family's close friends—about 200 of them. Sixth, there was the tradition of the red underwear. Let me explain. Throughout Italy, there are two New Year's Eve traditions that are thought to bring a person good luck throughout the coming year. The first is eating a dish of lentils and sausage at midnight, a guaranteed gastronomic charm. The second is wearing red underwear, and that particular package of luck, from my point of view, is not long in manifesting itself. In fact, by the time we joined the party, the celebrants were just approaching this stage of chivalric concern, checking each other out to see that no one had forgotten to prepare themselves for forthcoming fortune. The sights were heavenly—a flip of a skirt, a breathtaking flash of a butt mantled in red silk.

Seventh, there were all those kisses, many unforeseen, welcoming me into another new, and better, I hoped, year. Starting with Miss F., progressing to the glamourpuss Nina, then on to the uncle, the aunt, Rosso, Fabio, Maria, Lucia, Teresa, Helena, Barbara, and countless other angels whose names I never knew.

Oh lucky man!

In Sicily and throughout Italy, no one pitches out the old and rings in the new without lentils, which are regarded as a sort of gastronomic fairy dust, bringing good luck, prosperity, and—one hopes—plenty of lip-swelling kisses throughout the coming year. God only knows what might happen if you choose to double your prospects with red underwear, which must be verified by the crack Red Underwear Investigative Unit of inspectors—membership automatic at midnight, December 31.

LENTICCHIE E SALSICCE
(LENTILS AND SAUSAGE)

2 cups lentils (soaked overnight)
4 cloves garlic, minced
1 bay leaf
½ cup olive oil
6 sweet or mild Italian sausages
1 pound rapini, trimmed (optional)
¼ cup red wine
1 can plum tomatoes
Salt and fresh-ground black pepper to taste

After soaking, drain lentils and run them under cold water. Put lentils in a pot with enough water to cover them adequately, add garlic, bay leaf and a pinch of salt, then bring to a boil and simmer until tender. Add water if necessary during cooking. Drain and set aside. Discard the bay leaf and dribble two tablespoons of the olive oil over the lentils. Salt and pepper to taste.

Prick sausages with a fork and boil them in water for about 20 minutes, remove, slice lengthwise and sauté sausages in a skillet in remaining olive oil. Cut rapini into strips and boil under tender. Add lentils, red wine and rapini to the skillet. Toss and cook over medium heat until flavors blend. Correct salt and pepper seasoning, drain tomatoes and slice into skillet. Cook for 4 minutes longer, and serve on plates (not bowls)— 2 halves of sausage with lentils and greens per person.

SERVES 6.

LOST

During the days that withered after Christmas, and the ten or so that cantered ahead into 1990, D. H. Lawrence's golden, peaceful, blossomed Sicily was not the one we found, Miss F. and I. It was nevertheless a Sicily we seemed to deserve, one that suited the increasingly bleak landscape of our relationship. The south winds were indeed fresh, carrying the leathery scent of Africa, but they backwashed with the gloomy European airs of winter and sealed the island with a low grey canopy, snagging and shredding on mountain peaks, obscuring Mount Etna—that "shrouded horror," the writer had called it—and Calabria lay misted past resemblance of the sparkling jewel Lawrence had described. We were perpetually damp and chilled under our many layers of clothing, often wet from lingering drizzle, sudden but not unexpected showers, and our love—no, not the love itself, but its vital context—had been unravelling for almost a year.

We had moved to Italy in late summer and for the first time had escaped the wretchedness of our caged lives at the American Academy, a most unaccommodating institution, more like a penal colony than famed sanctuary. Now we were ostensibly on R&R, attempting to recoup, make the best of things, deaf to our own common sense which for months had been imploring us to retreat, go home, back to America, and save ourselves from the great war of snobbery and negligence in Rome that threatened to defeat us.

"I have the feeling I'm making the biggest mistake of my life," Miss F. had told me on the eve of our leavetaking from the States. I had not rushed to disagree and, once in Rome, she had sunk into a depression the likes of which I had never seen from her, this sassy, smart, and lovely woman whom I had lived with for fourteen years. And although I knew full well her blues were justified, as the days went by I could not abide her behavior, which thus made it all the worse. She had let the carrion-eaters of high culture that haunt the Academy get under her skin; in the middle of her life, she had exchanged her modest home and budding career in Florida for a stark, unheated bathroomless one-room cell in Rome, where her privileged cohabitants loudly cared less for who she was or how she had struggled to make her way in the world. All these bad seeds rooted in ground already cultivated for dissolution, and in her depression she bedded down to float in and out of stuporous, despairing sleep. I was her best friend, sure, but now also her most unforgiving enemy, relentless in my disapproval.

And now here we were trying to manage a vacation, driving fast to and fro across the Sicilian countryside, guerilla tourists, raiding the sites of classical antiquity: Syracuse, Agrigento, Selinunte, this temple, that castle, those ruins. The plan, though, wasn't working. The mystique of Sicily was not a balm on our wounds; we were not drawing closer to one another, rather just the opposite. Behind my tight-lipped grimace and our monosyllabic conversations, was a vow: never again to travel anywhere with her. Miss F., from my perspective—all this from my perspective, only half a story—devolved into a spoiler; she had no stamina, no patience (or much too much martyred, guilt-inducing patience), an irrational fear on the roads, migraines, nausea, an endemic tense weariness, an incapacity to be energized by the riches of a history that gushed and fountained from the land.

The truth was, I felt ready to murder her. For a year, fate had been delivering straight-on knocks to the life we had made with our labors. First our beloved Irish Setter, Tyrone, had died, worn out by a disastrous holiday trip we had taken to the Utah mountains. Then Miss F., preoccupied by final exams in her second year of law school, was at fault in a traffic accident and could not bear the thought that she had injured two teenage boys, however superficially. Finally, the awful, pointless punishment of the Academy, crowned by my anger at her drift toward disintegration and my bitter lack of sympathy, since I saw her weakness as an enviable luxury that I myself could not afford. When she worried out loud that I was falling out of love with her, I had no answer but terrible, deadening silence.

On January 6, we got off the road and checked into a pensione in Taormina, on the magnificent coast north of Etna, for a three-day stay before flying back to Rome. January 7 we looked upon with dread. It was the first anniversary of the death of Tyrone, and the second anniversary of the death of Bob Thompson, a best friend in Missouri.

My own dire and prophetic warning had been issued on that date a year ago: "Nothing in our lives will ever be the same after this," I had told Miss F., both of us strangled by grief the breezy sun-swept day we buried Tyrone in a Florida pasture. Winding the clock of our days with the intimacy of dog-ritual, Tyrone had been with us since the embryonic stage of our relationship, a relationship without institutional sanction or family blessings, a relationship stubbornly asserting that love required no certification from church or state, as if it were a franchise to be licensed out. As the years went by, we passed into the *de facto* legality of common law without fanfare. We usurped the language of tradition, calling each other husband and wife, friend and mate and lover as we saw fit. Romantic, pagan, idealistic, and preposterous and yet it worked while all around us the formal marriages of our friends and relatives dissolved and reformed and dissolved once more. We were the sole inventors of ourselves, love's autodidacts, and we had endured.

Nothing could shake us out of the tree, we thought, and yet death of course did. Tyrone, so sweet a presence, had been our alter ego: the purest, simplest, and most viscerally consistent reflection of our joy in togetherness. We, a childless couple, were not and had never been two—always three. A week after laying him in his grave, I read in the newspaper that few couples survive the loss of a young child and separate within a year. And I thought to myself, This statistic applies . . . and goddamn anyone who laughs it off. By the time we set foot in Sicily, I had lost my tolerance for human shortcoming, lost my sense of humor, lost my ability to be tender, and believed my heart had disappeared, beyond my influence to recall it, under the earth. In this season of loss, I assumed the next thing I'd probably lose was my wife. I felt as if I had swallowed poison.

On the morning of January 7, I woke before dawn. We had avoided any discussion of the day's significance. Both of us were overripe and ready to burst with bereavement, sentimentality, maudlin gestures, a good cry. And yet the feverish, woeful bond induced by such emotions would be suspect, might prove sickening, unbearably transient, fraudulent. My job for the day was to drive south to Catania, return our rental car, catch the train back to the Taormina station and hike back up the mountain to town in time for lunch.

I dressed quickly in the darkness, fished a photograph of Tyrone out of my briefcase and placed it out on the desk, an impromptu shrine. Miss F. awoke and through a voice that forecast tears asked for a kiss. I bent over and gave it and left, unable to look into her swollen eyes, unwilling to be sucked down by the sorrow.

I remember the drive south for its short fabulous bursts of sunniness, the light skating across my fragile veneer of melancholy that hid a depthless, primitive mourning. I longed for the return of grief, the only perfect bridge across the darkness, for it allowed nothing to fade, nothing to be forgotten. On the train back north, I felt myself weakening. I read Lawrence's *Sea and Sardinia*, and on its end-page I scribbled, admonishing myself not to weep in Sicilian train stations. *Molte sentimentale*, I wrote. And then, *Tyrone, our heart, how I hate the mornings, without you there*. The howl of emptiness.

I remembered suddenly and with surprise, as if learning of it for the first time, that across the length of the island, in its cold cathedrals one after another, Miss F. had made offerings to the dog star, Sirius, the brightest star in the sky, having me tug 100 lira coins from my pocket so she could light candles in the cavernous darkness, light honoring light. It struck me that in committing these strange but comforting acts, she was somehow preserving her most clear-headed and centered self; the image of her hand extended to light a wick, the flame leaping, now filled me with extraordinary sadness.

By the time I arrived back at the hotel, a lethargic rain had begun to fall. We put on our oilskins and walked up the street to a cafe. Reading my guidebook, I determined we were on the Lawrencean side of town, and that without too much effort we should be able to follow the road up and around through the village and find Fontana Vecchia, the old farmhouse where Lawrence and his wife Frieda had lived for two years, and where he had written *Aaron's Rod* and *The Lost Girl*. The appropriateness of such a pilgrimage seemed inescapable. Lawrence and Frieda had been a notoriously volatile yet loyal couple. He is said to have pitched a plate of fried potatoes at her in Fontana Vecchia. They had been known to conk each other on the head with frying pans. Perhaps Miss F. and I would be doing that ourselves before too long.

We finished our espressos and set off, but soon found ourselves confused by the labyrinth of streets and lost our way. Here we were again, standing on an unnamed street corner in a foreign land, arguing about whether to turn left or right or just give up altogether. We argued and we argued like assassins, precise and wicked, increasingly infuriated by mutual impotence, then she lurched ahead and I followed a half-step behind, seething as she made an obvious wrong turn down an alley twisting through a channel of silent, dour rowhouses and that, within the minute, dead-ended. We stopped, boxed in.

"Oh my God," Miss F. said, and we both gasped, goose bumps rising and, as I remember it, we involuntarily cheered.

Sitting in front of us from between two stone stoops, there was the red god she had summoned throughout our journey: a handsome male Irish Setter, studying us with an entirely familiar aloofness, the same reserve our own dog had preferred to show strangers. Although we were delighted to have seen the breed everywhere in Rome, we had not spotted a one in Sicily, and now here he stood, wondrous, and nothing on the street could compete with his color or radiance, Sirius shining bright, miraculous but not a miracle unless miracles are those moments of grace restored. And perhaps they are, for such moments have enormous power to check the momentum of despair, and this one sustained us, the way a trickle of rainwater will sustain a man trapped within a collapsed building, keeping him alive until the rescuers come.

We wanted to pet the dog—he permitted a perfunctory stroke from each of us, but that was it. On the hill above us, Lawrence had written, "How the dog-star Sirius looks at one, looks at one!" and so he did, with great ennobling dignity, before he trotted off, following his own inscrutable agenda. It didn't upset us to see him go, such an uncompromising message from the fates that had beleaguered us. We ascended the hill and found Lawrence and Frieda's house and relished the view across the Straits of Messina. It would be eight more long and brutal months before my anger subsided and I recoiled from the abyss.

"It will circle back," I said to Miss F., walking back to our room.

"What will?" she said, mystified. "The dog?"

I didn't quite know what I meant myself. "Yes," I answered. "The dog."

SOUP THERAPY

"O poor immortal comforts: Fish,
some bread and wine."

—Nikos Kazantzakis

February, and we are prisoners of woe.

At dinner some evenings ago, at a restaurant on the misty Via Benedetta in Trastevere, in Rome, we talked with visiting friends about the food of comfort and reconciliation. One must talk about such food, when you're sentenced to rain-haunted Rome for the winter; cloistered for the crime of writing books, alongside the innocent Miss Sniffley F. in a drab and damp one-room cell at the American Academy in Rome, command post for the ongoing Grand Tour, and the last institution I know of in the modern democratic world that takes the royal point of view regarding what might most successfully inspire and enrich the creative effort. Money? No. Pampering? Heavens no. Comfort? Nope. Discomfort? Ah. Suffering? *Ecco!*

It's beyond me, how this myth has managed to survive, here at the Academy, but persist it does and we were embalmed within it, Miss F. and I, victims of the gilded punishment called the Prix de Rome: freezing, aching, congested, claustrophobic, shuffling in our robes across icy tiles to the communal bathrooms, squinting in the dimly lit interiors. Eating Italian chaingang food at long tables, seated with the 30-odd scholars and artists who share, some complacently, some more gracefully, this backhanded reward. The low-budget meals are cooked by a mamma whose mamma instincts are in full flower in our parsimonious colony. With what little she has to work with, she struggles to comfort us with her pastas and frittatas; she slips me extra servings of lentils to reconcile me with the gods of this bleak kingdom who declaim: "Silence, insect, you're in Rome, ancient capital of gluttons, conquerors, and role-model martyrs. Thou shalt not bite the hand that barely feeds thee."

So, we escaped for the evening to Da Checcho e Carrettiere, an excellent and warm-hearted establishment where we would be daily nourished if either I or Her Flushedness Miss F. had been wise enough to be born with trust funds waiting. Our friend Susan, having just heard a tale in which I am cast as both angel and scoundrel, commiserated with the weak Miss F., half-recovered from a rampage of Post-Classical flu. "When I'm sick," said Susan, cutting her eyes at her husband Tom, "you bring me what I want."

Hear the threatening tone just right: Susan wasn't making a statement, she was issuing law. It seems that when she was last convalescing, Tom had confused her sickbed request for lemon ice and had brought strawberry. Or vice versa. Susan had never forgotten this cruel denial. Now she was rubbing it in, delivering a commandment from the domestic bible, one that a cook and husband, friend and lover must heed. No ifs, ands, or buts.

Myself, I heed slowly, but well, once I find the rhythm. As for the infirm, I would as soon lock them in a closet, which is where I take myself when sick, to lie in isolation and darkness, off the path of the world like an injured dog, until my strength returns. This is not the feminine style, and it is surely not Miss F.'s, when she feels punk. When Miss F. fails to rise in the morning, I am unhappy—because she is suffering with a temperature or migraine, yes; but also because I don't want to fool around with her. A sick, tormented Miss F. must be carefully nursed and nurtured.

In our former pre-Rome life as adults, when the Florida sun dawned and the dog stirred, Her Merriness Miss F. would spring up, of good will toward most men, to open the house and make coffee. A half hour later, there would come a huge, shaking sound of combustion as she fired up her old Volvo P1800 in the garage. Hearing her rumble down the street toward law school, I would then arise, a free man in an empty house, breakfast, walk the dog, then anchor in my study to write. If, however, for my alarm clock, there were no untuned engine sounds, but instead restless moans and painful sighs from the wifely side of the mattress, then it was I who popped full speed out of bed, selfish and annoyed, and hurried to the refuge of my writing room. Always, not much later, there would be this faraway groan of appeal: *Honey?* the syllables drawn out into a keening.

I would ignore her until, again, sadder and more helpless than ever, the plea: *Honey?* projected feebly, but not so feeble it couldn't penetrate two closed doors. To myself I would say, There's nothing you can do, let her be, she needs rest, she'll soon fall back asleep, or her condition will deteriorate, and then you can send her away in an ambulance and get some peace.

Hon-ey? Now her voice would be broken and pathetic, and I must shout back. "Could you hold it down, my love? I'm trying to concentrate."

Then, whimpering, and finally, this: defeated peeps, as if from a lost soul in purgatory: *Bob-bee*. There's a tacit agreement between us that Miss F. will never call me Bobby unless she uses her last breath to do it, so I must get up from my desk and go sternly to her side, size her up with the scrutiny of a coroner, see if she's dead, and if she isn't, then I have no recourse but to comfort the poor girl.

It is our mothers who train us how to be sick, and Miss F.'s had a southern mother's largess for the bedridden. First, a terrycloth towel—pulled fresh from the line, transmitting the sunny fragrance of health, and rough with cleanliness—would be spread across Miss F.'s pillow.

Every hour or so she would wake to her mother's cool hand on her forehead and have the sensual pleasure of a new towel replacing the old. She
would be irrigated with unlimited ginger ale, and when Miss F. felt a tad
better, her mother would bring her to lie on the living room couch and
swaddle her in a fresh sheet and quilt. Then, when Miss F. felt able,
would come the grand comfort: milk toast, to settle her stomach. Two
pieces of bread toasted and thickly buttered, set in a shallow bowl and
swamped with an inch of hot milk. The joy! The butter would melt
and swirl a child's crayola sunshine, the bread would sop up the milk,
and Miss F. would eat it, like a Dickens foundling, with a big silver
spoon gripped in her tiny fist. Oh, how Miss F. rhapsodizes about the
milk toast of the fevers of her girlhood.

I must say, malady-wise, those were Miss F.'s halcyon days. Under my care,
she has had to adapt to an entirely different concept of help. But you just
try feeding her milk toast today, or even a buffered aspirin, when she is indis-
posed; her, with a stomach more delicate than a Lebanese truce! In the wretched
bloom of affliction, she's all to and fro in the sheets, as if trying to shake off
an invisible bird of prey that's sunk its talons into her
skull, tearing her eyeballs out piecemeal with its beak
while the bells of Notre Dame clang in her ears.
Ailing, Miss F. is quite more than a handful.
It crosses your mind to simply shoot her
and let her be done with the agony.
Did her mother have to
deal with this? At these
times, it's not ginger ale,
but unlimited hot com-
presses she needs,
and all the brotherly
patience I can
muster.

To my credit,
I eventually
come around to

attending her with the love and tenderness she deserves—not that I'm convinced of the good I do, since food is the medicine I best understand. Like the former gastronome-in-residence at *The New Yorker*, A. J. Liebling, who once sent his convalescing friend and mentor, Yves Mirande, a pound of fresh caviar from Kaspia, it is the kind of medication I approve of. Liebling could comfort himself only with a feast, nothing less, plus a few Burgundies and Bordeaux, frosted with a bottle of Champagne, but he recognized the "reassuring tastes of infancy"— orange juice, tomato juice, chicken broth—that encourage the recovery of body and spirit (even more so when mixed with vodka).

Wringing a scalded washcloth and holding it to Miss F.'s forehead, I am aware that I would feel more useful if I were in the kitchen, where the healing arts were born. For wooziness, weariness, pit in the stomach, disorientation, wistfulness and vague tensions, I would prescribe softly scrambled eggs or the teas and cookies, breads and jams of a chilly twilight afternoon. For general malaise, cold in the bone, uneasiness of joint, slack blood or sadness, Miss F. is to be coddled with pastas bathed in rich cream sauces, baked potatoes broken open and glazed with butter, or a roasted acorn squash, or anything heavy and earthy to insulate her against these metaphysic inclemencies. But for flesh sweaty and burning, for the stormy onslaught of the stomach and hammering pain, nothing can be done, kitchenside, but the preparation of a hopeful soup for when the crisis has passed. Let it simmer and pump its brothy essence into the air hour after hour, let it humidify the house with its soothing promise of health. And then, when the patient is ready, prop her with pillows and move a wooden chair to her bedside, then fetch her a brimming bowl on a tray—perhaps with a camellia or a rose, or something bright, and a linen napkin (which you should tuck into the collar of her gown or nightshirt)—and sit in the chair by her head and feed your Miss F. Feed her and praise her for surviving such awfulness, and restore her vitality and bring back her colors, so she can maybe kiss again and soon, and life can proceed, as it was meant to, with her on the other side of town, a-lawyering, and you at your desk, tap tap tapping into the day.

•   •   •

Back at the Academy, unhoused, our lives held for ransom by the wicked Professor of Fundraising, we persevere, Miss Homeless F. and I, for the time being. But when the first autumnal cold front swept the Roman hills with vile winds, assaulting our immunological systems, it looked as though we were done for inside these walls without warmth. It was then that I commandeered the communal kitchen and mounted a soup campaign of resistance, and have remained vigilant ever since. The following recipe for chicken pasta soup had the power to moderate Miss F.'s urge to fling herself out our cell window, down to the courtyard below, to end her tribulations. Think of what greater wonders it might manifest for you, safe in civilian life.

MISS F.'S PRISONER OF WOE SOUP

½ chicken (1 ½–2 pounds a breast quarter and leg quarter)
1 pound sweet Italian sausage, cubed (optional)
1 large yellow onion
4–6 plum tomatoes, skinless (fresh or canned)
2 cups sliced mushrooms
2 cloves garlic, minced
1 sprig fresh rosemary
2 leaves fresh sage
1 bay leaf
Salt and pepper to taste
Water (no exact amount)
½ box pasta (elbow macaroni, or quill-shaped penne)

The day before serving: In a soup pot, cover the chicken and sausage with water, add minced garlic and bay leaf, and bring to boil. Turn heat to low and simmer for six hours. Allow to cool overnight, skim congealed fat, drain the broth, debone the chicken and tear into pieces, put broth and meat back into the pot on medium heat. Add onion, tomatoes, mushrooms, rosemary, sage, salt and pepper, and cook for two hours more. Add more water as needed, but not so much as to diminish the savoriness of the broth. Ten minutes before serving, cook the pasta, drain, put individual servings in bowls, and ladle the soup over it.

SERVES 4 TO 6.

Ross Anderson, the neo-primitive New York architect, thought he might enhance his perspective on the world last September by separating with his business partner, marrying a gorgeous girl (Miss N.), then two weeks later leaving work and wife behind for six months in Rome, chambered at the Academy. He may speak for himself about being the pride and joy of the Academy's president, but I can tell you, life without his bride made the boy blue, and when he announced that he was dying of sperm poisoning, I didn't know quite what to do, since I had sworn to his wife that whenever I saw him talking to a pretty woman, I would yell out, *How's your wife, Miss N., Rosso?* Finally, to get him through a particularly desperate night, I made him a soup, and made him hold the hot bowl in his lap, and meditate on the gaping clams and mussels within, before he ate it.

LIFE WITHOUT NINA SOUP
(ZUPPA DI MARE)

2 pounds mussels in their shells

2 pounds little neck or manila clams

1 pound squid

1 ½ pounds medium shrimp, heads on if possible

3 cloves garlic, pressed or minced

1 cup celery, diced

1 cup carrots, diced

2 cups red onion, diced

1 cup parsley, diced

2 cups mushrooms, sliced (porcini, if possible)

1 talespoon vinegar

1 cup red wine

Splash of olive oil
8–10 plum tomatoes, skinned (fresh or canned)
1 small red chili pepper, diced
1 tablespoon oregano
1 sprig fresh rosemary
1 teaspoon powdered ginger
1 whole lemon, sliced thinly
Salt and pepper to taste
Water

The day before: In a soup pot, sauté garlic, celery, carrots, onion, and parsley in olive oil. Wash and clean squid, slice into rings, add to the sautéed vegetables in pot, with water, vinegar and wine, bring to a boil, and simmer for an hour.

The next day: Wash mussels and clams, put in pot with squid and vegetables, add water, bring to boil, add tomatoes, mushrooms, red chili peppers, and spices. Simmer for two to three hours. Wash shrimp, but leave in shell, with the heads on. Ten minutes before serving, add shrimp, cook until pink. Immediately before serving, layer surface of broth with lemon slices.

SERVES 6 TO 8.

THE SANDS OF
THYME

The hurricane-force winds that have ripped Western Europe
five times in the last six weeks, killing almost 200 people
and costing upward of $11 billion dollars in damages, marked
the return of a weather phenomenon that has not often been seen
in the last two decades. Storms . . . battered Britain and the
Continent with winds surpassing 100 miles per hour.

—THE INTERNATIONAL HERALD TRIBUNE, MARCH 6, 1990

February 22, Rome. "Just believe in me," I said to Miss F., with all appropriate emphasis, for February, in the lives of sun worshippers, is the month of desperately consummated beach fantasies. When I must coax faith from her, she understands, obviously better than I do, that the limits of her endurance are about to be well tested.

I had proposed that we arrive in a notoriously severe foreign land and, without benefit of plates, utensils, grill, or fuel, proceed to create a romantic, elegantly composed meal, which we would consume on an uncivilized strand, under a canopy of unrelenting springtime. A barbarian seaside feast in "unconquered Sardinia," as D. H. Lawrence described the second-largest island in the Mediterranean. *Banditti*, wolves, and wild boars still haunt spectacular ranges of its volcanic peaks. There are wild horses on the austere plateaus. (The Italians filmed their spaghetti Westerns here.) Hawks and eagles own the air. It seemed to me like a place Miss F. and I could unwind in after a winter of genteel academic oppression in Rome, but she was regarding me with disheartening ambivalence—in her eyes, I was pushing my luck.

"You would think," I said, "that considering my culinary vigor in the out-of-doors, and considering the countless times you have gorged yourself like Catherine of Aragon around my humble fires, exposed to the fairest ocean airs, the sweetest panoramas and most provocative horizons underneath the heavens, you would think that an encore in the land of the Sardinians might be something you could say you were looking forward to."

"I might say that," said Miss F., warily watching me slip a garlic bulb into my shaving kit, "if you weren't so goddamned resolute about your cookouts. Now that it's in your head to do it, you're going to do it, no matter what, even if it means you have to defy nature."

She unkindly reminded me of the very last time we had dined on the beach, an entire crew of us in the summer past at Cape Hatteras. It was a squally twilight and I was forced to bunker under the lowered tailgate of our pickup, tending the brazier and its sad coals as the rain poured down.

"And what about the time," she continued, "when Hendrie and his kids visited us on the Outer Banks? The wind blew a steady thirty knots all day. The paint was sandblasted off the Subaru. We couldn't hear ourselves talk over the roar. The crabs took forever to steam. We huddled like a defeated army, gobbling our food so we could hurry away home. The kids wouldn't eat seafood and a gust of wind blew Arden's corn on the cob right out of his hands. He was so miserable, he walked into the dunes to cry. We all ate our recommended daily allotment of sand for the next ten thousand years. It was an awful, awful evening."

For better or worse, I was not inclined to be discouraged by these fractures in Miss F.'s confidence: she had supped well at my hands, lounging voluptuously, humming with contentment, on the beaches of the new world. Nor am I readily daunted by the variability of the weather, though I do in fact harbor a deep appreciation for its relevancy. I would take what the gods bestowed, and behave accordingly.

"*You?*" snorted Miss F. "Ha! Never."

February 24, Sardinia. Bright sun, balmy temperature. Disheveled as refugees from a night on the ferry, we picked up our rental car, began a ninety-mile jaunt down the infamously rugged eastern coast. The guide-book warned that it wasn't always easy to find your way to the sea by car—"erratic signposting." Within an hour, we were lost in the middle of an uninhabited nowhere, setting the tone for the week ahead. The coast was inaccessible without a parachute. Miss F.'s fear of heights was stirred by our slow weaving through the surrealistic peaks and gorges of the Sopramonte, the vertical vistas just off the road, thousands of feet down to tortured valleys spotted with Byzantine churches, decayed castles, and vineyards centered with odd cones of stone built by Bronze Age people. Past noon, we found a seaside village, embedded like an amber jewel in the harsh coast. A wearying search for an open shop. Finally, bread, Sardi cheese, and potent Cannonau wine for lunch on the water. I entered my gathering mode and bought a tiny box of plastic forks, a roll of extra-wide heavy-duty aluminum foil, a jar of capers, two tomatoes and a glowing head of *finocchio* (fennel). A worn-out Miss F. worried that I might indeed have energy left for a cookout when we arrived that evening.

February 25–26. Our itinerary shifted us back up into the untamed mountains to witness bizarre pre-Lenten village festivals, with origins unknown but ancient, as overtly pagan as animal sacrifices. Were served an equally weird meal: sliced pig's head marinated in sweet vinegar, a round steak of jackass and, most incredible to me, a raw artichoke. Miss F. happy with her discovery of *culingionis*: Sardinian ravioli resembling pierogi. Weather: perfectly lovely.

February 27. A morning's drive up the southwestern coast, head-ed for Oristano's medievalish carnival celebrations. Breeze fresh, sky a bit overcast; seas began to show a scattered lace of whitecaps. A weak cold front seemed to be passing through. Beaches perfect but we are compelled to move on. I assured Miss F. that the slight moodiness of the weather would play itself out by the morrow. That night, we lis-tened to the wind ripping the zinc sheeting off the roofs of the build-ings behind our hotel.

February 28. The western coast: The twentieth century is only a dim rumor here, according to our guidebook. Miss F. displayed a bit of anxiety about this as the gusts battered our Peugeot back and forth across the road north. We stopped at a wind-ravaged beach. Miss F. refused to leave the car. "Don't worry," I told her. "It'll blow itself out by dark." To keep my spirits up, I stopped at a market when we left and bought an onion and a lemon.

March 1. The Costa Paradiso. The tomatoes were ripening. I scoured the city of Alghero for an open fish market, but the boats had not put out to sea in three days. Headed north to round the tip of the island for the coves of the leeward side. Miss F. overly concerned that I will "make" her eat on the beach today. Unnecessarily sought a guarantee that I was on "her side." Found an open *pescheria* and liberated a pound of shrimp and two plump calamari, expecting fortuitous conditions in the afternoon. Incredibly, wind velocity increased throughout the day; Miss F. and I were obliged to slip on long johns. Much debris whizzing through the air. At Castelsardo we admit we are weatherbeaten and check into a hotel. The proprietor agrees to store my provisions in his refrigerator.

March 2. Our last day in Sardinia, awoke once more to the hellish, wolfpack howl of the wind. Tempest unabated, but by midday sunlight speared through the clouds and I felt we would soon be in a position to outmaneuver the worst of it. I spied an open *pescheria* and hit the brakes. Miss F. gave me a wild-eyed look. "For God's sake," she begged, "expel these thoughts from your mind." "Just want to run in here and see what they have," I said, hoping for some fresh red mullet. The fishmonger ranted about the *male vento*—the bad wind. I bought a kilo of wonderful razorback clams, found a *panificio* and bought bread. Saw a butcher shop and was inspired to buy a rope of fresh Sard sausage, just the thing for grilling up for a midnight snack on the ferry. Miss F. decided she had nothing more to say to me, but braced herself for a wretched afternoon of outdoor fun.

Some hours later, I finally managed to plant her behind the windbreak of an elephantine boulder. Though she had to wear a heavy jacket, she could stretch unmolested in a sudden wealth of sunshine and gaze out into the turbulent channel of the Maddelena archipelago and the island of Corsica, with mountains crowned by the brightest blue air. "Are you hungry, sweetheart?" I asked gently. Hurricane-force winds wear you down in five seconds—the poor girl had grown so weak the past few days. I was pleased to hear she was starving.

"Feeling relaxed now?" I asked, cueing her for words of appreciation. She told me to uncork the wine, a bottle of the dry white for which Alghero is famous; she had a long slug of it. I trudged off to collect driftwood, scattering a herd of cows on the beach. Back at the base of the boulder, I scooped a hole in the sand and concentrated on the architecture of campfires. Miss F. sucked the bottle of wine, sighed, meditated on her millionaire's view, found it satisfactory and lay back in the sand, taking a P. D. James novel from her pocket. The wind still cast little puffs and squirts into our hideaway, but we were doing okay, doing all right. I reached for the roll of foil. Aluminum foil is the secret to cooking a full-course meal on the beach. Prepare whatever

you want, however you want it—fish, seafood, pasta, sauces, vegetables, ragouts—double-wrap it in foil, loosely to prevent scorching (except corn on the cob and baked potatoes, which should be wrapped tightly), and toss it on the coals. I made up four packets, four little bombs of gastronomic pleasure: sliced fennel and tomatoes; shrimp, seasoned with fresh rosemary and doused with *bianco di Alghero*; razorback clams with chopped garlic, minced onions, and lemon juice; calamari stuffed with chopped olives, red sweet peppers and capers, painted with tomato sauce and olive oil.

I lit the fire, tended it reverently. The wind teased, flexed, slapped flames at me, singeing the hair off my forearms. Nothing to worry about . . . why worry? "Is the wind shifting?" wondered Miss F. "It is, isn't it?" I spread the packets across the coals. Miss F. roused herself, impaled a piece of sausage on a stick and began to roast it. The foil packets must be rolled every few minutes so the food inside cooks evenly. I flipped them over and learned a valuable lesson about beach cookouts in Italy— Italian aluminum foil ignites. Disappears. I snatched the bundles from the fire, swaddled them in more foil until they were as big as soccer balls. Miss F.'s stick caught on fire and snapped, dropping her sausage into the sand like a dog turd.

Finesse and brinksmanship are the *sine qua non* of cookouts: don't dare leave home to conquer Sardinia without them. Somehow, everything worked out, and a half hour later we were sprawled in the sand, well-fed and immensely relieved.

"Not bad, eh?" I ventured.

"Not bad," Miss F. conceded. "You outdid yourself with the calamari, but don't gloat."

The fire crackled, making magic. The ghost of our Irish setter, Tyrone, romped along the water's edge, bringing us a melancholic glimpse of all the happiness we had shared, on all the beaches of our life together. Then a rogue cuff of wind showered us with a confetti of dried seaweed. The sun disappeared behind a lengthening train of clouds.

No gloating from me. We packed up and got the hell away.

CALAMARI ALLA SARDINIA

2 pounds calamari (squid)

1 cup chopped black olives

1 cup chopped onion

1 sweet red pepper, cut into strips

2 tablespoons capers

¼ cup olive oil

1 ½ cups tomato sauce (your own, preferably, but since you're roughing it, you can get away with the bottled stuff)

Salt and pepper

2 sheets heavy-duty aluminum foil

Clean calamari: Take a knife and remove the head. Remove viscera from body. Turn body inside out, wash thoroughly, flip back and stuff with onions, olives, red pepper, and capers. Plug the cavity with the leftover tentacles. Place calamari in center of the double sheets of foil. Turn up edges of the foil to make a bowl. Pour olive oil and tomato sauce over calamari. Seal edges of foil together, making an airtight, spillproof packet. Place directly on coals, or on the grill of your barbecue. Cook for twelve minutes, turning frequently. Empty bundle onto a dish and slice calamari into rings.

SERVES 4.

GRILLED OYSTERS

4 dozen fresh unshelled oysters
½ stick butter
1 cup tomato catsup
1 tablespoon horseradish
Dash of Tabasco sauce

Nothing could be simpler. Cook oysters (or clams or mussels) on a grill until their shells gape open. Melt butter in a metal cup or small pot—even in a homemade foil boat. In another cup, make a cocktail sauce with catsup, horseradish and Tabasco. Dip oysters into whichever sauce you prefer. Lie back and complain about your sunburn. Get yourself another ice-cold one from the cooler. Ask yourself why you don't do this more often. Remember always, hurricanes are not your fault.

BURNT OFFERINGS

The restaurant is called La Estancia—The Ranch—and there are many like it in this city, in a country where campfires are a national obsession. Join the Argentines on their evening *paseando* down Lavalle, one of the glitzy pedestrian thoroughfares in downtown Buenos Aires, and eventually you'll come upon a most unusual gastronomic tableau, crackling with incongruity in the cosmopolitan night. A beautiful bouquet of flames, a roaring campfire. Behind glass, but a campfire nevertheless. The fire is centered on the tiled floor in the front of the restaurant, in a dirt and ash pit, stoked with fat round plugs of logs you couldn't reasonably ask a 12-year-old to lift. The flames rise chest high, spurting higher; it's a fine campfire, one of the world's simple wonders.

Encircling the flames are the sizzling carcasses of perhaps a dozen sheep, each crucified on an *asador*, a cross-shaped iron spit, staked vertically and leaned toward the heat, the legs of the animals splayed outward, mounted like grisly butterflies, succulent pennants of roasting flesh, golden and greasy. It's not so much the idea of food that intrigues as the idea of the campfire itself, I suppose you could call it a gimmick, a tourist attraction, but the *porteños* think of it otherwise, and so do I.

A *parrilla*—an Argentine grill—is an entirely ubiquitous and portable affair, as common in the barrios as it is in Amsterdam. But that's not what this is: this is an *asado*, a camp-style outdoor barbecue brought indoors, as if on a dare. Not country come to town, but city escaped to the countryside, a nostalgic gastronomic journey meant to evoke the lasting vitality of the Argentine romance with the pampas, *el campo*, life in the camp, camaraderie and freedom, love of the earth, an endless horizon. The aesthetic of survival, out here at the bottom of a hemisphere.

I had come to Buenos Aires for the first time from a friend's ranch, Estancia La Susana, in the province of Santa Fe, a place as midwestern to my eye as Iowa or Nebraska. We had ridden through unending pastures and paddocks, the two of us mounted on handsome but lazy horses, inspecting my friend's herd of Aberdeen cattle. The day before, the gauchos had fixed us an *asado*: a martyred sheep, *chorizo*, long strips of spare ribs, blocks of beef tenderloin. They had spread the meat on a raised grill that looked like a metal bedframe, then rigged a sheet of tin over it as a roof, so that they could cook the *asado* slowly and tenderly from above and below. The ranch manager built a campfire off to the side and, when the flames had retreated, shoveled coals beneath the grill and atop the tin, so that the heat came from two directions and radiated through the meat, leaving it juicy and delicate, fragrant with woodsmoke, not carcinogenically seared but not rare either. That is how they like their meat in the Argentine, unseasoned except by salt and smoke.

The day was cold and cloudy, a wintry summer in the southern latitudes, with a storm threatening to blow in from Patagonia. I appreciated the fire and its virtues, its warmth, its antecedents that echoed forth from the timelessness of Argentine history, the common denominator it seemed to present among us gathered round: the gringo, the Anglo-Argentine *patrino*, the Yugoslav overseer, the two gauchos, one young and cheerful, the other old and dark and a bit gloomy, each wearing a crushed-felt hat and wide silvered belt, a *facone*—wedge-shaped knife—tucked into their waistbands at the small of their backs.

We began with the *chorizos*. We ate as much as we could—almost everything, washed down with plenty of good local red wine. Argentines eat meat and little else: some fried potatoes, a small salad. Sometimes their intestines block up. Stomach cancer is a problem. Vegetarians are regarded as a screwball cult, like anarchists.

I had crammed myself to the top of my gunnels, so full that the heaviness stayed with me throughout the following day and made horseback riding all the more uncomfortable, though no less exhilarating. By the time I arrived in Buenos Aires, I had begun to fantasize about pasta. In Argentina for only five days, I had already consumed my yearly quota of livestock, even indulging in offal—sweetbreads and kidneys (but resisting udder and intestines). Nevertheless, walking down Lavalle, I stepped inside La Estancia, seduced by the campfire. Not to eat, mind you, though it was in fact dinnertime. I wanted only a pungent whiff of woodsmoke. I wanted to feel the warming of the flames on my face, I wanted the olfactory trigger that would propel the dream into my senses—a horse and rider cantering sweatily down the fenceline, the bulls scattering, the breeze autumn-sweet, the Andes barely visible off over the horizon. The magically real, latent in a campfire. All these smells and tastes of a heritage for those citizens of Buenos Aires who come through the door of La Estancia. It's like a visit home after a period of exile, which is the best way I know to describe the power of a campfire.

We hardly need Iron John or the Boy Scouts to tell us campfires connect us with what is primal and universal in our lives. Fires lure people this way; they are agents of artificial bonhomie, inspirers of metaphysical drift. They ask that we eat and sing; they want us to interpret life. They make love more fierce, solipsism more impenetrable; they make strangers risk revelation. They are soothsayers, fires are, and crystal bails reflecting a past that will always be mysterious. I suspect any fool bored around a campfire would find Pavoratti equally tedious.

It's August. By now Miss F. has slain the dragon of the bar exam, and we are off in the Northwest, the San Juan Islands, camping out, huddled by ourselves away from the world, to celebrate Miss F.'s release back into it. For a year there's been no time for play, but there's nothing better for us than to be out in the mountains or on the shore, setting up camp. We're addicts; we love to camp, love the perfect luminescent bijou of our domed two-man tent, our milk crate of gear (fire-blackened pots, Coleman lamp, tin plates); sigh with pleasure from the calming smell of our sleeping bag. It's not a covenant with adventure as much as it is the simplicity of the process, trading the civilized quotidian for an intimate immersion into nature.

The last time we went camping, though, it was with an underlying need for redemption. We had just returned from Rome and were living in Spokane, where I was teaching; our relationship creaky, fractured, in disrepair. We drove down through the wheat fields and crossed over into Idaho, into the mountains, and followed a treacherous dirt road up along the gorge of the Salmon River, finally locating an isolated campsite where the bank bulged into the river above a section of foamy, crashing rapids. The River of No Return, or something like that. We were fatigued, moody, cautious in what we said to each other, since whatever we said seemed to provoke defiance and led to an argument or tense silence. It had begun to rain. In a ring of stones, I started a pathetic fire and grilled a wiry chicken we had bought before turning off the paved road into the wilderness. Dinner was somber, perfunctory: Miss F. drank her wine, I found a friend in vodka. We crawled into the tent—her side, my side—and slept, a wet dog—Issabel—at our feet.

The following day was sunnier and promising, worth a measure of optimism, and we headed upriver, hoping to find a sandbar where I could fish, Miss F. could tan herself, and the dog could romp unhindered. The river was swift and cold, wild. Miss F. unfolded a camp chair, removed her shirt, and read. I cast far out into the river, into the slick above the rapids, praying for a miracle. Within an hour I had embarrassed myself with seven rainbow trout; they were fingerlings, barely longer than my index finger, to be exact, and unsuitable for dinner. When I hooked another, I reeled in only far enough to see what a minnow it was. By this time I was frustrated, losing patience. I called Miss F. to hold the pole while I rigged up better tackle for the conditions.

"It's tugging," said Miss F. a minute later. "What should I do?"

"Ridiculous," I muttered, and told her to reel it in and let it go or wait until I found the lure I was rummaging for.

"The rod's bending in half," said Miss F. drily. "It's really putting up a fight."

"Oh, baloney. Just hold on." My face was in the tackle box, and I wasn't going to bother turning around.

"It's hurting my arms."

"Jesus Christ," I growled. Why did Miss F. have to exaggerate everything? Why couldn't she do this little thing without making a fuss? I got up off my knees and stomped back to the riverbank to retrieve my rod.

"Okay, so you don't believe me, you ass," said Miss F.

There was a three-pound Dolly Varden trout, a sky-blue-bellied beauty, on the end of the line. It had caught itself, swallowing the fingerling, which I had been in too much of a hurry to unhook.

Miss F. gloated horribly. "I caught it," she cheered. "I caught it, it's mine. You can reel it in and you can cook it, but I'm the one who caught it. I don't know how you're ever going to live this down." It made her so happy, there was nothing I could do but let her rub it in. In an odd way, it was the gayest moment we had had together in a long time.

Back at our campsite, I lugged driftwood to a sandy pit scooped out among the rocks down by the water. At nightfall, I set our small bubble of the world ablaze, and cooked Miss F.'s gorgeous bull trout and roasted two ears of corn in tinfoil, charring the kernels a little, the way Miss F. likes it, and we ate it all with a cucumber and tomato salad, and then Miss F. got up from her seat on a rock and lay back between my legs in the sand, and Issabel turned in anxious circles and then scooched down beside us, and we sat with our drinks and watched the fire, beads of resin rising out from the wood, red as cranberries. There was a change of atmosphere that was the fire's fault, I decided. Campfires can turn on you like this, reversing serenity into real human seriousness.

"Are you happy?" asked Miss F., not at all sure if she should be asking, but wanting to know.

"Pretty much," I said after a while. We stared into the fire for another hour: there was plenty there to contemplate. Then we doused it and went to bed, no his side, no her side. Just us.

So reaffirming, these fires we build and put out and make again, elsewhere.

The following recipe is designed to be cooked over a campfire.

GRILLED RAINBOW TROUT WITH FRESH HERBS

2 1–1 ½ pound rainbow trout (or any other freshly caught fish)

Salt and pepper to taste

2 individual stainless-steel fish-shaped grillers

4 sprigs fresh rosemary, or 4 tablespoons fresh rosemary leaves

4 tablespoons fresh thyme

15–20 sprigs fresh parsley

10 sprigs fresh dill

4 sprigs fresh fennel

4 sprigs fresh mint

8 large fresh basil leaves

½ lemon

Remove the insides of the trout; clean well. Rub the cavity with salt and pepper. Lightly score the skin of the fish with a sharp knife so the flavor of the herbs can permeate the flesh. Combine herbs, then divide into four piles, one for each side of each fish. The grilling basket opens like a clamshell—open it and lay the fish on one side of it. Spread one bunch of herbs along the top side of the fish. Place the other side of the basket on top of the fish, so that the herbs are pressed between the grilling flange and the fish. Turn over, open the basket, and spread the second portion of herbs atop the other side of the fish. Clamp the basket shut. Repeat with second fish. Barbecue over a hot fire, 3 to 4 minutes each side or until the skin and herbs are nicely browned. Remove from heat with a pot holder, unclamp grilling basket, drop out the fish and serve immediately, sprinkled with lemon juice.

SERVES 2.

AFTER DARK (CHOCOLATE), MY SWEET

This month, upon either the twelfth or the seventeenth instance, is Miss F.'s birthday, which I have promised to celebrate with what she expects to be a display of uncommon, if not unprecedented, sweetness, disremembering all the flowers I've brought to her in the years we've been together, all the beautiful dinners I've cooked for her, all the lovely things I've given her, all the exotic places I've taken her, but forever mindful of the fact that for much of the past year I have often voiced the desire to go to war with her.

"Are you planning on leaving me?" she asked, miserable but also defiant and upright, upon our return to our home in Florida last summer after our utterly wretched sabbatical abroad.

"No," I growled, "I don't think my heart could survive the break. I'm merely planning on killing you."

"Fine," she said, her eyes sadly glistening, "only I wish you'd hurry up because I find your anger toward me unbearable. I'll admit that I haven't had a good year—"

Haven't had a good year! Her backsliding had been breathtaking.

"—but look what's happened to you. You've changed too. You're not a nice guy anymore."

I told Miss F. it's not a proven fact I ever was. Or ever wanted to be.

My subject here certainly isn't physical abuse nor wickedness nor the failing light of love, despite appearances. Rather, what concerns me are the obliquely opposed natures of niceness and sweetness—the former the processed meat of social intercourse; the latter the dessert of emotions, served warm, fresh from the heart's patisserie.

By way of illustration, I should address the discrepancy regarding Miss F.'s date of birth. I know the year conclusively, but I suffer from a small and inconvenient dyslexic confusion as to the actual day because my very first girlfriend from high-school days, Miss K., also has a birthday on either the twelfth or the seventeenth of January. Eerie. I still can't get it straight whose is whose, and I confess I've argued with Miss F. about the true date of her birth, accused her of trying to get away with having two birthdays in January, which she's perfectly capable of trying to get away with, and have gone so far as to demand that she produce her driver's license for my inspection. Was I appalled to learn that she was telling the truth? Well, sure I was. Ah, but was I contrite? Yes, I was, a little; at least I shut up about it. Did I apologize? Goodness, no. Why, what for? I pursued the issue without malice. Apologize for being a jackass? Please, have some respect for the mystery of personality. Miss F. had nothing to complain about, because sooner or later each January I always gave her splendid presents (which she adores receiving more than anybody I know). And therein lies the distinction between niceness and sweetness. Niceness is charm's poor cousin, the bulk supplier of saccharine convention. Sweetness, on the other hand, is affection's special delivery. In the gastronomic alphabet, tuna-fish casserole and jello are nice—comforting and risk-free. Sweetness, such as that of a magnificent *gâteau*, not only complements a good dinner but possesses the seductive power to make you forget about a bad one, and so is an exercise in brinkmanship that owes its virtue to finesse.

About being nice, I'll say this: I'm against it, both as a gastronomic standard and as an overall policy of behavior. This past autumn, the United States achieved the apotheosis of geopolitical niceness when, after lengthy consultation with Miss Manners, our leaders were nice enough to count to ten before annihilating Saddam Hussein. I much prefer our behavior in World War II, when we simply kicked ass and then rebuilt our enemies into global giants. That was very sweet.

No, Miss F.'s indictment against me was off the mark. Throughout the year we had spent away from home, I had been as unnice, as cranky and dyspeptic, as ever. The problem? I had stopped being sweet; the moments of grace just weren't there, and the reasons for this are manifold and shrouded in paradox. I have always been aware of the baffling reciprocity that exists between demand and supply of my own personal reservoir of sweetness. The more Miss F. requires it, the less I'm able to accommodate her, which suggests that sweetness is a shy and fragile quality that can't be extorted no matter how judiciously it may be deserved. And throughout the year, though Miss F. clearly needed—and occasionally deserved—truckloads of it, I was never able to summon more than a thimbleful, and that at irregular intervals.

We were crazy with unhappiness, the two of us, holed up and freezing in Rome, living an anti-domestic and dogless life. Miss F. became depressed, which was an absolutely warranted response to our circumstances, but she wallowed in the blues, she lay in bed and read trash novels and drank potions concocted by Capuchin monks. Her dissolution spiraled, and I hounded her about it and showed no sympathy, since I thought the texture of our life had become just as awful for me as it had for her. In her despair, Miss F. gorged herself on pasta, then constantly queried me about her subsequent gain in weight.

"I haven't gained weight, have I?" she would ask forlornly.

"Just at your waist," I'd answer without pity, "and in your thighs and butt. No more than a few kilos, though," and she would scream, rip off all her clothes, throw on a dowdy bathrobe and refuse to leave the room.

Her behavior became increasingly strange and infuriating. She took Italian lessons, but I never heard her speak a word of the *lingua bella*, although on occasion, five minutes after observing that I had no idea what a waiter or a portiere had just said to me, she would offer a belated translation. At dinner in the Academy dining hall, she would entertain the classical scholars by telling them retard jokes. She taped prayer cards to the wall of our cell and took a fancy to the most obscure and crackpot Roman saints, mumbling their beatitudes. And although the poor girl is tone-deaf and has refused to sing for as long as I've known her, at bedtime she began to moo out mournful Patsy Cline ballads, which would bring tears to both our eyes, though perhaps not for the same reason, and I would go hide in the bathtub down the hall or escape to my studio and labor throughout the night to improve my writing skills with a devotion reminiscent of Jack Nicholson in *The Shining*.

This venomous bubble that seemed to entrap me popped but once, on Miss F.'s birthday this past year, when I was somehow able to retrieve a vestige of my former self and surprised Miss F. by whisking her off to Siena, obeying her every whim without exploring her faults, allowing her to get us hopelessly lost (which was one of her favorite things). It was a grand day. Miss F. smiled radiantly for the first time in months.

While I'll submit to whatever censure is due me for the yearlong acidity that replaced what sweetness is in me, I also assert that this alone is the beginning and the end of my sins. Even as the top and bottom of our society seem to rot, our tumorous midsection has become so nice it reeks of the churchy perfumes of paradise. But I don't want to live in paradise, I want to live on earth. I want to be bad, and then I want to make up for it by being very good, and then I want to be bad again, and so on. I don't want to run for office and influence my fellow citizens, since I would have to do what politicians do, which is pretend to be a nice person when I was nothing of the kind. I want to have my Tivoli Torte and eat it too. But niceness! Niceness wants cake for breakfast, lunch, and dinner. Niceness is drinking a single glass of white wine and becoming intoxicated to the point of smarmyness. Niceness is anathema to the diet of well-rounded, if rough-edged, humanity; so unlike sweetness, logically placed, like dessert, at the end of more savory and toothsome pleasures.

I want to be like our new dog, Issabel, who is as sweet as hibiscus honey but an indiscriminate crotch-poker, and who chews up everything. I admire her immensely.

"Is the bloom off the rose?" Miss F. asked, once we were back in Florida, as we struggled to pick up the old rhythms, recover the lost chords. She had resumed her final year in law school and had a life of her own again outside of my withering shadow. She was fighting hard to reestablish her precious sense of independence, her self-confidence and self-esteem, and was finally secure enough to take a long look in the mirror and give a wink, let herself be.

"See for yourself," I said, and tossed a scarlet bud into her lap. I had just returned from walking the dog and, as I used to do, before we moved to Europe, I had stolen a flower from our neighbor's garden, an illicit rose of affection to carry home to my Miss F.

At our house, dessert was making its way back onto the menu again.

TIVOLI TORTE

TORTE:

½ cup softened butter

¾ cup, divided, plus 3 ½ tablespoons sugar

1 teaspoon vanilla extract

7 eggs, at room temperature

⅔ cup all-purpose flour

3 tablespoons cornstarch

⅓ cup semisweet chocolate chips

⅔ cup sour cream

½ teaspoon fresh lemon juice

FROSTING:

⅓ cup semisweet chocolate chips

1 ½ tablespoons softened butter

3 tablespoons sour cream

½ teaspoon vanilla

1 cup confectioner's sugar

½ cup whipping cream

12–14 fresh strawberries

So beautiful, delicate and elegant a torte, no one I served it to could quite believe such a ham-handed oaf as myself had made it. Though it's honestly easy to make, whoever attempts it should be unemployed, since it does take several hours to concoct, but then I've always found the labor factor in sweetness to be disproportionately high.

In a large mixing bowl, combine butter and ½ cup of the sugar, add vanilla, and beat until smooth. Separate egg whites from yolks and slowly add yolks to butter mixture, beating until creamy. Mix flour and cornstarch together and gradually pour into bowl, mixing until all ingredients are blended thoroughly. Divide batter in half, putting one portion into another bowl. Melt chocolate chips in a double boiler and mix into one portion of the batter. Set both vanilla and chocolate batters aside. Beat egg whites until they thicken and peak, then gradually add ¼ cup of the sugar, beating at high speed until the mixture stiffens. Fold half the whites into the vanilla batter, the other half into the chocolate batter. Preheat broiler. In a greased 9-inch springform pan, spread ½ cup of the chocolate batter evenly across the bottom. Place pan 5 inches below flames and flash-cook for 1 ½ minutes. Remove from broiler, spread ½ cup of the vanilla batter over the cooked chocolate layer and broil for 1 minute or until the batter turns golden. Repeat process until both batters have been used up, probably 6 to 8 layers. Combine sour cream, the remaining 3 ½ tablespoons of sugar and lemon juice and spread over top of torte. Broil for 1 minute. Cool for 20 minutes, then remove the side of the springform pan and set the torte on a cooling rack.

To make frosting, melt chocolate chips in a double boiler. Remove from heat and stir in the remaining butter, sour cream, and vanilla extract. Slowly add confectioner's sugar and mix with beater until creamy and smooth. Frost sides of torte, put remaining frosting into an icing bag and pipe a ring around the rim of the torte, then a smaller inner ring (about 3 to 4 inches in diameter) in the center. Beat the whipping cream until stiff. Clean the icing bag, fill with whipped cream, and pipe a second ring on the inside edge of the first. Fill inner circle with piped cream. Wash and hull strawberries. Crown center with a whole strawberry. tip up. Halve remaining strawberries and arrange between inner and outer circles, tips pointing inward. Chill at least 2 hours.

SERVES 10 TO 12.

An unpleasant side effect of serving this torte is that it inspires the chocolate addicts at the table to fawn and act unbearably obsequious.

Light up a cigar, start belting down brandy, and try to make the best of it. Now's the perfect time to offend your guests, if for some reason you've managed to restrain yourself throughout the evening.

FLAN DE NARANJA
(ORANGE FLAN)

1 tablespoon cold water

1 cup sugar, divided

2 tablespoons lemon juice

1 cup orange juice

6 eggs

2 oranges

Fresh mint sprig

In saucepan, stir water into ¾ cup of the sugar. Cook over high heat, stirring constantly with a wooden spoon, until mixture becomes a dark, amber-colored syrup, then quickly pour into a 9-inch flan pan, pie pan, or souffle dish. Swirl until mixture coats bottom and 2 to 3 inches up the sides of the pan. Let cool on a wire rack. Preheat oven to 350 degrees. Combine the remaining ¼ cup sugar, the lemon and orange juices and eggs. Grate the peel of 1 orange and add to mixture. Beat until thoroughly blended, pour into caramelized pan, and place pan in a larger baking pan; pour boiling water into baking pan. Water should reach halfway up the sides of the flan pan. Bake 30 to 40 minutes, or until a knife inserted into the flan's center comes out clean. Remove flan pan from hot water, let flan cool, and refrigerate for at least 6 hours. When flan is firm, remove from refrigerator and let stand at room temperature for 15 to 20 minutes. Run a butter knife along sides of pan to loosen the flan. Cover pan with a high-rimmed plate and flip the whole thing over as quickly as you can. The flan should pop neatly out onto the plate, if you're a good person who has tried to live an honorable life. Thinly slice the second orange. Place a full slice in center of flan and garnish with mint sprig. Cut remaining orange slices in half and arrange in a pinwheel design around center.

SERVES 6 TO 8.

PART THREE

CAVEAT CAVIAR

"With what do you associate plover eggs and *quails financières*, veal marrow and pike quenelles?" I asked my friend Scott, encouraging him to lay aside his bag of Doritos. Scott's stomach claims solidarity with the workingman's, though his aspirations have occasionally been sighted, in daylight, lurking around the thrones of royalty.

"With fat rich men and lean rich bimbos, both unabashedly anxious in their desire to raise funds of a deductible nature," Scott answered. "Why do you ask? Are you planning a foray into an environment where luxuries are consumed? That can be lethal, if you're ill-trained in the terroristic art of condescension. Besides, the rich, as we have come to know them, eat things that are inherently filthy, as if they suffer a nostalgia for the cruel and uninhibited behavior of their childhood. They yank snails out of shells with little tweezers. They force-feed geese and smear their mouths with the bloated livers. They serve Stilton cheese so ripe it's like eating a dead cat that's been in repose on the sideboard for a month, then rhapsodize about its naughty flavor. I advise you to stay far away from such exhibitionism of the golden varieties, especially if you've just won the lottery."

I hadn't won the lottery, no, but I had received a gift of beluga caviar—$300 for seven ounces—and before I decided what to do with it, I thought it might be helpful to solicit Scott's opinion on the ethos of prestige, which I've always found to be a rather tricky social dynamic. Take tuxedos: I'm suspicious of them. Whenever I rent one, it always fits perfectly, as if I were born in it, and I find myself thinking: "Wait a minute, my prospects for leading a life of privilege have undergone a vast improvement; suddenly, I seem to have risen to at least the rank of captain in the army of prigs that do battle in the world's salons, and it is all so easy that any fool or charlatan can do it." Scott, on the other hand, had been a spin doctor for some of the swankest sleazebags on Wall Street until one day he choked on a crouton during a power snack at Chanterelle, had a near-death experience, and walked away from the big top, making a new life for himself in Iowa with the waitress who had hoisted his not inconsequential self with the Heimlich maneuver.

"It's no use being against prestige," Scott informed me. "It's like being an anti-intellectual; you can never win at it. Prestige carries respect the way vermin carry disease, regardless of the fact that it is merely an affair of the wallet."

It would be naive and inexcusably dumb to think that prestige can't be bought. Prestige is exactly the sort of thing money can buy, yet it's a dangerous commodity, since it calls such acute attention to one's aesthetic integrity, and is a hollow, vulgar triumph unless accompanied by natural elegance of style (which very few of us seem to possess) rather than a Lucullan lust for extravagance, which, only yesterday, seemed to be our main national agenda. Just ask the Donald and the Ronald, those fairy vampires of American culture.

Besides, often the snobs are right, even if they are nothing more than the mannered rednecks of the culinary barnyard. Because unless you are a gastronomic *idiot savant*, the best is, after all, an acquired taste, cultivated by experience and education, and nothing is less democratic than excellence. In other words, snobs may not invent standards, but they perpetuate them—and that's why we let them escape with their lives. I offer as an example one of my former colleagues in Rome, a sneering historian of Renaissance art named Eve. Eve is a person who considers the higher aspects of culture most useful as bludgeons. "You are of an ignorant class," she would say to me regularly in every way but directly. One morning, she discharged volleys of contempt at my modest breakfast, lecturing me on the tragedy of consuming inferior goods, since conspicuous consumption of Only the Best was the traditional means of achieving reputability for a fledgling gentleman and scholar such as myself.

"Only eat prosciutto from Parma," she commanded. "It's the best. Only eat mozzarella made from buffalo's milk. It's the best. Only buy bread from Il Forno. It's the best. Only drink cappuccino from Sant'Eustachio's. It is, of course, the best, the very best."

After a month of tasting and exploring, I found it necessary to concede that Eve was right—a concession that gave me a rash. Her ability to locate the best was impeccable, but her delivery—nothing free-spirited or generous about it—made me itch with outrage, for she saw the world as a tidy package of absolutes. Eve, when you got right down to it, was a soft-spoken bully. She tainted appreciation by making appreciation an aristocratic obligation. Everything she consumed was divine, and she made the divine cut-and-dried, thereby sucking the joy out of it.

Scott, upon hearing this tale, moaned and rolled his eyes heavenward. "What's going on over there?" I asked, alarmed to see him wipe a string of drool from the corner of his mouth.

"Forgive me," he said. "I know it sounds absurd, but nothing titillates the decadent appetite to such a state of arousal and agitation as the company, even if only in the telling of a story, of a spoiled bitch. Unwholesome, but true."

"I'd rather take my chances with *fugu*," I told him.

"Look," Scott argued, "you can't waste grub such as you describe on your garden-variety cheerleader. It would be like deploying the 82nd

Airborne to hunt bunnies. Now that you've stirred my hunger with your tales of palatal combat, I am reminded of the *mets fantastique*, a little snack that I have slobbered over in my dreams ever since my tadpole days as a student of deconstruction: *la grosse anguille à la regence*! A gigantic eel, richly sauced, garnished with quenelles, truffles, and cocks' combs. It would be a petty transaction, selling my soul for a taste of that."

"Would you keep it all for yourself, or—"

"Oh, Christ, no!" Scott protested. "With that kind of meal, the palate requires the presence of a real world-class bloodsucker to achieve the full erotic effect. That fat boy Baby Doc's consort—what's her name? Michelle Duvalier. She'd do."

I said if she weren't available to grace his dream table of untold prestige, then perhaps I could suggest a satisfactory substitute: a torture queen who had recently made mincemeat out of an architect I know.

Adriana once gave her father a truffle for Christmas. It was a white one, which, unfortunately, was neither the color of Adriana's soul nor an emblem of her chastity. My friend Arthur was in love with her. They moved in together and began the dialogue of romance that customarily ends in vows either sacred or profane. Adriana determined it was time for Arthur to meet his future in-laws, her wonderful family, descended from a distinguished line of executioners, so she swept him off to Paris for the Christmas holidays. Unbeknown to Arthur, however, a famous English scribe, a notorious homophobe, had had the opportunity to eyeball him across a room at a soirée a month before and judged that since Arthur was fair to behold and given to flamboyant gestures, he must therefore be gay, and wicked, and of a low background. The writer communicated this opinion to Adriana's mother, with whom he was conducting if not an affair then at least a vigorously simulated truffle-rooting expedition between Mama's dusty thighs.

Arthur arrived bearing presents himself—not truffles but books. The gifts were accepted, but the unsuspecting Arthur was not. Within twenty-four hours, Mother made reference to Arthur's international reputation as a queer and banished him from that house of fine breeding. Adriana made no move to save her beau. Instead, she vanished into the recesses of the house, in preparation for an assault on the shops of the Champs-Elysées. Her sister merrily drove Arthur to the airport, where he caught the first plane out of the eugenic hell that is the special province of nouveau-riche expatriates living in Europe.

"Forgiveness will never do," Scott clucked, "not when it comes to the behavior of the upper echelons of society. Your Arthur seems destined to eat tuna on rye with cowgirls. That Adriana, though—*wow!*"

As for myself, my reading on Adriana is inextricably tied to that single white truffle she gave her father. What inspired this self-deluded child—it would be heinous to call her a woman—to nibble into her trust fund and buy Daddy a precious delicacy was, I have to assume, the iconography of prestige. Said a French gourmet, who would never end up on Adriana's or Mother's short list, "There are two types of people who eat truffles: those who think truffles are good because they are dear and those who know they are dear because they are good." Adriana, clearly, is one of the former, one of the elite scoundrels who pervert the art of eating (or loving) into the art of showing off. I suppose if Arthur were a truffle and therefore rare and valuable, rather than rare and valuable by virtue of being a good man, she would still be with him, flaunting the guy. Which would be terrible for Arthur, but it's no use telling him that.

Adriana's sin was that she took something rich and singular and made of it a fraudulent conceit, to service her masquerade of worldliness and refinement. Had the truffle represented an enlargement of her consciousness? Not at all. Had the truffle expressed her aesthetic vision? Yes, as a macaw repeats the simplest expressions of its trainer. Worldliness and refinement come first, on their own unhurried schedule; then the rewards materialize out of the smog of flummery and hauteur. To eat caviar is nothing; to enjoy it honestly and without self-congratulation is something else altogether, and who needs the false magic of prestige for that? It's the difference between vaingloriously possessing a truffle and being worthy of its delicate, subtle, sensuous flavor. Worthiness—now that takes a knack.

As a tool or ornament of success, the food of prestige leaves me a bit indifferent, although I agree with Scott that there's an irresistible side to its personality: the eroticism of its earthy flavors. We venerate French cuisine mostly, I think, because of its sensuality; its identity, as M. F. K. Fisher says, is the "simplest in the sense of primitive and natural." And what could be more primitive and natural—read sexy—than the two most precious gems in the culinary portfolio: truffles and caviar? Subterranean nodes of fungus nosed out of the oaky soil by swine, and a glittering sac of eggs torn from the belly of a prehistoric fish.

"Well, so," I continued to prod Scott, "what do you know about beluga caviar?"

"It is the Mozart of caviars," said Scott, licking his lips, "best eaten from the umbilical cavity of a person you adore. Failing access to such a person, only a vixen will do."

I phoned Miss F. and requested she ice up her button.

Remember, caviar is perishable and should be kept refrigerated, served cold, preferably on crushed ice. Refrain from squeezing a lemon on it, which ruins the flavor. The ideal way to eat caviar is to spread a bit of sour cream atop a blini, spoon on a dollop of roe, savor them, then recharge the palate and the soul with a shot of Polish vodka, flavored with bison grass. Might as well put out a slab of smoked Scottish salmon while you're at it.

BLINI A LA FRANCAISE

1 teaspoon dried yeast
2 ¾ cups sifted flour, divided
2 cups cold milk
4 eggs, separated
½ cup warm milk
Pinch of salt
½ cup whipped cream

Mix yeast and ½ cup of the flour (use semolina and/or buckwheat for more-savory blini) with the cold milk and allow to rise for 20 minutes in a warm place. Mix in remaining 2 ¼ cups flour, the 4 egg yolks and the warm milk. Throw in a generous pinch of salt. Blend ingredients thoroughly, but don't let mixture thicken. Beat egg whites until stiff; add, along with whipped cream, to mixture. Put batter aside for 1 hour, then fry small, thick pancakes in the smallest cast-iron skillet you have.

SERVES 4 TO 6.

CRUDE NOISE

*Eating is always at least two activities: consuming
food and obeying a code of manners.*

—GUY DAVENPORT

I happened upon a horizontal Miss F., in reverie beneath the dining-room table. It is a very primitive and shaky table, one we inherited from Vietnamese refugees—I swear—fifteen years ago, when they'd disappeared from their church-sponsored house in the middle of the night. One of us is always crawling under it to reinforce its legs, so it wasn't unusual to discover Miss F. down there, only odd that she should enjoy it enough to linger with a wistful smile on her face.

"Dare I ask?" I asked, doing a knee bend to facilitate conversation.

"Oh, it's nothing," she said and flashed a screwdriver so I'd understand she'd been motivated by a favorite Saturday-morning obsession of hers—the need to repair. "I've just been remembering how, when I was growing up, if you misbehaved during meals you had to eat under the table with the dog, the idea being that you belonged with your own kind."

"The brutality of it!" I said with enormous sympathy. "How it must have scarred your innocent soul!" I wondered if, now that Miss F. was about finished with law school, she would inaugurate her entrance into the litigious fray by filing suit against her parents.

"Oh, no," she protested. "I just loved being under there, because I could feed the dog what I didn't want to eat, and it was informative to have a good look at everybody's knees, and I could bite my sisters on the ankles."

I asked what crimes against good breeding had exacted this punishment, and I must admit they were severe: squishing Jell-O through her teeth, using her fork to make crude noises with her mouth, insincere compliance with the rules as a deliberate tactic to incite the barbarism of her sisters—*Fran, Fran, strong and able, keep your elbows off the table.*

I was appalled to learn what a little wretch she had been, destined for a life without standards among barristers and writers. As for myself, I carry only the dimmest memories of my own conduct as a junior member of civilization, which was not exactly centered at the dinner table in my house. I remember little more than the wet sounds of my father smacking his lips, sucking the marrow out of every bone in reach, and the noise of my mother weeping if we four kids hesitated to take a third helping of goulash or piggies in blankets, and I recall the rare occasions I was able to bolt from the table with my senses intact, grateful that for once no one had cut a fart.

If there were rules or conventions, I'm afraid I missed the briefing, which I accept with no real regret, since I can't really say my ignorance proved fatal to my rise in society, at least on this side of the Atlantic. After all, America is a nation where manners are at best a novelty. Many of us are howler monkeys who vote Libertarian when it comes to etiquette, though we nevertheless rise to the pukka code when it behooves us. Consider this bit of gastronomic apocrypha from the West, for instance. It seems one day a particularly rough-looking mountaineer appeared in the dining hall of a Colorado hotel, toting a viand wrapped in a bandanna. He marched toward the kitchen to instruct the cook how he wished the meat prepared, then retired to a table and waited with a Continental air of self-assurance to be served. When the meal was delivered, the desperado took pleasure in it as a gentleman, with all due and proper comportment, and upon finishing communicated satisfaction with a burp and proclaimed, "There, by God, I swore I'd eat that man's liver and I've done it."

I'm inspired by this tale, made to feel somewhat patriotic by its bottom-line recognition of propriety maintained under harsh circumstances. We Americans struggle in our hearts to do the right thing, if not to make the right impression, even as, given the opportunity, we are equally comfortable in our role as a thundering storm of wild men and wild women. If a year ago you had advised me there'd soon be full-scale war in the Middle East, that the Mother of All Battles would find herself engaged by the Father of All Broccoli-Busters, I'd have said it would come as no surprise to me. Yet if you further suggested that a half million Americans would camp out in the Saudi desert for six months without consuming a single can of ice-cold beer, I would have considered that outlandish speculation, no more likely than Moamar Gaddafi's getting on television to play the Prince of Peace.

Given the tenacity of the more loutish aspects of the human condition, we can hardly fault Miss Manners's continuation of a timeless campaign to push us up the Ladder Evolutionary toward the paradise of gentility. But, alas, there's a Catch-22 to her aspiration, since the folks she encourages us to model ourselves after—the gentry and the ruling

classes—have behaved like god-awful swine for millenia, though they certainly have dressed nice and kept their fingernails clean, haven't they?

Miss Manners's predecessors, too, had a dickens of a time reminding ladies and gentlemen of the court not to pick their teeth or scratch themselves with their knife while at the table, and to refrain from describing the results of the hunt while their maw was crammed full of it. In 1526, Erasmus wrote in his Treatise of Manners that noblemen and their consorts should try to wipe their greasy lips on a handkerchief and not on a sleeve or tablecloth. "It is coarse to put your fingers in your soup," he warned, "and it is unseemly to put chewed items back on your plate. It is absolutely not done to throw your bones under the table or lick your plate," although it was, of course, acceptable for your favorite wolfhound to do so.

When Henry III of the Holy Roman Empire, a monarch feared for his strict adherence to protocol, threw a dinner party, it was expected that his guests preface the event with a flurry of "idolatrous bows," not merely to his Royal Ego, but to the king's personal belongings as well. The pomposities were much more digestible when one dined with Louis XIV of France, who cannonaded the gals with little balls of bread and was most pleased when they chucked them back. In our own age, the open-door policy that has accompanied the triumph of capitalism has created a situation where any sockless oaf can infiltrate polite society and rain democratic abuse down upon the rituals of elegance. Actually, I have done it myself, in the days before I came to realize that good manners have their own aesthetic rationale and no pragmatic justification whatsoever except the aversion of gunplay.

But it's an unforgiving world if you falter.

In American cuisine, mussels are one of those things that divide the hawks from the doves on the gastronomic battleground. If your guests don't know how to handle these succulent bivalves, and are of no discernible social status, send them home immediately.

MUSSELS CHARDONNAY

35–40 fresh mussels
¼ cup finely chopped onions or shallots
¼ cup finely chopped celery
2 garlic cloves, minced
1 tablespoon butter
1 tablespoon olive oil
1 cup Chardonnay
1 bay leaf
1 tablespoon minced parsley

Remove beards from mussels and wash mussels under cold water, throwing out any that are broken or are open and smell iffy. In a large saucepan or pot, sauté shallots, celery and garlic in butter and oil. Add wine, bay leaf and mussels, and bring to a boil for about four minutes, occasionally shaking the pot so that the mussels become well flavored. Serve in soup plates with the broth, garnished with parsley. Crusty bread for dipping will be universally appreciated by your guests. Don't toss the shells on the floor, unless the hostess first leads the way.

SERVES 4.

HUNGER AT BAY

*"There is no shortage of good days. It is good lives
that are hard to come to by."*

—Annie Dillard

There are perfect lives to be snatched up out of the wardrobe of routine and worn like favorite hats, always being misplaced. Sometimes Miss F. and I have lucked onto them, not in any linear fashion, but in structureless, stalled, and luminous moments, sunny islands of weeks or months, self-dissolving cycles of time. In the early summer of '87, before we migrated to Florida to indenture Miss F. in law school, we had one (or was it two?) of those seamless, shining lives and then, as with all perfection claimed by humans, the wind came up, and we lost our grip and were released back to the more pedestrian flow of adult events, where we prospered for a year in brisk, familiar rhythm where perfection had no role, wasn't even an issue. Then, the year after, we watched as the world around us unraveled with separation and death, spent the following year in exile from our happiness, and then closed a year measured on a calendar of recovery, balance and possibility painstakingly restored.

It doesn't take much for the talk between us to travel back to that early summer on the Outer Banks of North Carolina, as if we were sure it's the place we come from, although it's only one of many. Crabs, a favorite food, are a favored topic. In language, at least, and on paper, a crab is not a beautiful swimmer until it's translated: *Callinectes sapidus*. So it often is with a metaphor and an irony to carry around in your pocket.

But those months on Hatteras Island required no translation. The mercy of nature is in its literalness. We arrived on Hatteras the same day as Hurricane Charley, more an annoyance than a killer storm. The domicile we had leased was a double-wide trailer on substandard stilts, so wobbly that water sloshed out of the toilet when the wind rose past 30 knots. Tawdry fish-camp decor: flood-stained plastic furniture, porno mags shoved under the mattress in the main bedroom. But it sat smack on Pamlico Sound and had a screened-in porch with a millionaire's view of the sunset and space underneath stacked with walls of wire-meshed blocks—crab pots, scavenged out of the marshes by our fundamentalist landlord.

Having grown up in tidewater Virginia, I thought about those crab pots the way a Texan thinks a lot about oil wells. Before the end of our first week in Hatteras, I'd rehabilitated four of them and talked Barris, the local fishmonger, out of bait—bluefish heads (less smelly than the chicken necks I preferred when handlining, and free). I waded offshore, trailed by my Irish setter, Tyrone, twice a day, dusk and dawn, to set and to pull the pots. The results were tantalizing but unsatisfactory. Three or four middling-sized crabs, all sooks (females), didn't square with my serious intentions—to learn if, by eating crabs day and night, it were at all possible to reach a saturation point, a place where I would beg "Enough! Gimme a goddamn hamburger!" The gloating blue heron posted at the mouth of a nearby creek was having better success, and I couldn't stand it. I needed to get farther offshore, where the flats dropped into the bay proper, but I couldn't afford to buy a boat, even a broken-down skiff to pole out into blue water. Fishmonger Barris, an unlikely source of sympathy, came to my rescue. He loaned me his canoe, and thus I made my mark in the world of back-bay watermen.

Don't believe anybody else if they tell you they have done this: I'm the only person in modern times fool enough to work crab pots from a canoe—barefoot, as well, with the scars to prove it. This was an exceedingly reckless accomplishment, on par with inner-city jogging in Newark, snapping wildlife pictures of Sean Penn or pinching a woman's ass in

Riyadh. I lost paddles trying to snag pot lines and would end up over-board myself. I'd paddle out on calm water, and then an offshore wind would kick up and it would take me hours to fight my way back in. If the waves stood up at all, I'd paddle in circles, unable to find the floats, but on perfect days I could paddle standing up, gliding over the transparent shallows, watching the shapes of sharks and rays below me, the silvery schools of mullet and sea turtles winging past. This was a low-budget operation, and the crabs had to be emptied helter-skelter into the hull of the canoe, clacking and snapping and generally pissed; but they were less a problem than the two or three monkfish that showed up daily in the pots, ugly, aggressive creatures that would flop into the boat and beeline for my toes, chomping on to the paddle I used to shove them away, refusing to let go until I dipped them back into the water. The boat would become splattered and filthy with decaying bait, but still I couldn't have been happier, and the effort paid off handsomely: four dozen crabs a day, a few of them peelers (molting crabs, about to achieve that state of gastronomic transcendence known as sautéed soft-shells)—this bounty of beautiful swimmers supplemented by bluefish, drum, croaker, and Spanish mackerel I caught off Cape Point, and by clams, oysters and scallops I harvested from the bay with my rake. I could pick a crab down to the succulent back-fin lump about six times faster than Miss F., but, you know, I liked her and would stuff them, one for one, into her mouth. We inhaled the treasures of the coast and exhaled con-tentment. We had been happy before, in other places, but we had never been so brown, so healthy. Or so fat.

If you heard the rockets bursting in air last month, that was the sound of a barrage of torts and briefs fired off in celebration of Her Royal Paleness, Miss. F., being graduated from law school. Alas, this month she finds herself locked in combat with a particularly bloodthirsty beast, notorious for its unsportsmanlike conduct: the bar exam. Life around the house couldn't be more stressful if I were bunking with Norman Schwartzkopf. Maybe Norm could deal with Miss F. at a time like this, but I can't: there's room for only one brooding, moody, volatile, exhausted person at our address, and I've got dibs on all the unsavory character traits, being a writer. Which means I issued Miss F. a thirty-day supply of domestic MREs (Lean Cuisine and Budget Gourmet microwave dinners), taped a communiqué on the refrigerator door (GONE CRAB-BING, GOOD LUCK. LOVE), and hit the road, with no inclination to return home until home returned to its former status. Me and the Emir.

I called Miss F. a couple days later, to check up on her.

"What, you're not here, really?" she answered in a zombie voice. "How long have you been gone?"

"Not very long," I said. "Are you okay?"

"Okay?" she screeched, turning fierce. "Do you know what your street address was when you were nineteen years old? Do you know how much money you made when you were twenty-one? Did I ever tell you that the most unconstitutional group of prying bastards and extortionist thugs ever assembled goes by the name of the Florida Bar Association? They make the FBI look like sissies dancing around the maypole."

Yes, she had told me, more than once, I said. But it made no difference—she was off on a rant. The real crisis, we both knew, was not the arrogant power of the Florida Bar, but something more subtle and open-ended. There was no way of knowing, once she passed the exam, what it would amount to or where it would lead. How much would she gain in her life, and how much would be taken away? The answers were unclear; only the knowledge that our life was approaching a threshold had certainty woven into it. Change would soon be underfoot, yet again, and would our lives be what we wanted them to be, afterward?

"Where are you?" Miss F. asked, calming down.

I told her—Hatteras.

"You rat," she moaned. It was exactly where she wanted to be on earth, this instant, right now, chop-chop, Miss F. and me and the dog, sitting on the backside of the ferry docks on Ocracoke, six lines in the water, a bushel basket for the crabs, a cooler of cold beer for the crabbers, the net swooping down upon the beautiful swimmers. It sounds like an elegy for a life that used to be, but it's not, it's not that at all.

Give the devil his due, I told her. I'd be waiting for her, out on the dock.

STEAMED BLUE CRABS

Steamer pot with raised rack
2 cups water
2 cups vinegar or beer
6 ounces Old Bay seasoning
2 dozen live crabs
Salt
Garlic salt (optional)

What could be simpler (though you'll probably have to live on the eastern or Gulf seaboards before you'll find a use for this recipe)? Get down to the fishmongers, buy a couple dozen jimmys (males) or sooks, whatever the guy has, depending on the season. Take them home, dump them in the sink (a few at a time, unless you're prepared for cheap thrills), and rinse them under cold water. Meanwhile, add the water and beer, or water and vinegar (for a tangy flavor) to the steamer and bring to a hard boil. Start layering in the crabs (the steam will kill them, though not as quickly as will salve a guilty conscience). After you've covered the bottom of the pot rack with 4 or 5 crabs, sprinkle generously with Old Bay seasoning and salt. Garlic salt, too, if you like the taste. Repeat the process—a layer of crabs, a fresh dusting of spices, until the pot's full. Put the lid on and steam for about a half hour, or until the crabs have turned bright red. Drain and cool for a few minutes in a colander, spread newspaper on the table, dump the crabs in the center, make sure your beer is right where you want it, and start picking.

WHEEL LOVE:
MUSINGS ON A MERC

MALE VOCAL: Well way out West they call me Barbecue Bill, And
if I can't do it, baby, you know my hot sauce will.
FEMALE VOCAL: Cook that sauce and put it all over me, Want so
much sauce that I can't even see.

—BILL WHARTON AND THE INGREDIENTS

Miss F. has a new car, sort of, and, brother, I'm telling you she had to get one, there was to be no discussion about it, because when her ivy-green '68 Volvo P1800 coupe died—which I could not psychologically afford to fix because I hated that piece of shit, no matter how alluring Miss F. looked in it, wrapped in a ball cap and sunglasses; hated especially driving it myself, because it felt like being dragged down the road on a sheet of cardboard while you sat slumped in a piece of cast-iron lawn furniture—when it up and died its spiteful death, Miss F. started taking off in my truck, on a schedule inconvenient to my inner need to feel that that there was *my* truck, violating my sense of being the primary and not-so-generous user of the truck and utterly dependent on its availability to, say, get the stuff we need for dinner, since we don't grow it ourselves anymore or raise livestock. When she started this "I'm taking the truck to work" baloney, I stopped celebrating the demise of the Volvo and let it be known that we had a problem of a fundamental nature, being that we are middle-class, not exactly urban, and over the age of 16 and that I am of a certain moral energy that might at any moment require me to drive to Fort Lauderdale to the Kathy Willets nymphomaniac trial, to see for myself what our world has come to, or to drive on a holy pilgrimage to Alabama for some Dreamland ribs, then on to Louisiana to prostrate myself before some etouffée.

You see my point. We're talking America and what can bring it up short.

So, Miss F. has a new car, another dinosaur, since she so prefers their style, this one dragged purring from the automotive tar pits of Detroit. A Mercury Monterey, twenty-fifth anniversary model, a paleolithic relic from that blunder year, 1964. Hey, 1500 bucks! Ninety thousand original miles, a few rust spots, droopy upholstery on the ceiling. It's white and long, long as a pilot whale, has seats like twin beds, uses more gas in a month than the nation of Burundi does and—its big claim to engineering immortality—features an inward-slanting rear window that powers up and down. Cool.

Miss F. tells me she earns compliments at stoplights, invariably from gap-toothed, white-haired old black men. "Oh, ain't she a pretty thing" they call across the lane to her. "Honey, that back window still ride up and down?" they ask, and Miss F. obliges them with a demonstration. "Oh yeah," they say. "Oh yeah. Mm—hmm."

It's that kind of automobile, the kind in which our parents once slapped our smirking pubescent faces, in those days when slapping still had currency as a disciplinary statement, back when gas was nineteen cents a gallon and only housewives used drugs. With a trunk as spacious as a mass grave, we'd sneak half the high school into a drive-in movie in a car like this; we learned anatomy in these cars, taught each other that fucking and fucking up were sometimes too close for comfort. We went real fast with these wheels, found out that the night and movement and no particular place to go were an infectious combination, met our first policemen thanks to these cars, puked out of their windows, slept luxuriously in them at the beach, cried and fought in them, pulled down our pants in them, went steady and broke up in them, did nothing and everything in them, including, finally, leave. We wanted all this to happen though, and while it happened, we were shaped and sculpted by the music that poured like bourbon out of their

AM radios and—let us not forget—learned, however frivolously, to feed ourselves in these cars. Cheeseburgers and fries and onion rings (and a fish sandwich for the nimrod in the backseat—me), pizzas and po'boys, grinders and gutbusters, tacos and chop suey, fried chicken and hot dogs and ice-cream cones and special secret sauces and all the other greasy, salty, dripping wonderful garbage the road set out for us like votive offerings to Speed, the guy in the chrome tennies, the god of youth and internal combustion.

It seemed not that we stumbled upon this class of food but that we invented it, and without us and the cars and the music, it wouldn't have existed. What dare you eat, after all, in a 1993 Saab? Nothing. Never. Forget it, Jack. Suck on an herbal breath mint, refresh your trendy self with a Calistoga or a Perrier, and get your sad-sack butt to the gym—and don't eat anything there either, lest they drum you out of Jazzercise, you backslider.

No, I am not mystified by Miss F.'s peculiar automotive desires, and, in fact, I encourage them as traits of a virtuous nature. She's not nostalgia-driven, as you might think, but motivated by preservation (and budget), and I consider her new beast illustrative of an ethos, a tradition at play, a vestigial grace warping through the cultural continuum. Oh, yes! This is ontology and metagastronomics I speak of, citizens, the music and the secret sauces that shift up to the surface of existence when Miss F. straps herself into the '64 Merc and fires it up, as if she were the delivery girl for the angel Gabriel's catering service. The Merc, in fact, reeks of sensuous down-home cooking and music, and if I'm not mistaken, that music is the blues, the blues like a nasty worm in the dry heart of the new-age apple. Now Miss F. adores her Merc and harkens to its sounds and smells, but we have among us friends who are appalled by her choice of transport and who advance the proposition that such an automobile, an environmental and fashion *faux pas*, is not a politically correct automobile, and all I can do is refer these friends to the proper authority for such cases, not for judgment but for enlightenment. That authority would be the Poet Laureate of Sauce, the Sauce Boss himself, gentleman by the name of Bill Wharton, a modern hero of the blues and a visionary who has seen the face of God in the hubcaps of vintage Chevrolets: a fellow who takes from the kitsch and gives to the pure, who would explain to them that the blues hath no fury like a Mercury scorned, that the blues, being duly occupied by its devotion to big-assed women in boat-sized cars and the food that placed the heft and the glory into those broad rear ends, has precious little time to waste being guilt-stricken by sex or color or imperfection or breakdown on the Utopian highway, amen.

Don't get confused—Dr. Wharton is no apologist for the Retrograde; he's a gumbo preacher with a slide guitar. He and his band, the Ingredients—these brothers are not slim—had provided Miss F. and myself with a culinary anthem, "Let the Big Dog Eat," from the sound-track of Something Wild, a cinematic treatise, as I recall, on the dialectic involving old cars, pretty girls, and the divine mess. A self-made gourmet entrepreneur-entertainer of the boy category, Wharton and his wife, Ruth, are actual Guardians of the Secret Sauce, members of the brave society of capsicum converts who have had such an uplifting impact on the flavor of our nation's gastronomic faiths; they are saints like Walter S. McIlhenny—Mr. Tabasco—and Bernard Trappey, creator of Trappey's Hot Sauce and a founder of the Original Ancient Order of Creole Gourmets. Bill and Ruth hail from the sect indigenous to Florida that tamed the demon pepper, the thermonuclear Datil, known in Mexico as the dreaded Habanero and throughout the West Indies as the Scotch

Bonnet (perhaps for the headgear they bury you in after accidental unadulterated consumption of the Datil). But Bill and Ruth, missionaries of the palate, grow these little boogers from hell on their four acres in Monticello, Florida, and brew them down into a sassy elixir that they bottle and ship coast-to-coast as Liquid Summer, sold at better sauce shops everywhere.

I don't want to overplay the theological side of the endeavor, but it's there, in spades, so why not? You take a look at Bill, who's sort of like a bright-eyed middle-aged Santa Claus, raised in the Delta, and you think, well, if the good Lord didn't get ahold of Bill Wharton first, with that presence of his he would've landed feet-first at the Vatican, in charge of financial operations, or at least charcoal-grilling. Because the thing is, and it's not just food we're talking about here, Bill Wharton wants to feed a lot of people.

"Man," he told me recently, when I caught his show at Margaritaville, "I mean a whole lot of people."

Well, Bill, that's nice, that's real nice. He and his band don't just perform the blues, they *cook* them, literally, whereas Miss F. just cruises around town in them. Wharton walks on stage and plugs in two things: his electric guitar and his hot plate. The drummer gives him a roll—"May I introduce the chef of the evening"—and the audience salivates.

"We gonna have to cook a little bit for you tonight," the Sauce Boss drawls in his raw voice, wet and raspy. "I've got my little pot over here and a bunch of shit I'm gonna put in it, and this is how we're gonna do it," and then the bass player whaps this thunderous idling-Mercury-muffler sound out of his guitar, and Wharton commences a gumbo, making vital connections and parablizing.

"Now, if you're building a house, you don't call the roofer first, y'all. You get the bricklayer. Same with the bass player and the blues. Same with the gumbo and the roux. Yeah! Heh-heh-heh."

He advocates heavy stirring. The bass thunders and bounces and dips; the keyboard checks in with the vegetables, the chicken, the chicken stock. The bluesmaster waves a judicious link of smoked sausage, he grabs for the sauce. "I'll tell you what," Wharton cackles, "Liquid

Summer is the hot sauce that makes making babies a pleasure." He's splashing that shit all over the place. "Ladies and gentlemen, this is something that will change your life, if not your entire digestive track." Behind him, to the side, the blues are churning, and Bill steps in to turn up the heat with his guitar. The damn gumbo's steaming; the gumbo bubbles, making the joint as fragrant as a bayou kitchen.

"Stir the gumbo," yells the audience. "Stir the gumbo."

Deep into the second set, the gumbo fumes; a tall blonde priestess comes forth with bowls of shrimp and oysters. "You wanna see a grown man cry, baby?" Wharton sings, sliding the seafood into the pot during the apocalypse of the final song, and then Wharton testifies as to the miracle of a blues-inspired gumbo, a loaves-and-fishes thing: "Come on up, y'all. It's ready. I've cooked in a lot of places, and it's always been enough."

And they come. Cook the gumbo and they will come, folks anxious to be fed by Bill and saved by the blues. I tell you, sinners, it beats going to a Ted Nugent concert and ending up with Squirrel Tartare, or being served rice cakes by that girl with the shaved head. They come, just like they come to Miss F.'s heavenly wheels for the Big Ride, and this all makes sense to me, these intersecting lines, these kindred things, for this is where I myself worship in these puzzling times, the Church of the Holy Gumbo, the irReverend Wharton presiding, the music pulling my soul heavenward like taffy and a '64 Merc out in the parking lot, waiting to take us all home. This is like the Ur-language of modern life, such as it is, in America—these cars, that gumbo, this sauce, those blues.

THE SAUCE BOSS'S GUMBO BLUES

ROUX:

1 ½ cups vegetable oil

2 cups flour

GUMBO:

2 green peppers, chopped

2 large onions, chopped

1 frying chicken (cooked), cut into pieces

1 pound smoked sausage, cut into ½-inch slices

2 zucchini, sliced

½ pound okra, sliced

1 gallon water

2 cups chicken stock

¼ cup Liquid Summer (or another appropriately devilish) hot sauce

3 tablespoons cajun seasoning

Salt and pepper

1 pint oysters

1 pound shrimp

3 tablespoons file powder

First, in a large pot, lay that bass line down: the roux. Heat oil; sprinkle in flour, stirring constantly over medium heat until the mix is just a white-boy's (with soul) side of chocolate-colored (don't you burn that shit). Reduce heat to low; add green pepper and onion; cook until soft. Add cooked chicken (boned or de-boned, doesn't matter), sausage, zucchini, okra, water, chicken stock, hot sauce, cajun seasoning, and salt and pepper to taste. Stir well; bring the whole mess to a boil. Reduce heat, add file powder. Simmer for one hour, about the time it might take you to get into serious trouble. Add oysters and shrimp. Return to a boil, cooking about 5 minutes or until the seafood's done. Serve over rice and let the big dog eat.

MAKES 10 TO 12 SERVINGS.

HOMECOMINGS

Miss F. speaks. Her never-ending dialogue with me, doesn't matter if I'm there or not—and lately I'm not.

I was lying in bed this morning thinking about you, thinking about how I wish you could spy on us, see us in our life without you. It's so different, a difference that would, I think, delight you. You would step into the trailer and know immediately that a girl and her dog lived here—do you know what I mean? JUST a girl—no boy, no couple. There's girl stuff and dog stuff lying around but no boy stuff at all. It's different than when you're home—different and comfortable most of the time. Issabel is different too—much more affectionate and attentive, more protective. Not to say we don't miss you horribly, but I do enjoy the difference.

This past year I've been on the go for, Lord, too long. New York, Amsterdam, London, Cuba, Argentina, Nepal; teaching in North Carolina, Utah, California, Hong Kong. While I have traipsed to and fro, Miss F. remained anchored in Florida, first to law school, then to the bar exam, now to the legislature of the state, hired as a high-heeled samurai in the trenches of democracy, the staff attorney for the joint committee on information technology. Copyright law, public records, privacy acts—Miss F.'s in the thick of it. Smack in the middle of her own life, I mean, which was always the point. And yes, she's right, I can't say I really know what it's like for her, that other individual, the one who functions splendidly without me, not the woman I know so well, the one I habitually kiss goodbye, the one who marks my frequent leavetaking with a measure of sweet ambivalence, wrapping herself in the silky robes of her independence.

Sunday: Please do not go away again without giving me some idea of how to reach you. Brian called about Buenos Aires; Sarah called about Hong Kong. La Bel has gone off the deep end—I bathed her this morning and she has spent the last two hours curled up on my leather bag with a towel pulled over her, licking the bag as if it were coated with chocolate. Pete is coming over tonight for black-bean soup.

What is this girl stuff anyway, and how is it so different from boy stuff? While I'm off poking through the world, trying to earn both a living and a scope of knowledge, just what is it—what picture—Miss F. wants me to see and so appreciate, should I indeed possess the godlike skill of omniscience (actually, spying on Miss F. doesn't interest me; I'd rather look in the windows of strangers)? What essences is she cultivating outside of my influence?

What I see is . . . well, I dunno. Although I'm a bit of a slob, and she's a tad fussy, cleanliness isn't it. Visiting old pals in Miami—Miss C. and Cigar John—a friend of mine remarked that it didn't look as if a man lived in their house: too tidy, too swept up and picked up, no pungent boxer shorts a-mouldering in the naves, no sprawl of nuts and bolts or greasy tools, no sports equipment permanently inhabiting the corners, no clutter of any type, as if clutter served as the signature spoor of the male specimen. But the grander truth is that Miss C. and Cigar John have achieved parity on the issue of fastidiousness, and I've known plenty of girls who were blueribbon pigs in matters of domestic hygiene. Miss F.'s private life may be less chaotic when I'm not around, maybe, but it is no more or less immaculate, I wouldn't think, although the rate of degeneration is perhaps slowed by my absence.

Monday: This is not going to be my week. No money. Issabel tripped me this morning, and I twisted my ankle hard. Car broke in mid-traffic, had to

walk home. Two birds have built a nest in the Florida room. Now what?
Someone keeps calling and hanging up when I answer. John called and wants
to go to Cuba if possible. Who aren't you taking—besides me? What hap-
pened to the clams—did you eat them? Where are you?

Girl stuff? What I see is:

Miss F. propped up by scented pillows, twenty or thirty of them, in a
canopied bed. The sheets are candystriped, peppermint and white. Her
hair is in curlers, there's some mortarlike paste drying on her cheeks and
forehead. On the nightstand are a jumbo-size bottle of Midol, a dish of
headache pills, an open jar of Tiger Balm, a half-empty tube of exotic
body lotion. The light is somewhat Victorian, queenly, and throughout
the room there seems to have been a lacy snowfall of lingerie. Around
her in bed she's built herself an osprey's nest of catalogues—fashion,
gardening, food, furniture—though she's actually reading a mystery by
Jimmy Lee Burke. Every one of her fingernails and toenails is painted a
different color; the same with Issabel's claws and there's a ribboned bow
stuck atop her head. The floor is littered with empty bags of goldfish
crackers, cheddar-cheese popcorn, hazel-nut cookies, and—unlike me—
she hasn't dropped a single crumb down into the sheets. (Myself, I-pre-
fer to eat tins of sardines in bed, late at night, and although I couldn't
begin to explain why, I think we're getting to the heart of the conceptual
problem here.) Issabel sits at ease on the boy side of the bed, which
remains tucked, unmauled, fresh. Miss F., who is holding, wrapped in a
washcloth to prevent her hand from freezing, a pint of Haagen Dazs
chocolate chocolate chip, is feeding both of them with a fork: one bite
for herself, one bite for the dog, and so on, till they eat the whole thing.
That's their dinner because, being girls, that's what they want, and I'm
not there to feed them properly, to invade their feminine indulgences.

Friday night: Issabel and I have gone down to the trailer on Cedar Key
again. I've just finished gulping some quick pasta (w/pesto) and putting
things away. Coffee's made and Patsy Cline is on the box. A beautiful
night—rain-cooled breeze off the water, which is slick calm, a coral
and deep-blue sky, one large pelican swimming large lazy circles just
offshore. I'm going to read a bit more and then will sleep like a rock.

I miss you—hope we can sneak down here for a couple of days while you're (briefly) home.

There's the biological wall, the little secrets answering to hormonal criteria—can't get around them and wouldn't want to anyway. If Miss F. wants to squander seven years aggregate fooling around in the bathroom, that's her business and hers alone. But have we been socialized into different corners of the ring? Nah. Is she so much an other that I'm obsessed with the mystique? In a way, yes, that's one of the Big Reasons it doesn't take me long to get homesick on the road, but Miss F. can't really expose these fundamental differences to me that make her or any other woman unknowable: they're intangible, no matter how much science and pseudoscience you use, like acid, to burn them away. If it comes to that, I just won't listen.

Saturday: Strong breeze off the water this lovely morning; strong sun to the east, double-white clouds in the west. Were you here, you'd be off in the boat by now. I've just finished breakfast (a little cereal w/blueberries, peaches, strawberries, and a banana), am having my first cup of coffee before carting La Bel to the beach for a run. This is the perfect place for you to work: it's quiet, so quiet I could hear the rainwater dripping out of the boat last night; so quiet I could hear the tide go out; so quiet I could hear the land crabs walking across the dock. That quiet.

What happens when I go away is that Miss F. loses weight. She starves, if you want to know the truth (how very modern of her). Thus the source of her mixed feelings about my leave-taking. Like anybody else, we can get momentarily tired of each other, but she's never wished me a fare-thee-well because I am a pain in the behavioral ass, but rather out of caloric desperation. Although we are two, I cook for four; I cook like a fat, happy Italian; I cook like a peasant, baby-factory mother; I cook like a French farm wife, like there's no tomorrow, like Elizabeth Taylor's chef when she's on a binge. Here's the main difference between myself and Miss F.: It's gastronomic. Sad to say, left to her own devices, she eats girl food, the cuisine that ruined California; lite pastas, fruits, grains. Her favorite meal is a thick steak, obscenely rare, with a neuromuscular twitch left in it, yet it seems without a boy around she backslides into a feeding pattern usually associated with the convent, a menu to harmonize with her temporarily smoke-free, sexless, loudly peaceful habitat. Am I a bad influence on Miss E.? Well, no more than she desires.

Sunday: The wind has finally died a little—bad news, I think, because it seemed to blow until it sucked in bad weather: gray, heavy skies this morning, hot and humid. Fish are popping out of the water like spattering oil in a frying pan. Mullets. We girls had a bad night—Issabel was hot and bothered, panting next to my head or draped over my legs all night long. Cats, cats, cats, the trailer park's filled with cats, and how they tantalize La Bel. What tantalizes me is the thought of cooking a homecoming dinner for you. Won't you find your way home? Out of the world, where it's easy to get sidetracked, and into the shelter of our life together. I've been waiting to cook you a steak. I'm ready. My appetite's ready. Come home, boy.

Steak Florentine sounds *très elegant*, but the foundation of elegance, I would remind the pretenders of the earth, is simplicity itself and an instinct for class inherent in all such elusive ambitions.

STEAK FLORENTINE WITH GRILLED LEEKS

¼ cup olive oil

1 cup white wine

2 garlic cloves, minced

2 sprigs fresh rosemary (optional)

1 huge, extra-thick T-bone or porterhouse steak

2 leeks

Salt and pepper

1 lemon

In a small mixing bowl, make a delicate marinade with the olive oil, wine, garlic, and rosemary. Pour most of the marinade onto a platter large enough to hold the steak. Marinate each side of the meat for 5 minutes. Heat a grill until it's blazing hot. Trim leeks, split each bulb vertically down the middle and wash under the faucet. Throw the steak on the grill, salt and pepper liberally. Put the leeks on too, off to the side so they don't char, and sprinkle with the remaining marinade. The Italians like their meat well-done; if you do too, cook each side of the steak about 15 minutes. About half that to satisfy the bloodlust of a reunited Miss F. Cook the leeks until they are limp and browning. Remove steak from fire, cut the lemon in half, and douse each side of the steak with the juice from each half. You have to pay a fortune for this meal in Florence; at my house, all you have to do is come in out of the cold, like a roaming but single-minded mutt who's finally found his way home.

SERVES 2.

THE COMPANY OF
CANINES

"The more I see of men, the better I like my dog."

—FREDERICK THE GREAT

For the past year, I have struggled to enforce a very few hard-and-fast rules around the house regarding matters canine, and the result, now evident, is that I've lost both the battle and the war.

Throughout our many years together, Miss F. and I have owned a dog, *one*, one moderately big dog, and as recently as six months ago, that one-dog role was nicely played by Issabel, a rather independent, willful and self-amusing Irish setter who believes it's funny to ram her missile-like nose into your backside if you bend over to tie your shoes and who burps so loudly and insubordinately when you try to lecture her, you have to stop and wonder where she picked up all this rudeness—certainly not from me. Since Miss F. is now, thank God, employed and because I traveled too frequently this past year, Miss F. fretted that we had abandoned Issabel out on the brink of loneliness, left by herself in the house all day, not exactly starved for attention but increasingly undernourished—and wouldn't it be kind and wise and fun to find her a companion? I didn't pause to think that this suggestion might be only a ploy of Miss F.'s in her lifelong campaign to surround herself with a court of dogs, she the loving queen of their affections, licked and panted over until the day she dies.

She's never made it a secret that she expects to one day have at least five of them—a couple of setters, a standard poodle, a Jack Russell terrier, an Irish water spaniel—and I imagine there are a couple more breeds on her list that she's hesitant to tell me about. I think, though, that she thinks I'd appreciate being the alpha male of my very own pack.

Whenever she's gone on this way, I've always invoked Hard-and-Fast Rule Number One: You may have as many dogs as you wish, applying the formula of one dog per acre, and since our fiefdom in its most current survey extends to only about a quarter of that landmass, I have told her repeatedly that she's already exceeded her ceiling on dogs by a factor of four. Any waiver of the rule, I argued, would be madness.

Well, this reasoning seemed to have made quite an impression upon Miss F. She dropped the subject until this past October, at which time she was, not so coincidentally, admitted to the Bar; after that, I must say, it seemed that court was always in session around the palace as we sought to refine and tune the domestic code, which comes under a singular range of pressures with any addition to the fold. Miss F. advocated compassion and generosity for the latchkeyed Issabel. Since I am the unshaven and ill-dressed member of the family, you might assume I would therefore represent the libertarian, populist, underdog side of this issue, and Miss F., having thrown in her lot with the Established Order, would espouse the conservation of sanity and reason in our own self-made universe, but the bare truth is we have a set, however limited, of hard-and-fast rules around here because *I* want them, hoping to preserve some illusion of rationality in the days of our lives.

Right. Well and good. By November, the verdict was in the door, and his name was Frankie. I can't even recall the moment I acquiesced to this, though I'd like to believe Miss F. is not one of those monarchs who go in for drugging and backhandedness. Frankie was a handsome nine-month-old male with dancer's legs and foppish ears, a bit developmentally slow, who was able to communicate to us that, were he in fact human, his identity would be not unlike that of a baffled poet, who disdained physical love for spiritual knowledge and whose interest in the opposite sex was not merely platonic but noble to the point of canonization. Which we took to be the absolute truth because Issabel, a three-year-old tart, was in the middle of her semiannual estrus when Frank showed up, took one fastidious sniff of her and asked for a copy of *The Complete Works of Robert Browning*. The threat of being bombed with puppies seemed deferred for another six months, at which time we could either expand the boundaries of the kingdom or have Issabel spayed. Meanwhile, as long as her heat continued, Issabel was allowed to receive only eunuchs and, of course, the asexual youngster Frankie.

Around the same time, I left town for a week, off to Miami to determine the gastronomic impact of the Noriega trial on the American judicial system (*arroz con pollo* has definitely infiltrated the U.S. attorney's office, though a Justice Department spokesperson vehemently denies this). While I was there, I got a frantic phone call from Miss F., who was in Cedar Key visiting friends and fellow dog owners. While Miss F. sat for tea with Miss Connie, the dogs were out back with their dog host, Hobbes, discussing the often-subtle difference between leaves and birds. A brown Lab approached, perhaps with an insight about wind. Despite being neutered, he nevertheless became enamored with Issabel and pantomimed what he would do to her if only he were so equipped. Frankie, the retarded child-poet in a dog suit, feigned a distaste for such crude display, stepping aside to look on in a dim-witted but ponderous fashion. However, when Miss F. next glanced out the window, she saw what I have a great deal of trouble believing she had never seen before in her life, since she has seen most everything.

"Frankie and Issabel got stuck together!" she cried into the phone.

Today I have to honestly ask myself: "What the fuck were we thinking?" Spring is on its way as I write, and, by the mathematics of my Hard-and-Fast Rule

Number One, we are now operating at the ratio of forty dogs per acre, at the current net rate of being a ten-dog household, thanks to Issabel's litter of eight. Wouldn't it be easier if we just had a kid? I asked Miss F., and, maybe, well, yes, I finally got her to agree, so we're working on that with all the tenacity—speaking for myself—of Piers the Plowman, but that's another story. But I suspect Miss F. remains sympathetic to the views, conception-wise, of the African bushman who wondered why he should take up farming when there are so many mongongo nuts in the world. Or, as Cynthia Nelms has said, "I'd get pregnant if I could be assured I'd have puppies."

In the meantime, there are a few new hard-and-fast rules at our house—they are, of course, my rules, not Miss F.'s—and the majority of them apply to mealtimes. For instance: No dogs on the table during dinner. At the table is acceptable, to a point. No climbing up on guests, unless they are foolish enough to encourage it, or too inert or simply too stupid to knock the infractor away decisively, best accomplished by a rap with the flat side of a butter knife. Also, food that sits upon a guest's plate or is in transit from a guest's plate to a guest's mouth is, *ipso facto*, the guest's food and not doggy food, so lunging and running off with something is out, with this single exception: In the case of any ostentatious, long-winded and tedious guest who, in the midst of fatuous monologue, continues to wave a sparerib or a chicken leg in the air like a baton and shake it aggressively at other members of the party while he or she advances such propositions as "The Japanese are predatorial little devils" or "We can save education in America without paying for it," the aforementioned sparerib or chicken leg may be torn unceremoniously from the speaker's hand and gulped down quickly, together with any fingers that come along as garnish.

I have also enacted an amendment to the above package of rules, to close a loophole wide enough for Frankie's tongue to have made its way through. Frankie is to tongue what Cyrano de Bergerac is to nose. The dog is perfectly capable of standing well back from the table, seemingly obedient, and, while mesmerizing you with the exquisite sensitivity and lugubrious soulfulness of his poet's eyes, curling his tongue out the side of his apparently closed mouth to discreetly bridge the distance between him and your table setting, laying this anatomical wonder down on a plate or into a bowl of soup with such surreptitious innocence that it's possible for you to think that he thinks that you think this enormous pink and pulsing slab of tongue nesting in your food is simply a part of the evening's culinary presentation, and no one need be alarmed. Once caught in this ruse, Frank seems quite satisfied to graciously reel his tongue back where it belongs with whatever trace of flavor or ribbon of sauce has adhered to its flypaper surface.

Frankie established his gastronomic agenda early on at our house by habitually eating the covers off Miss F.'s *Bon Appetits*, yet he snubs the same high-quality brands of canned dog food that pensioners seem to enjoy so much at the end of the month. On the other hand, when he's in his ascetic poet mood, the big Frank adores the blandest kibble, holding each single comforting morsel in his mouth until it melts like a communion wafer delivered by the pope. He's a queer one, Frank. In contrast, Issabel's aesthetic works off the theme of gluttony. She's been ravenous now for months, devouring, devouring, devouring, and begging constantly for treats, her two current favorites being hot pickled okra and Max's Italian Style Dog Snacks, all natural ingredients—as if she cares.

Back to the rules. There is no need to legislate the ownership of food that hits the floor, seeing as how there's been plenty of precedent since the dawn of time, that this food is fair game for man or beast.

Understand that I realize not everyone wants to eat in the company of dogs, though most of our closest friends do, or don't mind, or perhaps are afraid to speak out. From my own perspective, once they've let it be known that the dogs are okay, I imagine if anything's going to put them off, it's the sight of Miss F. using these poor creatures to circumvent the one household task she is explicitly sworn to, no matter what, even though this job is the one she is worst at in all the world: washing dishes. (Listen, I cook, don't bother me with that.) So Miss F. enlists the dogs to help with the dishes. I'm sure if she had her way entirely, they'd lick everything clean, far cleaner than she ever manages to get things in the sink, and all she'd have to do is stuff the plates right back into the cupboard. Our more regular guests already conspire in this routine and simply pitch their tableware onto the floor for a preliminary scrubbing once they've had their fill. I have yet to come up with a hard-and-fast rule that addresses any potential abuse or embarrassment that might develop from this, since Miss F. tells me that the mouths of Issabel and Frankie are cleaner than my own, and although I know this assertion is part of dog mythology, in my case I tend to believe her. (Miss F.'s only hard-and-fast rule, by the way, if you were wondering, is that anytime they so desire, the dogs may eat the mail.)

It's true that we've been occasionally blessed with a dinner guest so important and uniquely fascinating, such a paradigm of culture, such an example of genius and manners and hygienic vulnerability, that we've wrapped the dogs from head to tail in duct tape and thrown them out into the backyard so as not to distract us from the utterance of the great man or great woman gracing our table. We'll do that for you, too, if you're that fucking wonderful and prissy. On the whole, though, Miss F. and I prefer our humanity rank and file, and for those of you on this earth, all of you nature respecters and admirers of things great and small, who find pets (or children) to be a vast annoyance, let me assure you that your invitation is not in the mail, and let me warn you that I have it from a pretty good source (the poet Frankie) that Saint Peter is actually a guard dog, a stern but nevertheless good-hearted Doberman pinscher, and he's going to want to know just what in the world it was you thought you were talking about, back on earth, when you talked about love.

FRUTTI DI MARE
(FRUITS-OF-THE-SEA SALAD)

1 pound each octopus and squid
(or 2 pounds squid)

4 cloves garlic, divided

2 pounds mussels in shells
(or 1 pound shelled and precooked)

1 pound bay scallops

1 pound medium-sized shrimp

2 lemons

½ cup oil-cured black olives

10 tablespoons extra-virgin olive oil

Handful of fresh basil leaves

Fresh parsley, chopped

Salt and freshly ground black pepper, to taste

I'm fully cognizant of the fact that this recipe has nothing to do with the text of this essay, except that I would like to salute the Italians, who, along with the British and the French, are the world's most passionate dog lovers. Compared to them, Americans hate dogs, spit on dogs, would just as soon see every dog dead or incarcerated. If you don't believe me, just ask the nearest elected official. It is to republican Rome, a city and culture nourished by the milk of a wolf, that we trace our modern regard for dogs, even though in the fourth millennium B.C., the Chinese emperor Fo-Hi did consider breeding tiny dogs to slip into his robe as pocket-warmers, and an ancient Egyptian would shave his head to mourn the death of his dog; and let's not forget that when Odysseus returned home after his twenty-year road trip, only Argus, his mutt, recognized him. Indeed, the rise of civilization and the domestication of dogs were simultaneous events, both inspired by mealtimes around the campfire. Dogs and food, hunger and friendship, are bound together in the roots of prehistory. Our appetites, not the least for affection, produced the dog; he's our creation, made in our image, a household hanger-on.

Also, I would like to suggest that this recipe is very handy if you happen to own a dog or dogs and they persist, as mine do, in crowding you while you work in the kitchen. If so, and you choose to cook this dish, you might find it worth your while, if you live near the coast, to go out of your way, down to the waterfront, to purchase the freshest ingredients—live, in fact, if possible. Because—here's the tip—nothing clears a dog out of the kitchen faster than sticking a live octopus or squid on its nose.

Anyway, if you do have an octopus and are brave enough to eat it, cut off its head (at the base of its tentacles; save the tentacles but throw away the head), then slice its tentacles into ¼-inch sections and boil in a large pot of salted water until tender. Drain in a colander and set aside. Wait, I forgot to say you should do all this the day before you plan to serve the dish, or at least that morning. All right. If the squid is not precleaned, cut off its head (same procedure as for octopus), remove the crystal feather that serves as the squid's spine, peel off the outer film of skin, then turn the squid's body inside out and clean away its viscera. When you're done, you should have something that resembles a condom made out of the same material used to mold the soles of tennis shoes. Cut squid into rings, then boil rings and tentacles in salted water (you can use the same water the octopus was cooked in) until tender, 15 to 30 minutes. Drain squid, then place in a large serving bowl with octopus. Meanwhile, mince 1 clove garlic and, in a separate pot, steam mussels with garlic until shells open; remove mussels from shells and add to serving bowl. Boil scallops in another pot (or the same pot of salted water you've been using) for about 4 minutes. Transfer to bowl. Devein and boil shrimp for 3 to 4 minutes, then add to bowl (you might cut them in half first, if they're large). Squeeze juice from lemons into bowl, add olives, olive oil, remaining garlic (minced), basil leaves, parsley, and salt and pepper, then toss, cover and stick in the refrigerator overnight (or for at least 8 hours) to marinate. Remove an hour before serving, to bring to room temperature.

SERVES 6 TO 8.

A CONSPIRACY OF
ICE CREAM

Miss F. likes to talk ice cream, discoursing beyond the simple declarative (I want some), the subsequent interrogatives (Is there any? How could you not leave me some, you skunk?) and the predictable, ecstatic exclamatives (Yummy! God! Double Yum! More! Gimme!) to wax nostalgic about the marvelous, magical ice cream of her youth. On and on she goes, pouring out a syrup of memories: the glint of the ice and the salt from her girlhood, the ripe turgescence of berries and peaches, the crisp succulence of cherries and pears, all of the sensual juice-bearing fruits of summertime harvested by a rose-cheeked, pinafored Miss F. with her sisters and mama, who would ceremoniously rinse and prepare this bounty and deliver it to Daddy, who would add the fruit to his bucket of cream and turn the hand crank for a minute or two in a ritual display of daddy-hood, then make the three girls take over the operation until their arms fell off. Finally, each rewarded with her bowl of slush, they would eat, and after managing to lift the last exquisite, best-ever goopy spoonful to their mouths, they would all faint, in hierarchical order, oldest first. Once restored to consciousness, the sisters would congratulate themselves for being so self-sufficient, ice cream-wise, and then sing "God Bless

America" and chase lightning bugs and have spelling bees and recite the Pledge of Allegiance, and then go skipping off to sleep in the sugar-frosted beds of their innocence. Or something. Gosh, what fun. Wish I'd been there at Miss F.'s house, where my ten-year-old self would have sneak-attacked Miss F.'s nine-year-old self, enslaved by her father to the ice-cream maker, and pulled up her dress. To see France, of course; at that age, I was still mulling over a career as a cartographer, whatever that was. "Why, that's not France," I would have said. "That's Thighland." Odds are excellent that Miss F. would have hated me as a boy.

Because Miss F. can also expound quite stirringly on the technological innovations that threaten First Amendment freedoms, it's only fair, I think, that I indulge her sentimentalities regarding ice cream, though I confess I'm much happier hearing about information resources and copyright laws. I don't know what it is about ice cream: I'm not ice cream's friend, though I'm occasionally its lover, and summertime homilies on the subject only feed my suspicions of a vast conspiracy of ice cream afoot throughout history.

"What! You never had homemade ice cream when you were growing up?" Miss F. seems to enjoy saying to me, feigning shock. "Poor dear. You were deprived. It explains so much."

Nope, no homemade ice cream in my childhood. At my house, we made kielbasi, which certainly speaks for itself. We didn't bore ourselves with berry-picking; we gathered eels and crabs, golf balls out of ponds, Japanese beetles off the rosebushes in the yard—armloads of weird crap more suited for the quorum of boys in our house than for our sister, probably not the ingredients she had in mind for a successful girlhood. Needless to say, I can't use any of this to square off, childhood against childhood, with Miss F.

"I seem to recall *bombe glacée* and *plombières*," I sniff back at Miss F.'s Norman Rockwell childhood, her Gallo-wine-commercial youth. "But I don't remember if the sous-chef made them in-house or had them delivered by courier from the city."

Miss F. snorts. "Liar. You never had hired help when you were growing up, and neither did we."

"Then who was that woman in the kitchen?"

"In all likelihood, she was your mother."

It all returns: the fish sticks, the pot roasts, the meat loaves, the potatoes in their many humble forms, the awful thawing brick of Neapolitan ice cream we lugged home from the A&P: that tricolor strata of better-than-nothing chocolate; insipid, mindless vanilla; and the ultra-sissy, perfume-tasting, baby-doll-pink strawberry that always seemed to get into the other flavors, no matter how vigilant you were, and poison them with cooties. I couldn't eat it. Even as a grade-schooler, I had an inkling that coffee, brandy, and tobacco were a more satisfying cap on dinner than dessert, which was for blubberers, snots, darlings, and people who were trying to pretend they were English—which I was definitely not, growing up in a house where English was not the only language heard.

"It's apparent," Miss F. says, "that you transferred the inescapable misogyny of your prepubescent boyhood to ice cream."

Oh, bull. It was a matter of class and tradition, which we didn't have. Miss F.'s family, which is a museum of Founding Uncles and Second Cousins of the Revolution, has a heritage, however attenuated, of sweet privilege. We, on the other hand, were serfs escaping the ice cream-less oppression of czarist Russia. If my ancestors wanted ice cream, they had to sell a baby on the black market for the price of a single-scoop cone, which they'd then have to share with the entire village.

"Get off it," says Miss F. "We both grew up in the suburbs, in adjoining neighborhoods, in similar houses, on identical streets. Our fathers were both government bureaucrats."

True enough, but at her house, they made delicate-flavored, rich-bodied tubs of their own ice cream. We poured Kool-Aid into an ice-cube tray and froze it. At Miss F.'s house, on the Fourth of July, they shot their Roman candles into the nearest body of water. At my house, on the Fourth of July, we shot our Roman candles into one another's hair, trying for the eyes. There are obvious sociological and, of course, sexual differences that provide us with our separate pasts and palates, but I often wonder if perhaps Miss F. herself represents the vestige of an ancient ice-cream cabal that has forever sought to control the earth, beginning in China long before the birth of Christ, when iced drinks and desserts were the refreshments of emperors: If you were born outside the royal chambers during, say, the Shang dynasty, forget trying to find a sno-cone on the streets in July.

Everything has its history, and the history of ice cream, *Larousse Gastronomique* reports, is closely linked with that of gastronomy and refrigeration. You and I and Jerry Brown understand that "gastronomy" means ruling class; "refrigeration" evokes the sweaty struggle of the masses to enjoy Fudgsicles after a hot day's work. As best I can tell, ice cream and its predecessors, as with armies and gold bullion, are some of power's trademarks and can be used to track its westward drift across the millennia. Thanks to someone in the imperial Chinese kitchens, the gastronomic art of eating ice was taught to Arab traders, who brought it home to the kingdoms and caliphates of sandy Assyria, where they mightily impressed their lords and masters by concocting *sharbets*, fruit syrups chilled with the unseasonable treasure of mountain snow.

Icy desserts popped up next in the court of Alexander the Great: spoils of war, traveling ever farther west through space and time, to the Roman Empire, where we find Nero on his knees in the vomitorium, having consumed a swinish excess of fruit salads and purées mixed with honey and precious summer snow. What the gods failed to provide, slaves did their cheerful best to compensate for.

The secret of chilling liquids without ice, by using a mixture of water and saltpeter, was one of the party tricks Marco Polo brought back from the Far East, and thus, in the thirteenth century, the great fashion of water ices took hold in Italy, if you knew the right millionaires. Catherine de Medici introduced the treats to France, 240 years later, when she married the future Henri II, a dweeb who hadn't even heard of forks. As royalty are wont to do, the court hoarded the secret for another century; by the 1700s, sherbet (ice cream's ancestor) was all the rage in Paris, with 250 *limonadiers* hawking Slurpees on the boulevards. Milk or cream ices themselves seem to have been invented prior to 1650 by a French cook in the employ of Charles I of England, but the king bribed the gastronome to keep his method a secret, which he did with great success, since no Londoner seemed aware of ices made with cream and eggs until around 1775.

"Stop there," Miss F. says, interrupting. "According to your date, you've just associated the discovery and popularization of ice cream with civilization's democratic awakening."

"Right."

"Let me see if I have your revisionist history of the world straight," she says. "First, the kings and emperors had all the ice cream."

"Yes!"

"Then they suddenly gave it away?"

"Well, not exactly—it was a preemptive strike. The monarchs saw those revolutions coming and released the recipe, hoping to pacify the downtrodden: Give them ice cream and they'll go away. The way I see it, the ploy is, after 200 years, finally gathering steam."

Miss F. looks concerned. "Oh, dear," she says consolingly, "you've been reading *The Nation* again, haven't you? What happened next?"

Next, ice cream made its transatlantic voyage, and, in Virginia, Miss F.'s people got ahold of it; they weren't as generous with their new dessert as you might think. In fact, it wasn't until 1851, in Baltimore, that ice cream became available for mass consumption, which as you know was one of the contributing factors to the Civil War. Then, of course, Teddy Roosevelt had a craving for banana splits, which resulted in the United States' invading Cuba, the Philippines, and most of Central America, and, thanks to ice cream, we were on the road to becoming an imperial power.

"You're getting yourself worked up over nothing," says Miss F., leading me to my favorite place in the house, a camp stool right in front of the TV.

Next, they invented television to keep us indoors. Now there are even microwavable sundaes you can order by phone and have Fed-Exed. In Cincinnati, they're glad to "cut up" your ice cream with M&M's and sprinkles and all manner of glittery toxins so that you'll forget about censorship and Charles Keating and Pete Rose. Miss F. turns on the tube, hoping to calm me down.

"Look," she chirps, "it's your favorite show." C-Span. "Alan Simpson and Jesse Helms are filibustering."

Something's happening out there, a rising tide of nationalism, everybody so chauvinistic about his own ice cream, those damn Italians, electing Mussolini's neo-Fascist granddaughter. Miss F. coos to me, spooning Haagen-Dazs into my mouth, trying to lower my temperature, to stabilize my blood sugars. Those guys at Haagen-Dazs, I know about them: They've gone global, they're up to something, follow the ice-cream trail. Miss F. thinks it's time we got an ice-cream maker, even if we don't quite as yet fit the royal standard.

"Ice cream," she says, hypnotizing me with the spoon, "deserves to rule the world."

You see, you see. She's one of them.

PEACHFISH'S FAVORITE
ICE CREAM

1 ½ cups peach nectar

4 large egg yolks

½ cup sugar

1 cup whole milk (not low-fat or skim milk)

1 cup heavy cream

2 cups chopped fresh, ripe peaches, peeled

4 tablespoons peach schnapps

In a small saucepan, cook peach nectar over medium heat until reduced by half. Cool to room temperature, cover, and refrigerate. In a large bowl, cream egg yolks and sugar until thick and light. In a large saucepan, heat milk and cream over low heat until scalded. Do not let mixture boil. Beating egg mixture slowly, add milk and cream mixture and beat until smooth. Return the entire mess to large saucepan and cook over low heat, stirring, until it thickens, coating the back of a spoon. Do not boil. Cool to room temperature, cover loosely with plastic wrap, and refrigerate about 3 hours. Add reduced peach nectar, peaches and peach schnapps to chilled custard, stirring well. Transfer mixture to an ice-cream maker, and freeze according to manufacturer's instructions.

SERVES 4 TO 6.

MOCHA ICE CREAM

1 cup whole milk

1 cup heavy cream

1 ½ tablespoons instant espresso powder

½ cup sugar

6 large egg yolks

7 ounces good-quality chocolate, broken into small pieces

In a large saucepan, combine milk, cream, espresso powder, and sugar; simmer over low heat, stirring frequently. In a medium-size bowl, beat egg yolks until blended. Beating slowly, gradually add milk and cream mixture to blended yolks. Return mixture to saucepan and cook over low heat, stirring slowly, until it thickens, coating the back of a spoon. Do not boil. Remove pan from heat. Add chocolate, stirring until melted and smooth. Cool to room temperature, cover loosely with plastic wrap, and refrigerate until cold, about 3 hours. Transfer mixture to an ice-cream maker and freeze according to manufacturer's instructions.

SERVES 4 TO 6.

MANGO SORBET

1 cup water

1 cup sugar

2 large ripe mangoes, peeled, pitted and puréed

2 teaspoons fresh lime juice

½ teaspoon grated lime peel

Combine water and sugar in heavy saucepan and cook over low heat until the sugar has dissolved. Cool to room temperature. Pour sugar syrup into a large bowl, add remaining ingredients, and stir until smooth. Refrigerate the mixture, loosely covered, until thoroughly chilled—at least two hours. Transfer mixture to an ice-cream maker and freeze according to manufacturer's instructions.

SERVES 4 TO 6.

THE WALLOPING
GOURMET

Contrary to the opinion of some of our friends and plenty of my adversaries, Miss F. is the hothead in our house, and as domestic violence becomes more and more fashionable across the country, a trendy part of life among the most respectable and accomplished families, she has seen to it that we at least have the appearance of making an effort to keep up with the Joneses. Admittedly, we are both emotional sorts with flashpoint tempers, yet when the shoe fits, she is the one you'll find wearing it, and because this is the topic currently on my mind, I've been sitting at my desk for the past half hour, trying in vain to recall where and why, sometime during the last year, Miss F. slapped me, seemingly out of the blue. Finally, I had to crawl out from my cell in the basement and journey upstairs to Miss F.'s domain. She was tearing apart a bathroom, claiming the colors were all wrong.

"Miss F.," I said, "do you remember where and why you slapped me, sometime during the past year, seemingly out of the blue?"

To her credit, I suppose, she takes questions like this in stride, even exhibiting a modicum of fierce Amazonian pride in the blows she delivers—encouraged, as it were, by the profound impression she makes on me when she loses control and goes berserk.

"No," she said, pausing thoughtfully from the labor of redecoration. "Could it have been in Vermont? Could it have been when we were having dinner with that poet?"

"I don't think so," I said. "I don't believe I have inadvertently humiliated you in front of any poets since 1979, at the faculty party in Missouri, when you threw your drink in my face."

"Well, could it have been in New York, when we went to visit Mark and Miss P., and Miss M. showed up suddenly, and you dallied with her down by the pool until 5 o'clock in the morning?"

"No, no," I said. "You showed great restraint and understanding on that particular occasion. I seem to remember this slap took place at a party in a wood-paneled room. You were wearing white, I believe. You had sun on your skin, which glowed. There was a cluster of distinguished-looking men in the vicinity, who seemed absolutely titillated by your brazenness, and for a moment I thought they were each about to beg you to slap them too."

"Gosh, I'm sorry," said Miss F., "but I really don't remember. Are you sure it was me? Are you sure it wasn't some other woman?"

This was enough to jolt my memory. "Come to think of it," I said, "it was another woman, a wealthy, intelligent, beautiful middle-aged woman from Belgium who smuggled diamonds for Hasidic Jews from Rio to Brussels. She was my student last summer at Bennington. She hauled off and slapped me in the bar, while I was having conversation with two nice elderly women, and for the life of me I don't know why."

"Probably," said Miss F., "because you were being an ass."

"Not at all!" I protested. "I was behaving like a gentleman. Her slap was wholly unjustified. I think she was operating off some hysteric impulse, something deeply Freudian. I had to throw my drink on her."

"That's not like you," said Miss F.

"But only fair," I said, "under the circumstances."

"Under the circumstances," said Miss F., "I would have slapped the piss out of her, if I were you."

I once cuffed a twit in high school, one Friday night at a football game, in a hormone-blind burst of utterly meaningless aggression. Looking back on that moment, I can only surmise that I poked this fledgling, bespectacled goose of a boy because he was so much my own mirror image, and by picking on him I had temporarily, for the first and I hope last time, elevated myself into the thuggish ranks of all the shit-heads who were picking on me.

Anyway, cuffing the twit is on my private list of Things I Am Ashamed I Ever Did, which isn't a very long list at all, I'll have you know, and but for that one half-hearted sucker punch to the twit, I can truthfully state that I have never, ever slugged somebody full-on in my entire life, except once, and the victim just happened to be a girl. Well, young woman, if there's a difference.

We were both Peace Corps volunteers on a Caribbean island, and for a very brief and stormy time—two weeks—lived together, though not as a couple, at least technically. A couple of idiots would be the extent of it. One evening we strolled out into the countryside with two friends to hop the sugarcane train and drink a bottle of wine as we rolled under the stars. We sat on a knoll beside the railroad tracks and drank the wine, but the train never came, as it was meant to. One of us walked to a near-by village and returned with a bottle of moonshine rum. My date, a corn-fed girl from Iowa, guzzled half of it and passed out. The other couple decided they were in an advanced state of lust and went off, I believe, to fornicate.

I wanted to go off with them, but it would not have been the decent thing to do.

About a half hour later, my date opened her eyes, gave me a very clumsy, slack-mouthed kiss, and then threw up. She passed out again, woke, puked, passed out, etcetera. Sorry though I was to spoil such a good time, it was now well past midnight and I wanted to go home. I stood her on her feet and led her, weaving and stumbling, down the rail-road tracks back toward town. Before long I observed that we were walk-ing straight at a single bright light coming toward us out of the darkness. Hearing the churn of an engine and a clanging bell, I steered us off the tracks onto the easement of the railbed. God knows what this girl was thinking, but she jerked away from me, back to the middle of the tracks. "Hey, stop fucking around," I said. "The train's coming."

It was an extremely slow train, so she had a grace period in which to get away with this crap, but it was coming ahead, regardless. I tugged her back to safety but she twisted away, attracted toward the approaching light. I tried to strongarm her off into the grass, she struggled against me, the train kept a-coming, the train was about two car lengths away, she wouldn't budge, she was trying to lie down, and so I punched her, right, as they say, in the kisser, and pretty hard, I must confess, because it knocked her cold, which wasn't so great because then there was nothing I could do but throw her over my shoulder and stagger under her deadweight two miles back home, whereupon I tossed her in the shower and left her there, sputtering and soaked. The next day, she had no recollection of me popping her, and I certainly wasn't going to mention it, and although I regretted the necessity of smacking her so soundly, and although it was terrible to watch someone collapse unconscious under the force of my own hand, this event does not belong on my list of shameful acts. That's it for me, violence-wise, except for walloping the dogs when they bolt out into the street.

Perhaps you'll find it revealing, as my friend Wilbur did, that I have never told Miss F. this story, thereby indirectly informing her that the passivity I display when she starts hammering on me might have a limit, and that I am fully capable of busting her in the chops, should the proper occasion arise.

"I think that's the right message to send," said Wilbur. "You wouldn't want your wife to think you were a total wimp, just because you never hit her."

We were having a long, early lunch together at the cafeteria in the mall, where Wilbur likes to eat because he can get fried green tomatoes and sweet-potato pie. We are both housebound writers, working at home while our mates—Wilbur's wife is a journalist—are out haranguing people in the workplace. I was taking a poll of my male friends, probing them about the issue of domestic violence. Of course, when you ask a fellow if he smacks his wife, inevitably his response will be no, whether he does or not. I'm talking about your standard issue, sensitivity-indoctrinated 90s type of guy here. Not PC. PC sycophants deserve to be beat up by their wives morning, noon, and night. I mean your normal guy, trying his best to behave and use his testosterone constructively. Ask, however, if during an abrupt intensification of domestic conflict, he's ever been pounded on by his wife and, I was finding out, the answer is likely to be yes. Wilbur confirmed the pattern: in a regular, non-abusive, non-criminal hetero relationship, women feel entirely free to cross the line, see red, let themselves go and kick our ass.

"They get away with it," said Wilbur, "unless you do something to establish physical parameters in these situations. Pee, for instance,"—he calls his wife Pee, *ee* not *ea*, a unique but definitely Southern endearment—"when we were first married, would occasionally find grievous fault with me, fly into a rage, and start punching. I would do the Gandhi thing, go limp, protect my face, and so on, but after a while I realized this passivity only enraged her further, and was counterproductive. Pee's a big girl, as you know, she works out all the time, she's strong, maybe she was getting delusions of muscular grandeur. There came a day when, as she clobbered away on me, I said, 'Enough'. I subdued her, threw her over my knee, and gave her a good spanking."

"Holy cow!" I choked on my iced tea. "This didn't turn into something sexual, did it?" I wondered out loud, perhaps inappropriately.

"Not at all," said Wilbur. "Pee was livid. She thought it was absolutely inexcusable that I did this. It had its intended effect though. She doesn't swing away at me like she used to, and now when she reaches the boiling point, all I have to say is, 'Somebody around here needs a good spanking,' and even though she turns livid all over again, she does indeed back off."

Frankly, I doubt I could spank Miss F. as wholesomely and with such firm resolve as Wilbur spanked Pee, and besides, Miss F. would probably giggle. In truth, she has only attacked me once with wildcat ferocity, pummelling me about the head and shoulders, scratching and kicking. We were in my skiff, out on the Gulf, wave-tossed, the weather was not to her liking, I got fed up with her whining and resigned my position as captain, abandoned the steering, hopped past her into the bow and said, fine, since she wanted so much to go back ashore, she should get in the stern, where the dogs were now huddled, trying to make themselves small, and fucking well take us there herself. Mistakenly thinking I had endangered our lives, she let out a blood-curdling war cry and jumped on me until I was forced to retreat, before we capsized, back to the helm.

As fighters, though, I have come to the conclusion that Miss F. and I are only second-rate. We know better, for example, than to dine together when we're embroiled in our worst disagreements, whatever they are (she generally knows, I can't remember), unless we've tacitly agreed to use the meal as a ceremony of reconciliation. Otherwise, she'll go to the kitchen first and bake a potato (to annoy me, I'm sure, since it takes forever; you won't see Miss F. eating baked potatoes unless we're spatting). When she's cleared out I'll slink in and grill a cheese sandwich, gnaw on a carrot.

How meager our fare is when there's trouble between us, as if during times of confrontation it makes the most sense to forage like soldiers or refugees, and eating becomes a gloomy physical extension of the psychological atmosphere of starvation.

I am of the opinion that things explode in our personal lives more often at the dinner table than anywhere else, or at least begin to unravel. Each of us has known since childhood that dinner has the potential to erupt into an absolutely terrible event, the locus of expression for all the rotten things that might have infused our day with the spiritual equivalent of toxic waste. After all, it's at the table where we first assert, in a drawn-out, quasi-public test of wills, our rejection of whatever brings us no pleasure. Initially, we are repelled by vegetables or liver or oysters. Then we graduate up the ladder of interaction until we have reached its most dangerous and hurtful heights. No longer are we turning off to particular foods, but to each other's behavior ("Amos hit me with a rock." "Don't chuck rocks at your sister," warns Dad), each other's opinions ("If you'd just listen to the album, Mom," says 16-year-old Colin, "you'd see what I mean about Satan being the Lord of the Universe"), and eventually, unhappily, to each other, period ("I've had it," Martha screeches at Dave, after three deformed years of marital ugliness. "You are an abomination. The sight of you makes me vomit blood." "Read my lips," sneers Dave, quoting his favorite sportsman. "You're a fat-assed, frog-faced, soul-sucking, ball-crushing, entry-level bitch who doesn't even know how to give an acceptable blowjob").

Time for everybody to leave . . . unless you're like me, fascinated to learn how other couples work beyond the volatility of the moment. When dinner turns to debacle, the social and emotional wreckage can be devastating, not to mention a lot of fun, as long as you're not paying for it. Which reminds me of the most stupendous, breathtaking, speech-robbing, dazzling act of violence Miss F. ever committed in our relationship, without ever laying a finger on me.

We've spent many splendid evenings at dinner parties, as hosts or as guests. Regardless of how brutally we have quarreled beforehand, it seems sinful to allow our tempers to pollute the food and fellowship. I suppose this means that our fights are frivolous to begin with, or that we both feel compelled to keep up appearances. Perhaps our only real agenda is not to squander an otherwise good time. Once though, when I was going to school in Iowa, no amount of socializing could leaven Miss F.'s anger or throw her off the track of her week-long frustration with me. On the drive home from a dinner monopolized by graduate student writer-types, Miss F. let me know that my overall lack of gallantry had been highlighted, instead of moderated, by my behavior at the table. I swear I didn't understand what she was talking about; from my point of view, the majority of my most dire crimes are unwitting, without shape or substance, and cannot be discussed between us except obliquely. Since I had no clear idea why Miss F. was on my case, I simply ignored her punitive tone and shrugged off her objections, the logic of which I failed to grasp. What she wanted of course was my attention, which impressed me as a rather abstract need. We were in my little pickup truck, driving out into the countryside, past the cornfields, headed toward our farm. Unable to get through to me, she started screaming like a hellion and, somehow contorting herself to raise her feet above the dashboard in the cramped space of the cab, she did something I didn't even know you could do, especially wearing only sandals. Miss F. kicked out the windshield of my truck. Naturally, I was dumbfounded. This tactic of hers did in fact attract my undivided attention, which I had to drive into a ditch to give to her. I wasn't actually mad, only excited, and all I could think, and still think, was, *Wow*.

What inspired me to ruminate about all this was a juicy and, for me, heart-warming snip of gossip I came across in the paper the other day, regarding an alleged tantrum in the White House, in which she-of-the-three-names smashed, in the midst of heated discourse, a lamp. *Hurrah*, I say. I'm grateful to the First Couple for their inability to be perfect, for being, shall we say, domestically challenged.

Back during the campaign and the Gennifer Flowers affair, when the press was self-infatuated with their unctuous capacity for hypocrisy, I was thunderstruck by the Clintons' performance on *Sixty Minutes*, the deft and adult spin they managed to place on the scandal-ball: We went through a rocky period in our marriage; we fixed it to our mutual satisfaction; we're moving on; grow up, America.

In a nation where about half the people who mouth the vows of matrimony land in court, symbolically murdering each other with lawyers, Bill and Hillary impressed me as rather realistic and uplifting role models, folks who hailed from Arkansas, not from a mountaintop, or Mars, or Heaven, or Hell. The wunderguy lost his bid for reelection, became depressed, and cheered himself up with a bimbo; Hillary found out he wasn't working late at the office, since there was no office anymore. She broke some lamps, he promised to be cool, she promised to change her name to Clinton, they both promised to be more attentive to each other's extraordinary needs, he promised not to hit on every babe that rubbed up against his leg, she promised to get a new hairdo and buy some power suits, they rejoined forces—hearts and minds—to conquer the world, etcetera, which is what, you must admit, in ways large and small (but mostly small), love was meant to do. A moment here. A moment there, and Congress when we're feeling up to it. Does somebody here need a good spanking?

SHRIMP SALAD BAHIA

2 pounds medium-sized shrimp
1 green bell pepper, cut into thin strips
1 stalk celery, sliced thin
½ cup green onions, sliced thin
4 cups spinach leaves
3 plantains, sliced into 2-inch strips
2 limes plus ¼ cup lime juice
½ cup unsweetened shredded coconut
¼ cup fresh cilantro, chopped
1 teaspoon crushed red pepper
1 teaspoon ground cumin
1 tablespoon sugar
½ cup olive oil

This is a Brazilian recipe, in recognition of a country where, if a husband catches his wife committing adultery, he may feel free to pitch her out the 10th floor window of their apartment, without legal consequence, unless, that is, she happens to land on somebody. And you thought American men were badass!

Devein and shell the shrimp, then cook in a little salted water until they turn pink; remove from heat, drain, and set aside. In a small glass mixing bowl, prepare a lime dressing by combining lime juice, red pepper, cumin, sugar, and ¼ cup olive oil. Blend well. In another bowl, combine shrimp, green pepper, celery, onions, and cilantro, stir in dressing, cover, and refrigerate for 2 hours. Bring to room temperature before serving. Arrange spinach leaves on individual salad plates. In a frying pan, brown plantain slices in ¼ cup olive oil. Drain. Divide shrimp salad in portions on each bed of spinach. Cut limes into wedges; squeeze two of the wedges on fried plantain slices. Arrange plantains and remaining wedges around shrimp salads. Sprinkle with coconut shavings.

Get a grip on yourself. Take a bite. If you've got an attitude problem, this salad is the first step toward a safer, saner you.

SERVES 4.

DO YOU WANT TO
KNOW A SECRET?

At a dinner some years ago in San Francisco, where Miss F. and I resided at the time, one of our dining companions turned to Miss F. and asked how she managed my many absences, since I seemed to be so often on the road. Was Miss F. lonely, etcetera, and how did we as a frequently bicoastal or bicontinental couple handle the issue of trust? I opened my mouth first, my tongue, as it happened, having something urgently smug and unforgivable it wanted to say. The previous Sunday, I had been back East, interviewing neutrodynes on Capitol Hill, and Miss F. spent the weekend at her sister's house in the Marina District. When I telephoned at 7 A.M. (Miss F.'s time), her sister told me Miss F. couldn't speak to me because she wasn't there, she was doing something, she was out.

Out where? I wondered. I have sworn to Miss F. since the day I met her I'm not the jealous sort, and though in my opinion that thesis has been proved again and again, I had to ask, with what I suppose was a frown, out where?

Miss F. might be an early riser, but she wasn't, in those days, a jogger or anything else that might take her out of the house by seven on a Sunday morning. I was not anxious, but I must say I was damned intrigued.

"Um, she's down at the corner getting the paper," said her sister.

I said, "Okay, tell her to call when she gets in," hung up and thought, Hmm, but left it at that, until the dinner I'm referring to here, at which time, in response to the aforementioned question, my tongue proclaimed, during a certifiable mental lapse, that I wasn't the least predisposed to worrying about Miss F.'s behavior throughout my periods of absence, except in regard to her ability to enjoy herself and have a good time and so forth when I wasn't there to take her by the hand, since she seemed vulnerable to social unimaginativeness and tediously loyal to the wholesome traditions of her personal mainstream and probably wasn't very brave anyway except within the invisible fence of our relationship.

Oh, I went on and on like that in the most stunningly boneheaded manner. In retrospect, I feel like Walter Raleigh pontificating to Queen Elizabeth the First that dames aren't quite cut out for the throne. When I finished, Miss F. was—perhaps *steaming* is the right word—though it fails to express a certain bloodthirsty light that flashed from her eyes. I must say, though, that she delivered, in the most civilized way, the absolutely perfect response to any imbecile stupid enough to say what I had just said, libeling certain traits in her character that one dare not mess with, upon penalty of comeuppance.

"As a matter of fact," Miss F. said, seething, "I have, since I started living with you, three very large and very shocking secrets, and you would fall over dead if you heard them, which you never, ever, for all eternity, will, you fucking asshole."

Given my propensity for being a snoop, and Miss F.'s for being a blabber, this was the lowest, most devastating of underhanded blows; it transformed me instantly into a groveler, apologizing madly, ingratiating myself to Her Royal Unfairness. The truth is, I can't stand anyone having secrets but me, a Knight of the Information Age. I demand to know what's cooking, not to moralize but simply to know, and lack of access drives me crazy, starves me. I need to be gorged with juicy facts and piquant rumors or I shrivel right up.

"Aw, honey," I said, dropping to my knees, "please, please, please, come on, tell me just one, even just half of one, a quarter of one, the first letter of one, just tell me if it's animal, vegetable or mineral," and all the while I'm pleading with Miss F., referring to her former generosity as a spiller of secrets, the girl is shaking her head no and gloating. Lord, how cruel she was in her revenge upon me, and then she did that thing that I hate, and that she had never before done to me, a little pantomime I believe she learned long ago on the playground from mafioso playmates, the ultimate gesture of intractable silence: She zipped and locked her lips shut and then threw away the key.

Every year since, I have badgered Miss F. to feed me at least a tidbit of one of her Three Big Secrets. Every year since, she has refused, silently, except this year, at a dinner we hosted for our friend Pete the professor, when she shook her head no, gloating as usual, and revealed she now had a fourth! How merciless she is. One must pay for one's tiny peccadilloes again, again and again.

It's not as if I regard secrets the way the French once regarded sauces: as something meant to conceal the putrefaction of spoiled flesh. Miss F. hasn't a wicked cell in her body, so I don't think it's likely any investigation of her life would turn up that which is heinous or chilling: I don't think she's been running a wholesale parts business with Jeffrey Dahmer, or voting Republican, or eating Cheez Whiz straight out of the can. Nor does it really matter to me if she was up in Mendocino, having a tryst with Robin Williams, over in Reno playing Texas hold 'em, or walking around the Castro District with a ring through her nose. Although revelation is a natural form of intimacy, curiosity is also the beast that kills the cat, and as much as I say I want to, and feel I want to, the fact is, I honestly do not want Miss F. to tell me everything—I don't. It would be antithetical to my sense of who this woman is: an independent, wholly capable person, irrefutably entitled to her own life within or outside of the parallel life of togetherness that is us. She's not my dog, she's my lover and equal; she came into this world without me and will leave it the same way, and if she wasn't independent, and didn't have a Secret Life all her own, I must say I'd feel suffocated and probably wouldn't put up with the way she eats ice cream with a fork.

The bottom line is, I want her to have her secrets, I just don't want her to flaunt them, which, as you see, she does, but I suppose I have it coming. Which brings me to our friend Pete the professor, who in the several years we've known him has been mostly single—I like to think at my expense, seeing as how I elate in the company of women just as much as he does, and yet he has regularly brought only his bachelor self around to dinner, without regard to tit for tat, since in addition to whatever gastronomic satisfaction he may have encountered tableside, he has also enjoyed the equal or perhaps greater pleasure of feasting on the likes of Miss F., and in fact I will concede she is 67 percent more worth listening to than I am. It reached the point where I said to myself, The professor's got a great deal going here, but *what about me?* I said, and let Pete know that, for my sake and the sake of balance at the table, perhaps the time had come for him to move beyond this unaccompanied phase he'd been indulging in and in the future consider his meals with us to be on the potluck plan. As in, bring your own tasty dish, to complement the one provided. I was perfectly frank about this: I wasn't actually thinking of his welfare, I said. I was thinking only of mine.

I readily admit that when any friend, single whether by fate or by desire, suddenly succumbs to an irresistible attraction in matters of the heart, I look upon the affair somewhat capitalistically, a small and benign opportunity to enrich myself. So when Pete stopped by this month with what we shall call a hormonal bounce to his step, to announce that he had fallen in love—or fallen close enough, at least, for it to be a gimme—I thought, Hot dog, this is pretty darn good news, a long-due improvement on an already rich relationship, and only fair to me. It wasn't long before he came by to present his inamorata. She was gorgeous, and I thought, *Hey!*, I thought, *Bravo*, and I immediately wanted to have my conversational way with her.

I will also admit that my chatting skills are slightly journalistic; that is to say, I grill people, though I would like to think not without some boyish charm, and I am not the Gestapo. Blah, blah, blah, I said to this woman, Miss X., and she informed me, not in effect but rather explicitly as she marched past me out the door, that her life was unequivocally none of my business. Of course, I agreed, yes, that's right, shame on me for being so nosy, but by the following morning I had reconsidered the proposition, asking myself why the hell it wasn't my business, and was thus confronted by the essential question mark of existence: Just what *is* my business, anyway?

The short answer is, *everything*. A through Z (allowing for Miss F.'s Three or Four Big Secrets and the private life of most individuals, especially folks like the late Arthur Ashe, as long as they're not standing in my kitchen, talking to me). All the famous advice on secrets is the same: As Napoleon said, don't wash your jockey shorts in public. But I'm a card-carrying busybody, a professional voyeur. When Miss X. showed up, I had just finished a novel that took ten years to write, which meant that, for a decade, without anyone ask-

ing me to, I had flayed myself raw to the point where I would be forced to stand intellectually naked before a jury of anybody who wanted on. I hadn't tried to strip-search Miss X. but to rev her up to the usual badinage, via info about her ex-husband(s), since she was bold enough to state that when she'd first met my friend the professor, she thought he was arrogant and not the least bit sexually attractive. Oh? I said and was off and running.

What it comes down to is this: I want to know the ingredients of a personality, and I've never been one to waste time in this respect. I wanted to know Miss X.'s "normal" taste in men, I wanted to know her politics and hobbies, her eating habits, reading habits, TV habits. Does she dance like a white girl or like a woman with a soul on fire? Is there enough wildness in her to keep her honest? I wanted to know her social range and geographical tracks. Is she a shoe freak? Is she earth, wind, fire, or water? What does she want in fine print and what does she want in ALL CAPS? Does she have a brain and a heart and has she paid attention, taken risks? Does she have dreams worth dreaming and can she take a joke? Stuff like that.

I call this "making friends," though sometimes it seems to be the identical process one uses to make enemies, which still works out for the best, according to Longfellow, who once wrote: "If we could read the secret history of our enemies, we should find in each man's life sorrow and suffering enough to disarm all hostility."

It's of course up to Pete to discover the handling and care of Miss X., how to prepare her for his own banquet of affection, and how long she has to cook before she's ready. I do know the nature of my business after all, and it is not unlike that of any earnest cook's, to connect with the flavors that most make us appreciate our humanity, in all its dimension, hurrying to get the dish on the table before the true endless silence overtakes us.

For M. F. K. Fisher, and Elizabeth David, and all the tasty, thrilling secrets they've shared with us over the years, this dish is for you.

GRILLED DUCK WELLINGTON WITH PORCINI MUSHROOMS

4 duck breasts (2 whole magrets)

2 tablespoons olive oil

Salt and pepper to taste

1 sprig fresh rosemary

1 ounce dried porcini mushrooms

1 sheet frozen puff pastry, thawed

1 egg

1 teaspoon milk

What we have here, basically, is an *encroûte* recipe, in which the essential ingredients—duck breast, fish, tournedo beef, goat's head, Nike Cross-Trainers, Sharon Stone's panties, or whatever—are anxiously (or prankiously) concealed within a pastry casing, and the guests can't possibly know what it is they're being served until you, the cook, in a grand, magnanimous (and gratuitous) gesture of good hostmanship, relent to reveal the content of your little treasure boxes. O Disclosure! The table seems all the better for it, when cooks (and friends and governments and even imperfect strangers) take us into their confidence.

It's not necessary to precook the duck breasts on the grill, but that process makes them all the more tasty, and in any case a few minutes' precooking, by whatever form you can manage, is advisable, so that in the long run you can avoid a situation where you know the pastry's done but you have your doubts about the meat filling. Rub flesh side of breasts with olive oil and salt and pepper, then chop rosemary and sprinkle it on. Grill breasts (over a fruitwood fire, if possible) for 3 to 4 minutes each side (about half the time you normally would to cook them through). Remove from heat and allow to cool. Meanwhile, rehydrate dried porcini in 1 ½ cups of water for about 45 minutes. Drain off porcini stock and save for sauce (recipe follows). Slice each cooled breast into halves, vertically. Lightly flour a cookie sheet, a large cutting board or a countertop area. Unfold thawed pastry sheet and press it out with a rolling pin until its length and width are each about 4 inches longer. With a butter knife, cut pastry into four squares. Place the halves of one breast in each square, with a line of porcini between the two pieces. Blend egg and milk, brush edges of squares with mixture, then fold edges over, pinching them together to form a pocket. Flip each pocket onto a large baking sheet or dish so that the seams are hidden, then glaze the round pastry top with egg-and-milk blend. Bake in a preheated oven at 375 degrees for 15 to 20 minutes, or until pastry shells are golden brown. Serve with Ripley's Secretive Sauce.

SERVES 4.

RIPLEY'S SECRETIVE SAUCE

1 cup red wine

2 cloves garlic, chopped

1 bay leaf

1 tablespoon chopped shallots

1 sprig fresh thyme

4 to 5 leaves fresh basil

4 to 5 leaves fresh tarragon

1 cup porcini stock (see recipe above)

1 teaspoon salt

¼ cup heavy cream

Ripley's Secretive Sauce is a variation on Bordelaise, its savory *what-is-this-ness?* and mysterious velvety texture the product of the porcini stock and the cream.

In a large saucepan, bring to a boil over low heat the wine, garlic and herbs, and boil until the volume is reduced by half. Add porcini stock and salt, return to a low boil and again allow the volume to reduce by half. Remove from heat, blend in cream, arrange Duck Wellington on a serving platter, pour sauce on platter so you have an archipelago of pastry islands, and serve.

THE DIVINE MISS F.

*"The fiercely oppressive, mean-spirited ageism in this
country . . . [has] corrupted middle age, when the
best part of life begins."*

—FRANCES LEAR, PROFESSIONAL OLDER WOMAN

"I think," Miss F. offered during dinner, her soup spoon halted in
midair as she paused, introspectively, "that with each decade, I get
incrementally better."

"Better *as what*?" I wondered out loud, because what people have in
mind isn't always obvious, even if you've been shacked up with them for
1.675 decades, and though it wasn't my intention to confront her on
this, how could I be sure she wasn't referring to her steady improvement
as, say, someone who can carry a tune, which would not be true, or to
her increasing skills as a cook, which would be debatable and would have
to be discussed on a dish-by-dish basis?

As for her time frame, I don't know about you, but I don't particularly like to hear an individual's betterment posed on such a grand and
scary scale. The political packaging of the calendar—Are you better off
now than you were four years ago?—is good enough for me and just
about at the frontier of my ability to remember what it is we've been
doing with our lives. What gets better by the decade, except the very
finest spirits and wines? (And age, Larousse wisely suggested, "is in itself
not necessarily a virtue, [as] a wine can lose its freshness when allowed

to get too old.") Seafood, on the other hand, won't last overnight without refrigeration or curing, and I can't think of much else on the face of the earth that appreciates qualitatively after a decade's worth of man-handling—not farmland, not cities, not air travel and not, in the modern mythology of gender, females.

The occasion for Miss F.'s modest bit of congratulatory self-assessment was her fortieth birthday. *Hmmm.* Well, it had to come, one way or another, and I never really gave serious thought to the idea of icing her down at the more virginal age of twenty-six or twenty-nine or thirty-two. Frankly, despite a vague assumption that we would simply carry on, I had never actually planned this: middle age with Miss F. If our life were a dinner, it would be, by the very illusion of its suddenness, potluck, bring whatever you can, *although it better be good*, because, like any other couple who have struggled together through their twenties and thirties to compose a worthy life for themselves, we have had our fill of shit, without ever acquiring a taste for it.

Certainly, Miss F. has battled hard and endured much to earn the right to the pride in herself she expressed, and although I think it realistic that the nation measures its advances in bundles of ten, I have to say I felt uneasy to hear Miss F. doing it in regard to her own personal count, as these tens tend to mount up at a subtle but eventually mortifying rate, and the difference between two of them and four, as Woody Allen surely realizes, can be mathematically deceptive.

I suppose there's a knack to aging, though I don't imagine I'll ever do it well, especially since I regard nutritional health as the gastronomic equivalent of the Christian Far Right: taking aim at the decadent, libidinous passions inherent in good food and drink. When I confessed to my doctor I still butter my bread, he barely restrained himself from cuffing me. Still, because I am a man, society has promised to lubricate my unseemly journey to the geriatric ward and not make too much fun of me and not be overly appalled by my dissipation. On the other hand, if our culture were a cop, as some seem to feel it is, it would arrest every woman over the age limit of fifty for being, *ipso facto*, unattractive and, therefore, useless.

Which is why I've always shown more than a little skepticism toward Miss F.'s assertion, which I first heard her make when she was twenty-three and that she has often repeated in the intervening years, that she looks forward to growing old, being a cuckoo old lady who wears tiger-striped clothes and kitty-cat glasses and drives recklessly and shouts out advice to the characters on the screen in a movie theater and breeds a variety of huge, slobbery dogs and in restaurants slides the silverware and condiments off the table and into her purse and does whatever the hell she wants—and whoever doesn't like it can go get soaked. I thought, *Yeah, sure*, this was just an odd version of the more standard female fantasy, an adolescent's romantic vision of what it means to grow up, girl-wise, but I've since learned that not only did Miss F. mean it, but her desire for dotage was grounded in tradition, coming as she does from an old Virginia family whose matriarchs have had a certain reputation ever since the seventeenth century for being like time bombs, concealed within the status quo, suddenly blasting forth with independence at a certain ripeness of age, acquiring the most unpredictable habits and generally scaring the dickens out of the commonwealth's menfolk. I've heard about them all: Miss F. is always mentioning this one or that one as a Great Inspiration, like her Great Aunt So-and-So.

"Isn't she the one who answers the door nude?"

"Not at all," Miss F. says. "She always wears a feather boa."

Miss F. is intellectually and emotionally devoted to screwy old broads because, like Katharine Hepburn, whom she claims as a role model, they are women who have always, and without hesitation, embraced their age and aged triumphantly.

Age. We recognize its special quality when we taste it on our palate: the incomparable richness of a prosciutto *di Parma*, which takes eight to ten months to mature, or Scotch whiskey, which by law must sit in its oak cask for a minimum of three years. But when we taste age in our lives, or in the lives of our lovers, the first bite releases a dry and penetrating flavor, with a bitter aftertaste, and many of us doubt we will ever accustom ourselves to its gritty texture . . . but we do, because we learn to feed the appetites that youth, in its impoverishment of experience, never trusted, or never recognized as a source of happiness.

"To be happy you must have taken the measure of your powers, tasted the fruits of your passion, and learned your place in the world." George Santayana wrote that, and M. F. K. Fisher used it as the epigraph for *The Gastronomical Me*, a book that speaks sparingly and symbolically about cuisine but generously and literally about "wilder, more insistent hungers," as Fisher takes the measure of her powers as a woman, a writer, a witness: a sensualist testing recipes not found in cookbooks. And in the measure is the refrain that binds her work together, that charts her hunger for life and its feeding, the refrain that points to her place in the world. If the best part of life for a woman truly begins at middle age, I suspect it's because, like Miss F., she has located and secured that place that had once seemed elusive, shifting, when the door that love was meant to be seemed to open upon shadowy corners or suicidal ledges, when a woman's ambition seemed like the antithesis of togetherness, rather than what it actually is, which is the antidote to inequality and a more reliable aphrodisiac than the mass-marketed images of the flesh and their faceless, wearying parade.

"Better *as what?*" I asked at dinner, because if I pamper Miss F. (which I do), or if I am solicitous of Miss F. (which I am, though no one could possibly know it but her), these perquisites of loving me do not extend to conversation, public or private, because, conversationally, they are gratuitous, harmoniously deployed among only the boring and the dull, the witless and the rawly oversensitive; these niceties are an allowance for weakness, and believe me, if there's one advantage Miss F. craves as a woman, it is to be underestimated, at which time she will hammer some poor son-of-a-bitch into the ground. In the past, that's often been me, but I've learned my lesson, mostly; now I can sit back and enjoy watching her nail hapless bureaucrats and lobbyists and snakes in the legislative grass.

"Better as what?"

"As a girl," Miss F. blurted, almost coyly, in her Gracie Allen voice, and her forty-year-old face, which is and isn't her thirty-year-old face, brightened, you could say girlishly, and I was forever charmed.

As a girl. Of course. We live in the South, where people don't necessarily forfeit their status as either a girl or a boy until they are well-fossilized, but, Southernisms aside, Miss F. has never been more of a woman—more willful, more serene, more ideologically preoccupied, more competent, more fearless, more sexy, more independent, more enterprising, more composed and confident, more ambitious, more athletic, less complacent and needy and compulsive, more determined to engage herself to the world—and it may not be fair to say (though I'll suggest it, anyway) that until these past few years, her real life had not begun but had been hanging around, not exactly poised but nascent and formless, there to guess at, there to be prodded and poked at by an impatient mate, ready to rise only if it stepped into the fire and got itself heated up.

I can't pretend to understand the female rites of passage. When I first met Miss F., she was doing what I suspect to be the actual occupation of every interesting twenty-three-year-old female in history— breaking up somebody's marriage. After taking eight years to get a college degree in pottery, she was in turn a waitress; a bookkeeper for a travel agency in Palm Beach, a university alumni foundation in Iowa, and an alternative college in San Francisco; then a ticketing agent for a small airline in Virginia; then suddenly and strangely, the director of a degree program in travel (?) at a small college in the Midwest; then someone lying around the house for six months; then someone who fueled boats at a marina in North Carolina. Then, at age thirty-six, proclaiming she never wanted to practice law, she became a law student; and now, at forty, she's helping to draft landmark legislation for the state of Florida, she has just published her first law review article, and—this I really can't believe—she jogs three miles every evening after work. This is a woman who spent thirty-nine years thinking of herself as a spaz.

I look at her and I marvel. I look at her and I think, *Holy shit!* Maybe I won't give her back to the Gypsies after all, now that she has dared to turn forty.

Ernest Hemingway once said what he learned "constructive about women is that no matter how old they get, always think of them the way they were on the best day they ever had."

Oh, boy, am I glad I never said that, although I suppose I once might have, until Miss F. suggested I was holding the map upside down and reading it backward. Then the journey became remarkably clear.

If you want to know what I fed Miss F. for her fortieth birthday, the answer is seafood, always seafood. We celebrate everything around here with seafood; congratulations are offered with a dozen Apalachicola oysters on the half shell, pats on the back supplemented with a tray of clams Casino; every kudo comes with its own spiced shrimp, and if you've done something very, very special—like redesigning a problematic copyright statute—I'll even peel it for you.

APALACHEE BOUILLABAISSE

¼ cup olive oil

1 large onion, chopped

8 plum tomatoes, chopped

2 cloves garlic, minced

1 small chili pepper, crushed

1 teaspoon fresh thyme, chopped

¼ teaspoon grated nutmeg

2 cups water

½ cup dry red wine

2 bay leaves

Juice of 1 lime

2 dozen littleneck clams

2 dozen mussels (optional)

1 ½ pound grouper, amberjack or red snapper

1 pint shucked oysters

1 pound jumbo shrimp

4 8–16-ounce lobster tails, split

12–16 stone-crab claws

Pinch powdered saffron (optional)

Salt and pepper to taste

Fresh parsley for garnish, chopped

In a large casserole, heat olive oil and sauté onion, tomatoes, garlic, chili pepper, thyme, and nutmeg. Add water, wine, bay leaves, and lime juice, and simmer for 10 minutes. Add clams and mussels, and cook over medium heat for 5 to 8 minutes. Cube fish, add to casserole and cook for 3 minutes. Add oysters, shrimp, lobster tails, and stone-crab claws and cook for 4 to 5 minutes longer. Add saffron (or don't, if you don't want to bother with it), check broth for saltiness, season to taste with salt and pepper, then ladle into large bowls, garnishing with chopped parsley. Arrange some crusty bread on the side, for sopping.

SERVES 4 OVEREATERS, 6 NORMAL FOLKS, OR 8 DIET CULTISTS.

I forgot to tell you, you'd better crack those stone-crab claws before you serve them. Use a hammer, or the butt end of a butter knife. Nutcrackers won't do.

THE COMMITMENTS

*"Couples. I hate them. They make me puke . . . Why
don't they just slap me in the face?"*

—CYNTHIA HEIMEL, PROFESSIONAL SINGLE WOMAN

At 4 A.M., in one of those midtown Irish bars run by portly, raw-faced souses, insomniacs since birth and lyrically gifted with intolerance, I found myself conspiring in a most extraordinary pact with my friend Mark, who is not an Irishman but an insane Southern boy from Virginia. Mark is also a writer of great wit and insight and sensitivity—a talent which has of course made him selfish, as it must—and he apparently is a lover uncommon in his genius for over-complication, splintering the bold pure light of his passion for the delightful Miss P. into something resembling the display over Baghdad, two years ago, that first night of bombing that we all watched with such morbid fascination. So this is war, we said to ourselves, sinfully titillated. So this is love? I said to Mark as we slumped on our barstools, both of us pickled in the numbing analytic juice manufactured whenever two guys stay up all night in a foolish attempt to figure out the one thing in their lives that has no explanation—their relationship with women. Even God and U.S. foreign policy are easier to explain.

I seem to remember playing the drunken father-confessor, so essential to the Celtic traditions we were being encouraged in by the bartender, and

THE COMMITMENTS 295

with every bit of advice I dared offer Mark regarding the byzantine intrigues of his romance with the perfectly swell Miss P., he would order another double scotch, stare morosely into the purgatory of love, and brood.

The big deal was, the utterly charming Miss P. was a bit of a flirt, and this was eating at Mark, this was grievously troubling to his patriarch's sense of romantic propriety. He could name all the people she had flirted with during the past week, month, year. And it was true: the entirely adorable, filthily rich Miss P. was indeed a flirt, a terrific one—it was in her blood, if not her pants—and she wasn't fucking anyone but Mark, so what was the problem anyway? When Miss F. and I first met her, she flirted with me, she flirted with Miss F., she flirted with the dogs. It was irresistible, she kept a tingling spritz of sexual tension suspended in the air. I flirted back, definitely. So did Miss F. I believe the dogs did too. I didn't know it at the time, but it drove Mark crazy. He couldn't seem to grasp the overriding truth that in all matters of consequence, Miss P. was nunnishly loyal to him. She was, in the manner of which I speak, his. What did he want? I asked. His answer wasn't clear, though it did have a slight echo.

Mark felt that his inamorata's behavior was dishonoring him. Hmm, I thought. A writer's life is wired with a thousand and one seductive impulses, and I get the same message, couched in different language, sometimes from Miss F. who, without mentioning such noble and militaristically absolute emotions as honor, will nevertheless explain, with moody petulance, that if I persist in playing around with this or that female, people will misunderstand our—mine and Miss F.'s—relationship.

To which I always respond, "Naaa-aah." I do not make an exemplary penitent, sorry to say. But I wish Miss F. would stop fretting about people misunderstanding us. Of course they mi understand us. How could they possibly, in a million years of scrutiny, not. We're a couple, for crying out loud. Shit. We've made some very queer and exhilarating decisions about who we are and what we think we're doing, not that we're so out of line with the rest of the pack. Miss F. and I know dozens of other couples, we know a zoofull of couples, each and every one of them as weird as giraffes, with behavioral patterns so complex they give us vertigo, and I don't pretend to understand any of them for a second, although sometimes Miss F. seems to have a clue. Still, I realize that Miss F. feels it's her problem if other people misinterpret us because I'm on the loose, running around the planet, being mildly bad, but I'm not sure what she wants me to do, seeing as how I am totally hooked on Miss F. She might as well be heroin; my life with her speaks for itself and can't be destroyed from the outside, though it has occasionally taken direct hits from within the castle walls. When all is said and done, there are many ways to measure fidelity, and plenty of them are trivial. That's neither a confession nor a justification, but a perspective on survival.

So . . . back at the bar, Mark was muttering on about Miss P.'s transgressions of the flirty sort, the liability she presented to the chivalric anachronisms so dear to his heart. This had been going on for hours and, since Mark was a Southerner, I knew the only medicine he'd respond to was a good ass-whipping, but rather than have me administer it, I thought it would make more poetic sense if he gave it to himself.

Miss P.'s behavior was driving him batty. His behavior was making her nuts. They were in love with each other and unnaturally obsessed with each other's peccadilloes. He had moved out but had constructed a bridge of irrationality back to her, winding up at Miss P.'s place across town on nights when it seemed he should wind up some *place*. They were both generally flabbergasted and miserable, and Mark, who could probably keep picking at and unravelling this thing for years, was in danger of becoming a very bad entertainment—some shameless, pathetic form of moralizing windbaggage, like a televangelist, and it was clear to me, despite the hour and the booze, that he should avert long-term disaster now by running headlong into its toothy maw.

I thought he should marry Miss P. Immediately. He and Miss P. would be wintering at her family's compound near Sarasota. I asked when they were headed south and Mark said next week.

"Well," I ventured, "the week after that, why don't you and Miss P. meet Miss F. and me at our trailer in Cedar Key. I'll get a preacher or a judge or the captain of a shrimp boat or something, and you and Miss P. can get married."

Mark's lips expanded into his trademark coyote smile and his eyes filled with a devilish gleam. He thought about it for like three seconds. It was too outrageous of a scheme not to be taken seriously.

"Okay," he said. "Okay. Yeah, okay." He hadn't yet heard my reasoning, but this was the sort of screwball plan he could throw himself into. "I'll do it," he said firmly.

"Atta boy," I said. "Do it, then the week after that, get divorced, flush all of this nonsense out of your system, then try to behave as decently and empathetically as you can toward Miss P., and see if things don't get better, once you've de-ritualized yourselves. Or, failing that, at least you'll both have enough momentum going to stay the fuck away from each other forever, which may in fact turn out to be the highest expression of your love for the poor girl."

Suddenly, something about the whole idea struck Mark as questionable. "Wait a minute," he said. "If we do this, can we still have a big church wedding in the fall, with family and an orchestra and gifts of cash plus wonderful presents?"

"Sure," I said, "but the important thing is to act now, make commitment pronto, get this major hurdle out of the way, so at least you'll have an adult context as an excuse for your bizarre behavior."

"This sounds right," said Mark. "Okay, I'll do it. *But you've got to do it too.*"

"Okay," I said dishonestly. "That's not a problem. We'll have a double-ring ceremony at the trailer, you and Miss P. and me and Miss F. Only, no ring for me—I hate wearing jewelry. Maybe I'll carve our name on a tree or something."

"That'll be okay," said Mark, very pleased with himself for negotiating such a coup. "When Miss F. hears about this, she's really going to thank me."

"Probably not," I said obliquely, but let it go at that, not wanting to discourage the man in his triumph over ambivalence. He'd get married as a joke, and only if he could drag me down into the institutional depths of church and state with him, and I was going to let him do it, manipulate quid pro quo, because I'm tired as hell of only retrograde lizards like Bruce Willis and Demi Moore being the ones making the big commitments these days. I thought it would be nice if some of the progressive, smart folk I know stopped being so goddamn self-indulgent, or at least figured out a more constructive way to have their cake and eat it too, even if accepting responsibility for someone else's happiness is a lot trickier than simply being responsible for their unhappiness. Not to mention that the job can quickly turn you into a bore.

Having crossed the last threshold of maturity, we shook hands on the deal and went home.

Two nights later I saw Mark at a party downtown. He was chatting with Miss N., who almost thoroughly enjoys her life as a single woman, except for the past seven years she's been gnashing her teeth over Joe, the movie director, trying to decide whether or not to marry the guy. She was sure she loved Joe. Apparently Joe loved her. He'd say yes if she ever made up her mind but she wanted a few more decades to mull it over.

"So," I said to Mark. "We still on for Cedar Key in two weeks? Double-ring ceremony, etcetera?"

"Absolutely," said Mark. "Count on it."

"Have you told Miss P. yet?"

"Haven't seen her. Have you told Miss F.?"

"She won't want to hear it. We're going to have to spring it on her, get her caught up in the moment."

"She's really going to thank me," said Mark with great confidence.

"She's really going to kill you," I tried to convince him.

Miss N. was looking pensive. "Now, Bob," she said with increasing interest in the topic, "is this event going to be catered?"

"I don't know about that," I said frankly. "Mark and I will be out fishing all day, so there's a possibility we might grill some redfish. Or I might make a meatloaf the night before, for sandwiches."

"Will there be a band?" she asked, furrowing her brow.

"We have a portable CD player we can plug into the trailer," I said. "And there'll be a campfire. It'll be nice and cozy."

"I wonder if Joe would go for this?" she said.

"I was under the impression that he had already agreed to marry you countless times."

"I guess I should shit or get off the pot," Miss N. concluded. "I guess I should jump aboard with you guys, if you're serious."

"We're serious," I said. "Commitments are nothing to be afraid of. Right, Mark?"

"Are you kidding?" said Mark. "Commitments and drive-by shootings are the two things that make contemporary life so scary."

"Still?"

"Still, we're serious."

"Okay," said Miss N., "I'm in. What a relief, all that procrastination, all that self-doubt, all that feeling that I'm too selfish to live with anybody else, all that dread about domesticity—right out the window. Only, I'm a bit concerned that the three most important people in this equation aren't here to give their consent."

"No way," I said. "If Joe were here he wouldn't believe you for a second. If Miss P. were here, she'd flirt with somebody and break Mark's concentration. And if Miss F. were here, she'd tell you that after living with me for 17 years, she knows damn well I'd make a very unsuitable husband, that to marry me would somehow be like bringing a barnyard animal into the parlor to try to be kind to it. I don't know what Miss F. wants except what she's got. Which is not a husband, by any conventional stretch of the imagination. And I certainly have no interest in having a wife. Miss F. could never be my first wife anyway. She'd have to be number three or four, the one that stuck. There's some once-fervent but now vague ideology behind that but I can't remember what it is. In fact, housewise, I prefer to be the wife, except for washing dishes and cleaning up and taking shit out of the blue. And if we have kids, I get to raise them. They'll be trained to sit and speak and go lie down. She gets to name them and take them shopping, but not grocery shopping. That's my bailiwick."

"But now I'm really confused," Miss N. confessed. "Why are you doing this then?"

"I'm going to do this," I tried to explain, "to demonstrate that it can be done, that people our age and with our sensibilities can actually, without unnecessary hue and cry, make a commitment. Lightning will not strike, nor will a curtain of banality close on your life. Next, Miss F. and I will get divorced, the sooner the better, to demonstrate that people always break the commitments they make, depending on how you measure the breakage, and you can always measure it to fit catastrophe, if that's what suits you. Then, we'll go on as we always have, with short intermissions for complaints and fault-finding, and there you'll be, you and Joe, Mark and Miss P., trapped by biology and the screwball logic of love and some vestigial nostalgia you harbor about tradition and whatever wild rationale you can summon forth, still in charge of your life but *married*, and nobody, but nobody, knows what the fuck that's supposed to mean but you, and you better start inventing a playbook, fast. It should be a lot of fun to watch."

"Well, dammit, I'm going to do it," swore Miss N.

"I'm going out and buy a ring tomorrow," vowed Mark.

We adjourned to a bar, and by four o'clock in the morning the two of them were still swearing and vowing away. Then we decided we were starving, we'd go get a pizza and eat it at Miss N.'s apartment and refine our plans for the big day. By the time we made it to Miss N.'s place, though, I was losing consciousness fast and had just enough energy left to eat one slice before passing out on the couch. When I awoke in the morning, Mark was gone, Miss N. was snoring in her own bed, and there was a half-empty bottle of bourbon and a half-filled ashtray in the middle of the living room floor, between two chairs facing each other. That was months ago, and I'm still wondering what those two chicken-shits said to each other after I crashed.

Two days later, Miss N. called to tell me she had cold feet. I still haven't heard from Mark.

What I remember best, though, right after I had pronounced myself unable to carry on, as I was spinning down into sleep, I was still aware enough to know that Mark had come over to the couch to untie and remove my shoes, and Miss N. had brought a quilt, to spread over me and tuck me tenderly in.

What sweeties, what dears. So many of the moves they make, the things they do, foreshadow the lives they have hesitated to make with their lovers. One of these days, perhaps. I know it wasn't the thought of my meatloaf that turned them back from the altar, but that's all I know. I can't even say I know that what we risk with our hearts is worth risking, given that whatever we have made with our love will one day fall away from us, and be lost and buried and utterly forgotten, and that's that, and too bad for everybody. I only know that I thought I'd go along with the scheme, take the risk, gamble on meaning, live life that way even though a profound restlessness grips me too, sometimes when I unsuspectingly lift my head from the lap of domesticity. Even though sometimes I tell myself, "Beat it, get out of here", and I do, until I tell myself, "Go back! Go back!" and I do that too.

TONY'S MEATLOAF

2 lbs. ground beef (sirloin, round, whatever)

1 cup Italian breadcrumbs

3 eggs, beaten

½ cup onion, chopped

½ cup bell pepper, chopped

½ cup carrots, grated

½ cup celery, chopped

½ cup fresh parsley, chopped

½ cup sauterne wine

4 cloves garlic, minced

1 tsp. oregano

4 tbsps. grated Romano

Salt and pepper to taste

Never trust a meatloaf recipe that hasn't survived at least a decade of household warfare among wonderful, creative, deeply caring homicidal people. If you can fight like cats and dogs, yet still return to the loaf, year after year, something's really working, most certainly the recipe. Tony and Miss B. just celebrated their 15th anniversary. God, who would have believed it. "It shocked us," said Tony—which is only fair, since they've spent all this time shocking everybody else.

As for how to cook Tony's meatloaf, get a big mixing bowl, put all the ingredients in it, mush everything up with your hands, add a dash of water if it seems to dry, then, in a roasting pan, shape it into a form of your choice—like a valentine heart, with carrot slivers spelling out *Mark + Miss P. = ?*—and bake the thing in the oven at 350 degrees for 45 minutes to an hour, or until done, or until the person you live with starts to complain, "I'm hungry," or until you can't stand it anymore, and in that case, just walk out the door and keep going. The meatloaf, you can be sure, can take care of itself.

SERVES 4.

POT ROAST FLORENTINE

Pot roast is a ubiquitous dish; a recipe for it can be found in virtually every cuisine where there are no taboos against eating beef. With its lack of pretense, pot roast is comfort food, but it can be elegant as well as earthy. Pino Luongo's *stracotto alla Fiorentina*, adapted here, is a soothing synthesis of both styles.

4 pounds of eye round (or chuck or rump) roast

2 cups beef broth

1 bottle red wine

1 can tomatoes

2 tablespoons olive oil

2 cloves minced garlic

1 cup each of chopped carrots, celery, parsley, and red onions

2 cups sliced mushrooms, or 2 cups dried
porcini mushrooms, soaked in red wine

Salt and pepper to taste

Preheat oven to 350 degrees. In a saucepan, sauté the garlic, carrots, celery, and onions with a little olive oil. Trim extra fat from the roast, and sprinkle with salt and pepper. In a suitable casserole pot or covered pan, heat the olive oil and brown the meat almost till its surface is burnt, then remove the roast and set it aside. In the same pan, brown the sautéed vegetables; add ¼ cup of wine and stir vigorously, scraping the bottom of the pan. Turn the heat to high and cook the meat, flipping it frequently, until the vegetables begin to stick to it, then add wine and broth until they cover the roast. Add mushrooms (or porcini) and bring to boil. Cover the pan and cook in the oven for two hours. Remove and slice the meat. Slice the tomatoes and add them to the sauce in the pan, bring to a boil, then return the sliced roast and cook for five more minutes.

SERVES 4.

HOMEWARD BOUND

*"Once food was love. Now it's just
as likely to be fear."*

—Ellen Goodman

Home is where *what* is? I ask myself, disoriented, displaced.

I was in our cramped, claustrophobia-inducing kitchen cooking pasta for dinner a few weeks before Thanksgiving. Miss F. and I both had suffered frequent and severe bouts of *kouxinaphobia*—fear of kitchens—since moving in as first-time homeowners two years ago. Clearly, the kitchen had great possibilities and, clearly, those possibilities would not be addressed expeditiously, given the major, more urgent work to be done in other areas of the house. The place was what certain realtors, one notch up from slumlords, smilingly call a "handyman's special," and I was the designated handyman, and I was sick and tired of the state of perpetual renovation in which we lived. Still, for lack of a better word, it was home (although a better word might be camp), and I had made conditional peace with the kitchen, even though Miss F. refused to sign the treaty.

I don't know what she hated more: the kitchen's obnoxiously merry wallpaper, its huge daisies, their bright mindlessness circa 1955, booj as could be, and peeling; the sunny yellow cabinets and countertops, straight out of the fantasy life of a high-school cheerleader named

Susy; the enormously ugly white-brick linoleum floor, designed, evidently, to showcase filth, or produce its own; the cracked and sagging plaster ceiling; the plywood I had nailed over a door that once led to the master bathroom; the refrigerator that produced stalactites in its freezer and occasionally, most often in the middle of the night, would emit a sound like a car's burglar alarm; the narrow alley separating the counter and sink from the stove and refrigerator, a perfect space for fights, since it was impossible, if you were not the cook, to do anything you might reasonably want to do in the kitchen without interfering with the cook—*me*—who is usually not gracious and wants you out of the goddamn way, now, please. I want to reveal, though, that when Miss F. is cooking, she doesn't abide the smallest trespass, her humors are, at best, pugilistic, and her manners better suited to the Medellin cartel. More than once I'd found her in the kitchen viciously hammering the utensil drawer with the mallet whose proper use is for tenderizing meat. The drawer's joints had come unglued, the wood had splintered and warped, it came apart in her hands, knives and spatulas clattering to the floor. Miss F.'s hair is wild, her face reddens, she shrieks—well, it's part of the way she cooks, which is one of the reasons we don't mind if she doesn't, since she is also not above throwing her elbows, and shoving, and somehow she always manages to injure herself.

Anyway, it was a few weeks before Thanksgiving, I was at the sink rinsing mushrooms, staring ahead at the wall dividing the kitchen from the Florida room, saying my goodbye to that wall, because my friend Bill was coming from Austin for the holidays, as he had both Thanksgivings we'd spent in this house, and when Bill visits we engage in manly, handymannish-type things. The first Thanksgiving, we'd built a carport; the second, we framed out the Florida room into what would eventually be an extra bedroom and bath and, most welcomed of all, an expansion of the kitchen. This time when Bill came we were going to knock down that wall and get on with it. Then, say in a year or two, when all the work was done and we could recover our investment, we'd sell the house and move on and, one always hopes, up.

I dried the mushrooms and sliced them for the marinara sauce simmering on the stove. Our two dogs are apparently fascinated by my expertise in the kitchen; they crouch at the end of the alley, slavering, never taking their eyes off me unless they are called away by Miss F., who has plopped herself down on the living-room carpet demanding to be licked, or if the doorbell rings, when they fire off like Tow missiles toward the front door, berserk with the promise of jamming their crotch-level noses in between the legs of our guests, whom neither Miss F. nor I will rescue, since we think having your butt poked by a big dog is not at all an unreasonable price to pay for letting you into our home.

The doorbell rang; the dogs leapt up, delighted, and charged off. I heard Miss F. greet a pair of visitors, I heard the visitors whoop as they were being goosed by the dogs. I heard Miss F. escorting the visitors on a tour of the house and I thought, not for the first time in my life with Miss F.: What's going on? Eventually, the tour entered the kitchen. I was stoveside, fiddling with the sauce, and looked up as Miss F. made perfunctory introductions and then blabbed on about the kitchen's manifold potential while the visitors surveyed the room from corner to corner, top to bottom, and I stood there, wooden spoon in hand, puzzled, until it finally dawned on me that what Miss F. was doing was making a sales pitch.

"Don't mind me," I said as Miss F. ushered the couple into the Florida room. "I'm just the dumb blonde housewife around here. I'd make the babies too if I could borrow a womb."

Twenty minutes later I saw the three of them out in the driveway, leaning against Miss F.'s old Mercury, making the gestures people make when they're cutting a deal. Unlike myself, Miss F. is extraordinarily fond of The Deal, and out there in the drive she seemed to me to be among her own kind. Dinner was ready and I called her in.

"So, honey," I said, fixing her a plate, "what's this all about?"

"We just traded houses with them," she announced, thrilled.

"We did?! Jesus, are you kidding?"

It's not as though she was acting entirely unilaterally. For six months we had talked about moving: the remodeling seemed never-ending, and on the bedroom side of the house, we didn't have neighbors, we had student party-terrorists living in a quadraplex, guys who bellowed even when they were trying their hormonal best to keep it down; guys who couldn't understand that blasting 2 Live Crew at 4 A.M. on Tuesday morning was somehow an invasion of our privacy. And then there was the kitchen, bane to cooks who would go about their business with some level of serenity and good will. I wanted to move too, and had told Miss F. if she found the right place, and if we could finesse some sort of arrangement, seeing as how we were broke, then okay. Otherwise, we were better off where we were, staying put until the house looked a little less as if it had been creamed by Hurricane Andrew. I don't know why I tell Miss F. these things, though, since she is never in the least daunted by unrealistic criteria and is, in fact, downright stimulated by the improbable. Only two days earlier she had badgered me to take a cursory glance at the house in question: a 1930s Bauhaus, 90 percent restored, salt-box ugly on the outside, absolutely idiosyncratic and just plain weird on the inside, with a park for a backyard.

"Do you like it?" she asked, wanting me to love it.

"Sure," I said, knowing there was no way in hell we could ever afford it. Now, two days later, she had negotiated a swap.

"But I thought you wanted to move," she said as we sat down to eat.

"Yes, but . . . " I said. "I'm too busy now. Let's do it in the spring." The day after Thanksgiving I was to leave on assignment to Miami and Haiti; I'd be back for Christmas and New Year's, but then had to leave for South America until the end of February. It was absurd to think that we could close on the house and move out and move in, all in a mere three weeks.

No way in hell, I kept saying to her. No way in hell, I said, throughout the week. No way, I muttered, as our status as human beings was certified by the bank. No friggin' way, I protested keenly, when Miss F. told me we would close the day before Thanksgiving, and move Thanksgiving Day. I was still desperately copy-editing a long overdue novel. We had two sets of out-of-town guests coming for the holidays.

Was Miss F. out of her mind? Was I? Were our guests, who, adequately forewarned, said "Oh, that sounds like fun," and came ahead?

I rented a U-Haul truck and moved Thanksgiving Day. Miss F. remained in bed, sick, no mystery there, and didn't help. Somehow, in the middle of it all, I cooked a turkey with all the fixings for eight. Even the dogs were too exhausted to beg. That was about a month ago. I haven't been home since, and it still irks me that, for the first Thanksgiving ever, I didn't have time to smoke the turkey, but just threw it in the oven and forgot about it, until it was as dry as every turkey our mothers cooked for us growing up.

So here I sit in a hotel room in Miami, wondering, Home is where *what* is? The answering machine? Even as a place where we can count on getting in touch with one another, home seems like an anachronism, its structure eaten by electronic termites, Voice Mail, computer modems, conversations via outer space.

Home is where Miss F. and the dogs are? Well, surely, but the sentiment carries a strange absence of comfort, it brings me no nearer an actual place, a reliable address, and in fact there have been times when Miss F. and I have felt most "at home" in a tent, far away from whatever building temporarily housed our worldly goods. Frankly, I can't seem to keep an address on this notion of home, it doesn't actually strike me as a tangible location that I could give directions to. At best it's a region, though these days even regions have a tentative aspect about them, as if you better not count on the North or the West or the South to mean what they're supposed to mean, once you settle in. Perhaps our mobility has so diluted, and paradoxically expanded, the notion of home that any geographical definition of it is chancy, a conditional act of faith. We're all over the map; the cartography of home is in constant revision. The rootlessness is more than physical; it's peculiarly patriotic. Where do you live? Umm . . . the United States of America. Where are you from?

I don't remember.

How would you know where home is? Miss F. sometimes chides me. You're never there.

Since we began living together, seventeen years ago, Miss F. and I have moved, in chronological order, from the West Indies to McLean, Virginia; to Columbia, Missouri; to Coconut Grove, Lantana, and West Palm Beach, Florida; then trudged off to Iowa City, Iowa; then on to Walnut Creek, California; then did a transcontinental bounce back to Barboursville, Virginia; Columbia, Missouri, again; Iowa City, again; Cape Hatteras, North Carolina; North Florida; Rome, Italy, to which we moved from Florida by way of Montana. We moved from Italy to Spokane, Washington, and, for the past two years, back again to Florida. Sixteen times we've unceremoniously unhoused ourselves, chasing opportunities, climates, impulses. The quest always seemed inevitable. It still does.

If, as Don DeLillo wrote in *Mao II*, home is a failed idea, then perhaps food as well, now that we've overlabeled and overdefined it, is vulnerable to the same fate, and I fret that what we eat will succumb to the same super-charged mix of cultural pressures, whatever they are, that have devolutionized the place where, in the past, we claimed you could find our heart.

Food, I can see by looking around the kitchenette of my hotel room, is one of the ways we have of locating ourselves, of telling ourselves where we are, both physically and emotionally. And, as defined by the food I have at hand, where I am is away from home.

On the kitchen counter are three plums. I ate a fourth yesterday and was mildly disappointed it did not ooze with the purplest of juices, as it would have had it been M. F. K. Fisher's plum. It was merely okay, left no memory, and neither stirred my sense of taste nor satisfied any

craving but the shallowest, and yet I doubt the plum, in its listless supermarket plumness, is wholly to blame.

On the counter are also a half-dozen tangerines, but no radiator in the room to dry them out on, section by section, until they achieve some sensual level of transcendence and gastronomic immortality.

There's a can of honey-roasted peanuts. I would never have these in my own house: they'd be superfluous, a desire that never clicked. In the refrigerator are two Styrofoam containers, one containing a glob of white rice, the other an unpleasantly orange-flavored serving of black beans.

There's a stove in the room but I feel no compulsion to cook on it. I'll walk across the street for a roast beef sub, eat it while I thumb the *Herald*. Or I'll go to the Cuban grocery on the corner and return with a *cafe con leche* and an empanada. Ample evidence that I'm in Miami, experiencing the undercurrent of homelessness I always sense in urban environments. Feeling single, too, though not in any urgent way. When I open up the refrigerator and find nothing there, for me the sight of that clean, well-lit emptiness evokes my bachelor friends who live in Manhattan, who might love food, but seek its pleasure, as they seek love, somewhere other than home.

When food is more than biological survival, what we eat is either at the center of domestic tranquility, or at the luscious surface of erotic tension. It's no surprise to Miss F. that I'm incapable of choosing one over the other, though it might interest her to know that when I'm alone, the place food occupies in my life is very compressed and functional. It is simply base fuel, primitive, and it never satisfies as it does in company, because the hunger it suppresses lacks, I suppose—or has forgotten—its own eloquence.

It expresses little of what I need it to express, those essential desires. Home. Love. Passion.

I can't get that mouth-parching turkey out of my mind, and I'm not going to feel at home in our new house until I master the unfamiliarity of its kitchen, effuse its newness with the soothing aroma of garlic, and cook a beautiful meal.

CHURRASCO (MARINATED GRILLED TENDERLOIN)

1 pound beef tenderloin, trimmed and cut lengthwise into four strips

MARINADE:

½ cup Italian parsley, chopped
2 cloves garlic, minced
¼ cup sherry
½ cup olive oil
1 teaspoon white pepper, freshly ground
½ teaspoon salt

CEBOLLITA
(PICKLED ONION SAUCE)

1 large onion, sliced thin
1 fresh jalapeno chili, sliced thin
¾ cup white vinegar
¼ cup water
½ teaspoon each salt and sugar

On the road, some travellers steal towels, I swipe recipes. The recipes here are Nicaraguan, a national cuisine one restaurateur in Miami thinks of as "Central American health food," because of its disdain for frying. I adapted them from the Food Section of the *Fort Lauderdale Sun-Sentinel*, where writer/cook Steven Raichlen said of the 175,000 Nicaraguans who have beat feet to South Florida throughout the last decade: "[L]ike any immigrant group, they have brought with them a longing to re-create the foods they left behind." Need I say more about the relationship between food and home?

After you've cut the tenderloin lengthwise into strips, lay them out on a cutting board (covered with a sheet of plastic wrap, if you're less messy than me), and flatten them with a mallet, or the side of a cleaver, until you've formed steaks about ½-inch thick and 8 inches long. Combine the ingredients for the marinade in a shallow glass dish, then marinate the meat for 30 minutes. On a barbecue grill, cook the meat medium-rare, 2 to 3 minutes per side. Slice meat crosswise into strips. Serve with Cebollita Sauce, which you make by marinating the sliced onion and jalapeno in vinegar, water, salt, and sugar for 2 to 3 days.

SERVES 4.

LIFE WITH
DOGBOY

Whenever you're on the road as much as I've been throughout the past year, parachuting in and out to drop off laundry, and to reap whatever benefits one's absence might have fostered in the heart, you begin to notice that, increasingly, you're not returning to quite the same home, or quite the same equilibrium of domestic affairs, that you left however long ago.

For six months now, Miss F. and I have communicated almost exclusively by phone. The dogs, she informs me, trying to control her voice, are behaving like wild Indians. Frankie ran away—she claims he'll listen only to me. The phone never stops ringing with callers attempting to track me down. The house is a mess. She can't keep up with the yard. She's too exhausted to cook by the time she gets home from the office. The truck needs a tune-up, the roof leaks, the lawn mower won't start, etc. Thus goes the litany of chores I've dumped on Miss F. in my extended hiatus from the hearth.

Okay, so I've been on the road, gone—out of the house, out of this magazine, out of it, period—since spring, adrift in the larger circulation, a wandering slut of the Life Literary. A slut not so much by choice, I would point out, but by vocation. It seems to be the true nature of a writer's calling. I say no only to her, Miss F. accuses; everyone else gets what they want from me upon the asking.

As for the inevitability of my comings and goings, early on in our relationship it became painfully clear to both of us that there was in effect a three-month ceiling, max, on our ability to be separated from each other. Beyond that, the accumulated time and distance created a red zone in which we each, independently and out of necessity, began to construct ever-more-autonomous lives, apart and alone. When this happened, getting back in the door of my own home wasn't as easy as you might think. For a week or two, the loudest sound would be the grind of the domestic gears as I waited for Miss F. to get reaccustomed to the smoky, smelly fact of me, returned in the flesh to bethrone myself in her kingdom and generally fuck with its laws and order.

It was three months into my most recent and still expanding absence, the calendar of my leave-taking at the threshold of the red zone, when I phoned Miss F. for my nightly check-in and heard a rather youthful— and male—voice answer the phone. "Who are you?" I asked, and the fellow said, "Mace."

"Well, Mace, is Miss F. there?" I asked.

"Yep."

"Do you think I could speak with her?"

"Who shall I say is calling?"

"Her husband."

"Hey, Bobbo," said this Mace, perking up. "What it is, my man? Hold on."

Miss F. came on the line with cheery greetings and asked how my book tour was going, but I of course was more interested in the mystery of Mace.

"You remember Mace," she said with undue confidence: He was "that cute guy who helped Tom build the wall along the patio."

Tom was the inscrutable landscape performance artist directing Miss F.'s rejunglefication project in our backyard. Mace, my memory would have it, was his starving, beragged assistant, limber as a spider monkey and with a similar body type and the shaved head of a refugee.

"What's he doing," I wondered, "hanging around at this time of night?"

"He's not 'hanging around,'" explained Miss F. "He walks the dogs after dark so you don't have to worry about me becoming a statistic in America's blood trade."

Mace the Dogboy. I thought, How nice of the lad to lend a hand.

"By the way," Miss F. added, "he lives here now."

"Who lives where now?" I said, momentarily confused. "Mace? With us?"

"That's right," said Miss F. "He's also painting the basement, and I don't want to hear any crap from you about the color."

"Wait a minute," I protested. "What color is he painting it? That's *my* study."

"So come home and work in it," Miss F. said, not with the tone of compassion and yearning she might have used a month earlier. But the strain on her tolerance of my life on the road was of secondary importance to me in light of this most alarming development: Miss F. had gotten herself a houseboy.

We hadn't cohabited with unscreened members of the public since the Early Cambrian period of our relationship, when Skip the insomniacal surfer fraud—who, in his glacial journey into adulthood, had yet to grasp the ethic of silence as it applied in a communal setting—held a continuous, twenty-four-hour-a-day tequila-and-pussy marathon in the spare bedroom of the condemned house Miss F. and I occupied the first year we were together, the trumpeting elephant-like shrieks of Skip's playmates popping us straight up awake at inconvenient hours. I realized, that year, that I had lost my collegiate zeal for roommates (unless they were sleeping with me), as well as the endless intramural diplomacy they require, and that thereafter I would subscribe to the old adage that houseguests, like uncooked fish, begin to foul the air after three days.

Given the lack of financial resources in our life, a fact that has only recently been corrected, hired help of the domestic variety had never been an issue, though I had intermittently confessed to Miss F. that I harbored a special dread of strangers' invading my house to sweep up after my mortal self, and I took comfort in the fact that Miss F. was an annoyingly compulsive cleaner, and that her habits would forever pre-empt the inclusion of domestics into the everyday fold. Let them wipe the butts of the better-off, I pontificated to Miss F., but as for ourselves, we're better off without them poking around. Besides the uplifting but foolish virtue of self-reliance, of not paying somebody else to do what you can sufficiently do yourself, the issue was, and is, privacy, unavailable in an urban context but nevertheless a condition, some anthropologists argue, that distinguishes civilized humans from savages and celebrities. If I'm going to reflect the natural world in my domestic environment, I prefer mimicking solitary beasts rather than swarming insects, and I have always insisted to Miss F. that I would no more live in an apartment complex than I would fetch pollen for the queen of the hive. As for the royal order itself, to which all Americans seem to aspire, the Life Literary implicitly forbade the pursuit of such genteel luxuries as butlers, carriage men and groundskeepers, allowing you ambition, hard work, success, honor and minor fame without any obligation to reward you a dime more than was necessary to finance a life-style of high impoverishment.

Even if, like Zoë Baird, we could have afforded extra hands around the ranch, on or off the books, I didn't know how I could swallow the sociopolitical pretense of it all, which I had observed among my egalitarian-minded peers. A few years back, as Miss F. and I stood chatting with our rich friend Margaret in her kitchen, in dragged a large, weary black woman dressed in a white uniform. "This is my friend Roberta," said Margaret by way of introduction. Miss F. and I felt helpless to do anything but nod, but Roberta seized the moment. "Shee-it," she responded, taking the liberty of sitting down and fixing herself a cup of coffee. "I thought I was the maid." Enlightened boomers make unbearably smarmy employers, and I understood I would be only a crankier, more grumbling version of the same.

It's probably perverse, but the classicism inherent in the hiring of domestic help operates more as an attraction to me, a type of moral challenge, than as a deterrent—an attitude that I suspect Miss F. is right to ignore. When she finally hired one of the fast-talking toolless and carless characters who regularly knocked on our door asking for yard work, I objected, dishonestly claiming that in the not-too-distant future I was going to rake the leaves and mow the lawn myself. Every weekend for the next year, whether there was work to do or not, there was Jimmy in the backyard, scraping around, and at the end of the day, there was Jimmy in the liquor cabinet. Unfortunately, even though he was a pain in the ass, I liked him, and we became friends, which made me detest our boss–field-hand relationship all the more openly. Which, Jimmy pointed out, was my problem, not his.

"Have you ever thought about medical school?" I said to him one day. We were both in our cups, sitting at the kitchen counter.

"What the fuck for?" Jimmy said.

"They teach you how to be a doctor."

"Get real, man. I don't wanna be no godddam doctor. What the fuck's wrong with you, Bob? I'm a yardman, I keep the place looking good, save you from your white-trash self."

"This isn't *My Fair Lady*," Miss F. advised me. Jimmy didn't want to be reformed, patronized or shamed into betterment; he simply wanted to do his job, be appreciated for what he was and then hit on us for a twenty-buck loan. Leave him alone, Miss F. warned me.

Which is exactly what I tried to do with Lois—the gospel-singing, Lord-praising terrorist who began to appear in our house every other Saturday morning once Miss F. graduated from law school and started working for the legislature. Not so keen on doing the dusting and vacuuming myself, I conceded to the hiring, and to Miss F.'s unilateral stewardship of the house. I did my best to stay clear of Lois. But being alone in the house with her—Miss F. would be out running errands—was like sparring with Mike Tyson.

"It takes all kinds to make the world," Lois said with a cynical laugh, setting her eyes on me for the first time.

"Yes, it does," I agreed, trying to get past her into the kitchen for a cup of coffee so I could escape to my study.

"I know you, oh, yes, I do," she said, clucking her tongue.

"I don't think so."

"I know how to deal with you, oh, yes, I do."

"You won't have to deal with me, really. I'm going to my room."

"Can't please a man like you," Lois declared ruefully, shaking her head.

What was going on? Why did I have to defend myself to this strange, bossy, God-struck woman on the threshold of my own kitchen? "Wait a minute," I said. "That's not the kind of person I am."

"I expect the Lord will forgive you," she allowed, adding that she had just mopped the kitchen floor and I couldn't go in there. Then she burst into hymn, belting out pieties at the top of her lungs, and I fled, cowering, to my sanctuary, listening to her singing penetrate the walls. I came out hours later for lunch; Lois, wild-eyed and sweating, descended on me.

"Lois," I offered innocently, "fix yourself a sandwich if you want."

"I know what you're up to," she said. "Oh, yes, I do. You can't fool old Lois."

I let this go on for six months, enduring Lois's vague accusations and equally vague threats, like spending Saturday mornings with a black, female, pissed-off Kafka, until I begged Miss F. to can Lois, or at least hire me a police escort, so on cleaning days I would have the opportunity to travel from the bedroom to the kitchen to my writing desk, unmolested.

Anyway, eventually I got off the road and returned home to Miss F. and Mace the Dogboy where, ever since, I have become a student of this new science spawned by the mid-life requirements of my generation, the developing symbiosis between boomers and their retainers, mapping its pathologies, marveling at its variations and mutations, its hybrid of bourgeois stratification and multicultural compromise.

For one thing, Maceism has suddenly become fashionable in the neighborhood. Up the street, Jerry and Miss M. have acquired Tim the

Shedboy, and at a recent dinner party, I overheard a woman complain to her husband that if Miss F. could have a dogboy and Miss M. a shedboy, then why couldn't she, a painter, have a paintboy? Only if he could have a 19-year-old live-in Swedish golfgirl, her husband countered, and that was the end of that. Despite the possibility that it might address the local housing shortage, as a trend, I can't decide if Maceism is a new spin on a very old tradition or just plain weird.

As for Mace himself, I knew even before coming home that he and Miss F. had established an affectionate rapport, though it wasn't clear to me just how this compatibility was established, on what basis it had evolved, or if what worked for her would work as well for me. And I fretted that no matter how charming, helpful or trustworthy this Mace might be, I would still find his daytime presence in the house intrusive, since my writing habits require a solitude so strict that even Miss F. is banned from the premises from nine to five. What I immediately discovered, however, was wholly unanticipated: For the first time, Miss F. and I were of an age where it was mathematically possible to enjoy the company of adults who were young enough to be our offspring. For a childless couple, this was a profound and intriguing revelation and, whether Mace would agree or not, I would say that there's a proxy texture to his relationship with us. Given the shifting circumstances of any particular day, Miss F. and I are his friends, his employers or his you-know-whats.

Mace's tenure in the house, as with one's own grown-up kid's, has a provisional quality to it—he hasn't said how long he plans to stay; we have yet to ask—much unlike the presence of Jimmy or Lois, who made you feel you were stuck with them for eternity. Miss F. pays Mace for the work he does as if she were doling out his allowance, a little at a time, with an occasional advance upon request. Like myself, Mace works haphazardly, in fits and starts, trailing chaos behind him, yet with an eye toward perfection—the critical difference being that I am self-employed and Mace is not.

His wit is superb and through it he contributes an odd conviviality to the household; but if conversations are like basketball games, whenever he's passed the ball, he shoots, then retreats to the background, showing no interest in dribbling a point or in the stylistic techniques of team-work. He seems distracted by the postmodern flood tide of competing viewpoints, and he has worried out loud to me that he's too reflective. He feels entirely free to be moody and nonverbal around us—as he wouldn't with his peers—and we return the compliment. As much as Mace might sometimes see me as a mentor, I also sense him wondering just how much he should be rebelling against my authority and values.

As for the daily routine, though he fixes breakfast and lunch for him-self, I cook dinner, which he invariably eats, sometimes probing me about ingredients and recipes. By unspoken agreement, room and board are free and, like any kid at home, whatever he consumes he doesn't replace. "Is there no more mayonnaise?" he asked me one day last week. I told him I had finished the jar that morning. There's still no mayo in the fridge, and although I could have told him to go out and get some, and he would have, I suppose I'm half-waiting for him to take the initia-tive, as he does with walking the dogs and tidying up the kitchen. The love of Mace's life is music, jazz. Animated by creativity, he spends a lot of time in his room playing his wooden recorder. You can hear him throughout the house; when I'm in the basement, writing, or pondering what I'm about to write, the fluid notes annoy me, but I haven't men-tioned it to him, because I know he could not live in a place where he couldn't play his music and although I've no intention of signing an eighteen-year contract with Mace, I'm also not prepared to have him leave just yet.

The domestic algebra, the reciprocity between charity and exploita-tion, is confusing: What the three of us are doing together, I don't quite understand. But I must confess I like it, because what Mace really brings to this house, besides a posture of slothful vitality, is the fine, fresh, imprudent perspective of youth; he's an emissary from an equally self-absorbed but altogether foreign generation and, like any foreigner, what he shows me most successfully is a different way to see myself.

He was out of the house last weekend when Miss F. and I hosted a dinner party, fraternizing with three couples from our own demographic slice of the pie. From start to finish, the table conversation was all too safe and sane—middle-aged—to hold my attention. No one was bawdy, no one was bad, no one had a theory to offer about the universe or our place in it, and I was soon bored to tears. When everyone wanted decaf coffee to cap the evening, I mumbled under my breath "Lord, deliver me from the suburbs," and, sitting back, I found myself involuntarily thinking, Where's Mace? Maybe he'll come home and liven the place up with his excess and irreverence and his wild canine heart.

Before too long, I imagine, he'll be out of here. I suspect that's the way it is with dogboys.

Upon interrogation, Mace finally admitted to me that once, long, long ago, when he was in art school, back around '89 or '90, he loved to cook and had even considered going to culinary school but had since abandoned both the art and the activity and moved on to other things, like drumming and piping, *Star Trek* and starvation. That very night, I put him back in front of the stove, where he conducted himself brilliantly, I think, creating a southern grunger's version of a fish burrito he swears is popular in parts of northern Mexico. Though he's never set foot in those parts, I'll trust him on that, given the evidence he provided for the palate.

MACE'S TUNA BURRITOS
WITH TOMATILLO SAUCE

2 eggs

1 tablespoon milk

1 cup cornmeal

1 teaspoon cumin

1 teaspoon salt

1 teaspoon pepper

1 cup peanut oil

1½ pounds fresh tuna, cut into cubes

3 tablespoons mayonnaise

1 cup shredded red cabbage

8 flour tortillas

2 tablespoons chopped cilantro

Sour cream (optional)

Guacamole (optional)

TOMATILLO SAUCE:

8 to 10 diced tomatillos

3 diced shallots

1 clove garlic, minced

2 serrano peppers, minced

1 teaspoon salt

1 tablespoon cornstarch

1 cup chicken broth, cold

In a small bowl, beat eggs and milk. In another bowl, mix cornmeal with cumin, salt and pepper. Set both bowls aside. Meanwhile, make tomatillo sauce. In a large saucepan, combine tomatillos, shallots, garlic, serrano peppers and salt over low heat and let simmer, stirring frequently for 10 minutes. In a bowl, mix thoroughly cornstarch and cold chicken broth, and pour in with tomatillos. Bring sauce to a boil, then reduce heat, letting it simmer.

Heat peanut oil in a large frying pan. Dip tuna chunks in egg batter, roll in cornmeal until coated, and fry until golden-brown. In another bowl, mix mayonnaise with cabbage and set aside. Warm tortillas in a skillet, in the oven or in a microwave. On each plate, lay two warmed tortillas; add tuna chunks in a line down the middle of each, spoon on tomatillo sauce, add a thin layer of cabbage, sprinkle with chopped cilantro, and roll tortilla, tucking in the ends. Serve with sour cream and guacamole, if desired.

SERVES 4.

PLANTING
THE SEED

When Miss F. arrives home from her office at the end of each work-day, her custom is to look in on me in my basement cell, at which time we reacquaint ourselves and engage in spousal debriefing. How was your day, et cetera? Who called? Did the dogs behave? What have you been writing about? One afternoon this week, it so happened that the answer to the latter question was sperm, a substance that has made an intrepid dash to the forefront of our domestic dialogue this past year, since we, like many thousands of our biological peers, have invited science deep into our reproductive lives.

"Oh," she said, brightening. (Women, I've noticed, have no trouble with the legitimacy of sperm as a subject of conversation.) "Is it fun?" she asked, half-seriously.

Sperm and fun certainly seem like a foregone conclusion, but, frankly, the pleasure inherent in the stuff is probably better expressed in something other than words. Miss F. assumed, incorrectly, that I was having a good time with my topic, one half of the agenda that recently has dominated our private life—fertility, or rather infertility (as in *undi-*

agnosed). As in, if we're ever going to make a baby, it's time to get cracking. But for 40-year-olds, conception's narrative has been revised; just fucking no longer gets the job done. The river of luck must reverse course. A couple's customary ménage à trois with technology undergoes radical redefinition, and for everyone who has spent their postpubescent lives trying to dodge pregnancy, all failed attempts to conceive are, at best, ruefully ironic.

Let me make this clear to those of you who have never experienced the dubious pleasure of ejaculating into an empty peanut-butter jar: It's not that easy, and only a champion onanist would check it out as fun. Consider the furtive shift in erotic concentration from warm fantasy to cold glass cunt, the unexpected difficulty in aiming, the instant pathos and inadequacy of the absurd specimen, definitely not a butterfly. At least in the modern quest for fertility you can produce your offering to the goddess Technologia in your own home (though a nurse on hand would be nice). Then, however, you're the pizza delivery boy, committed to chauffeuring these thwarted figments of an incipient imagination to the medical lab across town in a half-hour or the deal's off. This is not time to be pulled over for speeding, subjected to a routine search for illegal substances.

Once I'd ferried my cargo safely to the lab, I was forced to wait in line behind an emphysemic old man who couldn't get his words out and a woman who'd misplaced her insurance card. The contents of my peanut-butter jar had an abbreviated shelf life, which I was acutely aware was ticking away. Also, the fact that I was the only one in the crowded room toting a brown paper bag was a source of some anxiety for me. Finally, I was confronted by the receptionist, a stern-faced, middle-aged black woman who wanted to know what was in the bag. Well, come on, what is it you're supposed to say? Hot stuff, baby, the real thing? Honey from the rock? Love juice? A burning wad? My already tenuous composure failed me.

"I don't know," I said stupidly and blushed.

"You don't know," she repeated, impatient, in a slightly mocking tone. "Let me guess. Is it your lunch?"

"Fertility test," I managed to croak, and she shook her head, *uh-uh*, looking over her shoulder at the wall clock.

"Too late," she said—the oracles of the bodily fluid had apparently retreated to their smoky cave for the day, not to be disturbed in their deliberations. I'd have to come again, ha-ha, which meant three more consecutive days of abstinence, which would provoke a prison riot in my hormones, never well disciplined, even under the most liberal of circumstances.

I begged her to accept the bag. *Please, please, please.* I was five minutes ahead of deadline. "You don't know," I whined, "how hard this is to do."

"Oh, I *do* know," she said, so knowingly and with such apparent sympathy that my libido took a compulsive leap forward against the bars of its cage and I found myself repressing the questions, the rather shameless lust for imagery that was so integral to my reason for being there. All the unacceptably delicious prurience behind this thing we were almost not talking about.

"Okay," the receptionist acquiesced, "who's your doctor?"

I hadn't a clue. My wife's gynecologist, whoever that was, had ordered the test, the first step in an updated Druidic ritual that would end with Miss F. and me viewing a videotape of her uterine wall as it was seared by a laser scalpel, inserted through her belly button, while Garth Brooks sang about betrayal on the OR boom box. Little wonder that Miss F. had dragged her heels in her decision to procreate.

From the lab, I phoned Miss F. who, amused by my predicament, reported without delay to the other women in her office. "They don't want to take his sperm!" Titters and giggles at the other end of the line. "Some problem with the expiration date."

Finally, I was allowed to deliver my brown bag and its not-so-secret contents to the receptionist, a most bizarre exchange of gender intimacy between two strangers. No matter how you package it, or to what purpose, giving someone a dollop of your semen seems to automatically raise the issue of their trustworthiness. And, of course, yours. Conceptually, if not in fact, you have just signed on for eighteen years of child support.

Several days later, Miss F. rang me at home with the results, relayed to her by her plumber. I stood accused of manufacturing a brat pack of lazy sperm, layabout lads with minimalist tendencies and a lethargic bioattitude. Disciplinary action was prescribed: I must sacrifice my beloved hot baths to the elusive future, wear boxer shorts like television dads do, ingest large doses of vitamins B and C to compensate for smoking. After ten days of ball-coddling and three more of restless chastity, I was ordered to have at it again with another peanut-butter jar.

Again, I heard the news from Miss F.: motility up there in the big-boy range, fist-fights breaking out among the albino troops, the lads clamoring like barbarians for an assault on the cervical gate; drawing DNA straws to determine who among them would thrash like chinook salmon up the Fallopian headwaters to give Miss F. what she most wants in the baby department—a little Oriental girl. It beats me how that's supposed to happen, since we are both Caucasians, but she has her heart set on it. If it's a boy, we're giving him to Rush Limbaugh or Limbaugh's alter ego, Howard Stern, possibly the only two assholes in America who will get out of the twentieth century alive. Survival skills galore, which your run-of-the-mill parents haven't the slightest idea how to impart to their male offspring in these unfriendly times.

Back in the early Eighties when I was 30, 31, I looked around our rented Iowa farmhouse and said to myself, There's the wife, there's the dog, where's the kid? Miss F., however, for her own irrefutably good reasons, had decided to steer clear of pregnancy until further notice, date and circumstances unspecified, at which time the subject of children would be resolved, or so it was hoped.

The rationales for having a kid all seemed primitive and murky to me, or indescribably selfish, sentimental and utterly deluded. The personification of love, the biological imperative of the species—these are tricky motives, prone to vicious paradox. My joy in watching a miniature Miss F. crawling around the house, eating out of the dogs' bowls, would be ineffable, and yet . . . yet what? That's just one scenario, albeit the best. I don't know how I've managed this over the years—certainly not for lack of stupidity—but I've never knocked up anybody, which makes the boy part of me wild with itch. Perhaps you understand about this, perhaps not.

In the big chill of the mid-Eighties, one of Miss F.'s girlfriends—a former lover of mine, I should add, who had in fact introduced me to Miss F.—came to visit. At dinner, our guest revealed that, since she had been unable to encourage any of the chain of ne'er-do-wells she had romanced throughout the years to evolve into an even marginally accept-able husband, she had now decided to get pregnant our of wedlock, as soon as she located a willing male who could match his socks and hadn't voted twice for Reagan. When Miss F. and I retired for the evening, I cleared my throat and ventured out onto the ice.

"How about if . . . ?" I proposed.

"Absolutely not," said Miss F. "I'll leave you if you do."

I didn't quite see the problem—and still don't, actually—but never mind. Having Miss F. walk out on me isn't worth *anything* anybody else could possibly provide. Although what I feel compelled to provide for myself is another story. Honestly, I wanted a kid and didn't feel entirely obligated to any given set of particulars. I was under the impression that progeny was a vital clause in the contract, not necessarily between man and woman, but between an individual and life, a millennia-old game of tag leading back to whatever divine hole humanity had popped out of. Not that you were a deadbeat if you didn't stick to the plan—not at all. Could lead a full and life, sure. I didn't postulate procreation as the be-all and end-all of existence, but I did think it was a profound and mar-velous opportunity, and why drive past a major must-see attraction on the suggested tour? Order everything on the menu; be prepared to take what you get, eat what you can. Then get the fuck out, because some-body else is waiting for a seat.

As the years passed—the Year of the Pill, the Year of No Insurance, the Year of the Peanut-Butter Jar, the Year of Corrective Surgery—it became increasingly evident to me that my desire for offspring coincided with my first breaks as a writer and was no coincidence at all. I had begun publishing—"leaving a trace," as Charlie Baxter would say—but for whom exactly? If part of the answer was "future generations," that meant your kids but not mine, because they didn't exist. I was stripping myself bare in a rather durable form, and, for reasons selfish and vain, I felt enormous envy for my invisible heirs and hungered for the possibility of the afterlife they could bestow. Into the silence that haunts the distance between a parent and a child would roar the hurricane of my writing, and I wanted to observe—or at least contemplate—that dynamic of the flesh and the word, since I had inherited only the scantest record of my ancestors, and even my own parents are, and have never much attempted to be anything but, strangers to me. Parents, period—ultimately a forgivable shortcoming. (What really makes me love my mother, though, are her letters, their scattered but poignant moments of depth and honesty.)

Kids as a metaphor for immortality was a soothing thought but existentially moot, and wanting children was just a wish—not a demand or an obsession, not an emergency, not an absolute need, especially in light of the modern devaluation of innocents. Life, I must confess, had gone on splendidly without them, and Miss F. and I seemed to have a tacit agreement to wait and see what happened, what turned up in the flow, regardless of what either of us intended. It seemed a reasonable intermediate stance, halfway between the promiscuity of fate and the professionalism of self-determination; between animals and gods. Yet what Miss F. intended wasn't always clear to me, and we floated in an illusory cloud of faith, the expectation that somehow, someday, there'd probably be a child underfoot in our lives. That an alarm clock would go off, and we'd actually mate.

The cloud darkened, as clouds do, and burst forth with a downpour of tears on Christmas Eve, 1988. Miss F. and I were snowed in, alone with our dog, in a backwoods cabin in the Uinta Mountains of Utah. The dog—ersatz child—was sick, and we were just beginning to intuit that the poor old guy was dying, and I blamed myself for his condition, for selfishly exposing him to this onslaught of winter. Outside, a blizzard piled snow above the roofline; we huddled in the freezing cabin, heart-sick, numbed by the curtain of sorrow being drawn across Miss F.'s favorite holiday. But Miss F. is tough, and she battled against the surrender of her spirit. She commanded that we cheer up, drink a bottle of good wine, be tender to each other and try to enjoy our dinner on this damaged but still special occasion, and then afterward, the Christmas treat she had been anticipating all day: We'd lie in bed together and listen to our friend Ron Carlson on public radio, reading his magical short story "The H Street Sledding Record" for Garrison Keillor's show, *A Prairie Home Companion*. It was Ron, in fact, who had lent us the cabin, and we considered him American's poet laureate of the crosscurrent passions and joys of domesticity.

But as the hour approached for the broadcast, the storm worsened; the radio's reception vanished behind squalls of static. We heard Ron introduced, and then we lost the signal. Miss F. howled. She would not abide, this final blow, this diabolical assault by nature on Christmas. She adored "The H Street Sledding Record" and needed to hear it in the air, resonating in the cabin, restoring precious oxygen to our emotions. There was a copy of Ron's collection *The News of the World* on the shelf and, inspired, she announced she was going to read the story herself, in ghostly tandem with Ron, out loud to the only audience she had—the brutal wind, a dying dog and me.

And so, swaddled in a blanket, she began: "'The last thing I do every Christmas Eve is go out in the yard and throw the horse manure onto the roof. It is a ritual.'" The story is about a man and a woman in Salt Lake City. A husband and wife. When their daughter turned 4, he got the idea to throw horse shit up on the roof on Christmas Eve—"Hey, look, Santa's reindeers pooped on the roof"—and even though his daughter is now 8 and his wife protests that he's fostering the kid's fantasies, he plans to keep throwing the shit up there every Christmas Eve until his arms give out.

Miss F. continued, glowing with pleasure: "'I put the brake on the sled in 1975 when Drew was pregnant with Elise so we could still make our annual attempt on the H Street Record on Christmas Eve,'" set on

December 24, 1969, the first year of their marriage. The ritual, of course, became sacrosanct, and now there was nothing about Christmas that their daughter looked forward to as much as the family's annual attempt at the H Street Sledding Record. Next year though, the husband hints, they might have to make room for one more on the sled. Who? the daughter asks. Your little brother, answers her mother. Miss F. kept it together until the last two paragraphs: " 'And that's about all that was said, sitting up there on Eleventh Avenue on Christmas Eve on a sled which is as old as my marriage with a brake that is as old as my daughter. Later tonight I will stand in my yard and throw this year's reindeer droppings on my very own home. I love Christmas.

" 'Now the snow spirals around us softly. I put my arms around my family and lift my feet onto the steering bar. We begin to slip down H Street. We are trying for the record.' "

There's another, final, line, but Miss F. never got to it. Her lower lip began to tremble, and I watched her expression contort with anguish. "I want my own daughter," she said, choking, barely able to speak. She lifted her head from the book and looked at me, collapsing into herself. "I want my own daughter," she stuttered. "God-God-God-*damnit*, where is my little girl?" and I jumped across the room to cradle her in my arms as she sobbed herself to sleep. This was the Christmas when our lives gave birth to a missing person.

Okay, so that was life before science. It's five years later now; I awake each morning to the *peep* of Miss F.'s digital thermometer, registering the relative scale of her heat. The days of peanut-butter jars and white-hot knives are past. To complete the late-afternoon vignette I began this with, let me say that Miss F. was kindly disappointed to learn that I hadn't titillated myself, writing about sperm.

"Too complicated," I had to tell her. "Too weird." Too microcosmic.

"Too bad," she commiserated. But the ritual was not quite finished. Before going upstairs to change into her jogging clothes, she had one more question to ask.

"So, what's for dinner?"

"Oysters," I said. This was not a big surprise, and the fact that the Apalachicola watermen were reporting their best oyster season in twenty years was merely serendipitous.

The following week, in mid-November, the debriefing took an extraordinary turn. Miss F. waved a little plastic stick in front of me, which it seemed she had just peed on.

"Do you see a blue line there?" she said anxiously, pointing to a tiny indicator window on the stick. *"Is that a blue line???"*

"Calm down," I said. "Yes, it's a blue line, but what's going on? What's it supposed to mean? What is this?"

Perhaps you've already guessed that it was a home pregnancy test.

"Company's coming!" said Miss F., hopping up and down. "Company's coming!"

My goodness, I thought—you can't ask for a better oyster season than that.

The oyster giveth and the oyster taketh away, and yet from the gastronomic point of view, to die in the saddle (à la Rockefeller), eating a well-iced dozen on the half shell, is not at all an ignoble fate. Nine Floridians succumbed in 1992 as a result of eating raw oysters. The culprit is *Vibrio vulnificus*, a naturally occurring marine bacterium that preys on weak livers. For those of us with healthy constitutions, the threat is nonexistent. My advice is to belly up to the raw bar and not step back until you're acutely aware of the improvement in your sperm count. If you harbor doubts, manly or otherwise, about eating it raw, heat it up. *Vibrio vulnificus* can't survive the cooking process. Think of it as foreplay.

OYSTERS CASINO

1 clove garlic, minced

1 tablespoon chopped fresh parsley

¼ cup chopped onion

2 dozen oysters on the half shell

¼ cup dry white wine

Hot sauce

4 strips raw bacon, each cut into 6 pieces

Preheat oven to 400 degrees. Mix garlic and parsley with chopped onions. Arrange oysters on a baking tray or cookie sheet and spoon onion mixture and white wine over each. Top with a dash of hot sauce, then a piece of bacon, and bake for 15 minutes, or until bacon turns crispy.

SERVES 4.

GOTTA
LIGHT?

I smoke.

Miss F. doesn't.

It's not exactly the Cold War Part 2, but let me see if I can evoke the magnitude of this difference with a suitable comparison: Whenever I feel the need to soothe my nerves, I slash my face with razor blades, roll in shit and bring rabid skunks into the house. Miss F. doesn't approve. "I pity you with all my heart," she might say, then order me into the yard.

In fact, she thinks smoking is a disgusting, filthy, miserable and indefensible habit (which is also what she thinks about my watching *Crossfire*), and yet in all the years we've been together she has mostly let me be. I suppose her behavior implies a somewhat healthy balance of tolerance, stubbornness and martyrdom in our relationship, one of the signatures of domestic stalemate. Miss F. is too sympathetic, or perhaps too clever, to be an outright nag, and because addictions do not gently open themselves to negotiation, cigarettes aren't something we actually fight over. Instead, we ritualize the conflict and lubricate it with civility, deference and tiny quid pro quos, which often seems to work quite well.

"Could you please not smoke in the bathroom?" Miss F. might ask.

"Of course, darling," I might answer and leave in the morning for Mexico City, where the air you inhale through a filtered cigarette is considerably cleaner than the air available on the streets; or Italy, where they are civilized enough to let babies cut their teeth on pretty good cigars.

In regard to tobacco, do I want to do the right thing, the correct thing, the decent, considerate and life-affirming thing? Sorry, the answer is *Fuck, no!* I want to smoke, preferably chain-smoke, preferably in day-care centers or small airplanes packed with state bureaucrats. I want to do this for many reasons, almost all of which have to do with my craving for nicotine; but I also want to exert my civic right to annoy my fellow citizens, as they seem to be exerting their right to annoy the hell out of me. Here I think I have put my finger on the one major accomplishment of the new world order, especially as it is interpreted on the home front: So that we might lead better, more fruitful and lasting lives, we are all now entitled to be absolutely sick and tired of one another. As Fran Lebowitz observed in a visionary 1981 essay, "Being offended is the natural consequence of leaving one's home.

"I do not like after-shave lotion, adults who roller-skate, children who speak French, or anyone who is unduly tan," Lebowitz wrote. "In private I avoid such people; in public they have the run of the place. I stay at home as much as possible, and so should they. When it is necessary, however, to go out of the house, they must be prepared, as am I, to deal with the unpleasant personal habits of others. That is what 'public' means. If you can't stand the heat, get back in the kitchen."

Like myself, Lebowitz once thought that smoking was the entire point of being an adult. It made growing up, she said, genuinely worthwhile. Now we both realize that the real point of growing up is to hire lawyers and engage in litigation. We both made the mistake of imagining that the personal was, well, a personal matter, rather than somebody else's political agenda. Sometime during the Eighties, it began not to matter whether you kept to yourself or not: If you were doing something in your own kitchen that pissed off the surgeon general, you were, ipso facto, a public nuisance.

One should always be able to count on one's home as the last refuge of sin, but this domestic promise has become increasingly tenuous. For most of the time we've been together, Miss F. has seemed able to accept my transgressions as superficial flaws to be overlooked in light of the bargain she was getting on the whole package—as if I were a used car that ran great but didn't look so hot. Then, over the past year or two, the issue of my smoking developed into what could be described essentially as a turf war. Suddenly, Miss F. was allergic to things: mold spores, red wine, overflowing ashtrays, obnoxiousness, the bar exam. We divided up the house. The top floor was to remain smoke-free, except during periods of sunspot activity, astronomical tides or magazine deadlines, when it was customary for me to lose control over my life. The ground floor was to be neutral territory, a live-and-let-live zone, where I was permitted to smoke in moderation and she was free to interrupt anything I was doing by shoving a fashion catalogue in my face in order to make me guess what dress or skirt or sweater would make her look terrific. In the basement, however, I could claim full sovereignty over the enjoyment of my peccadilloes. In the basement, the worst, most satisfying habits of boydom were given a green light, and Miss F. was not so foolish as to risk the perils of descent. I would like to report that we are living happily ever after under this arrangement, but that's not quite the case.

Since smoking is only one of the many ways I have insisted on killing myself, Miss F. has had more sense than to use that particular argument against me. On the other hand, throughout the past year the issue of my smoking began to spill over into neighboring issues, issues a bit more complicated than the puritanical premise that vice is wholly without virtue. (For a rebuttal to this notion, I refer you to Don Marquis's "Preface to a Book of Cigarette Papers," written in 1919: "All that is romantic and literary and spiritual in us holds by the cigarette. When we die and are purged of all the heavy flesh that holds us down, our soul, we hope, will roll and smoke cigarettes along with Buck the Romantic and Lying Cowboy and Ariel and [R.L.] Stevenson and Benvenuto Cellini and Jack Hamlin. We have never been the person on earth we should like to be; circumstances have always tied us to the staid and commonplace and respectable; but when we become an angel we hope to be right devilish at times.")

The auxiliary issues, as I was saying, became the real pitfalls in the smoky truce I had signed with Miss F. Take, for instance, social mobility. I will no longer accompany Miss F. to venues where I can expect to be criminalized for lighting up. Not so much because I am unable to survive without nicotine for a few hours but because, for me, an aggressively sanitized world is about as appealing as a date with a coed from Antioch. This is joie de vivre tucked into the fetal position. The world according to the high-school nurse. (Whenever I see Joycelyn Elders in her *Kommandant*'s uniform, I get a frantic urge to run to the boys' bathroom and hotbox a Camel.)

Or take the issue of finance. The government has helped jack the price of a pack of butts to around $530, and, given my high rate of consumption, Miss F. became justifiably appalled by the expenditure. "Wait a minute," I had to protest. "It's the patriotic thing to do. My country has called upon my resources in a time of great need." I had, in effect, been enlisted as a deficit buster; it was the least I could do for Bill Clinton, after all he'd done for my friends in Haiti.

Could it possibly be that I'm the only person left in the United States sufficiently depraved to be mortified by the phrase "sin tax"? There's a redundancy to this infelicitous pairing of words that might prompt any reasonable citizen to cry out "Lay off, for Christ's sake. I've always paid as I go." I've long considered a hangover a fair tariff for the excesses of the night before. And doesn't it strike you that in the art of collection, lung cancer is the superior player, surpassing the IRS at its own game? Taxing sin is a rather graceless, exploitative and hypocritical scheme, in light of the fact that *profiting* from sin is one of the mainstays of our economy.

If we're going to place a surcharge on human imperfection and common pleasures, perhaps it would prove equally wise to spread out the economic burden of existence with a parallel tax on self-righteousness—a "saint tax"—levied against smoke-free restaurants, universities that ban alcohol at faculty receptions and Catharine MacKinnon. Or let someone propose a tax on associating with bimbos and see how far that gets in Congress, despite its potential to rake in billions from politicians alone.

But back to the periphery and the one issue that seemed most likely to wield the power to reform. Miss F. formed a club with the intention of trying to get herself pregnant, and I was generously invited to join the enterprise. The club consisted of Miss F., two gynecologists, a host of technicians and me—though my membership was contingent upon my willingness to make, and keep, a vow to stop smoking. Smoking, I was informed, is not sperm-friendly; it wreaks havoc on count and motility, the male champs of old-fashioned fertilization. Like Eve Babitz, though, I never want to give up a sin until the last moment, hoping modern science will figure it out, and as Miss F. knows from the parties we've attended, I was born with a talent for prolonging last moments way, way past the appointed time (which, by the way, is precisely why condemned men and writers are so fond of cigarettes).

But this time, time had indeed run out on me; there were no rabbits to pull from the technological hat; and I had no recourse but to throw myself upon the mercy of the most sluttish, disheveled and unreliable part of my character. I am speaking, of course, of my willpower, the monarch of my inner life, the plump philosopher-king of procrastination, the patron of *mañana*. One dreads entering into any sort of constructive collaboration with one's pathologies, but when your manhood is on the line, what the hell can you do?

The first time I tried to quit smoking, ten years ago, I simply wanted to confirm that I could—only, as it turned out, I couldn't. After several weeks of gratuitous anger, crippling bouts of sadness, disconnected shouting, nighttime heebie-jeebies and, finally, a painful misunderstanding between my fist and the bathroom wall, I gave up trying to give it up and instead began immediately to smoke twice as much as had previously been my custom.

The second time I chose to quit was three years ago. Since the children of our nation had taken to shooting at themselves and us, I thought it prudent to be capable of running much faster than I was then able.

Also, I had signed on with an expedition to climb Mount Ararat, in Turkey, and I was convinced I would buy the farm on the ascent unless I made a concerted effort to refresh my lung capacity. From that experience I can tell you that scaling a mountain is not an appropriate time to undergo nicotine withdrawal. Hallucinations, mindlessness and vertigo make foot placement unnecessarily tricky. Also, in the purity of the air, I began to notice that everything smelled awful, especially my socks, and I yearned all the more for the olfactory camouflage of tobacco. Although I didn't die, I certainly wanted to, and when I returned from the summit to base camp, our Kurdish guides refused to be happy until I shared their celebratory beer and cigarettes. I could not bear their disappointment, and, soon enough, that was the end of that.

The third, and most recent, attempt to kick the habit occurred in October, and the goal this time was to make myself combat-ready for parenthood. I threw the dogs, camping gear and two weeks' provisions, plus plenty of booze, into my pickup truck and drove to the Outer Banks of North Carolina, where I hired a boat to ferry us over to the uninhabited island of Portsmouth. I also carried with me a single pack of Marlboros, to be rationed out on the following schedule: first day, ten; second day, five; third day, two; fourth day, two; fifth day, one; sixth day, none.

The first day, I recall, was pleasant. The second day, I recall, was also pleasant, but by that evening I had smoked all my cigarettes. The third day, I made myself hoarse, screaming at the dogs. The fourth day, in the throes of some serious metabolic crashing, I lost my ability to put noun and verb together in coherent fashion. The fifth day, I paid the caretaker of the fish camp on the island to radio to the mainland for a pack of smokes. As a result, I remember, the sixth day was a wonderful day to be alive, and the seventh day was pleasant. Since I had been a bit more sensible about my rationing, I was able to smoke my way back from the panicky ledge of the eighth and ninth days and endure. By the tenth day, however, the cupboard was again bare, and I stumbled around the beach like a lunatic, bumming cigarettes from the surf fishermen. On the eleventh day, I had a fine stroke of luck: I came across an injured pelican, wrapped up in a bottom-fishing rig, and as I was cutting it free, my fillet knife slipped off the wire leader and left me with a deep eight-inch gash in the calf of my right leg. A good flesh wound was just the thing to refocus my thoughts; I retired to my tent for two days to howl and shiver. On the fourteenth day, I was taken off the island, and I drove back to Florida in a stupor, arriving home at three in the morning. Miss F. took a whiff of me and, detecting not a trace of the evil weed on my lips, dragged me off to bed.

Two weeks later, we learned that I knocked her up that night. Two weeks later is also when I started smoking again. Perhaps recidivism, like the tropics, is a way of life.

Excuse me while I sit back, light up and think about that.

Native Americans, Marlboro men and cooks share a common belief: that smoke is an agent of transcendence. Regardless of whether or not you smoke tobacco, your life's missing something if you don't occasionally smoke a duck.

SMOKED DUCK BREAST WITH RASPBERRY-SWEET ONION RELISH

MARINADE:

¼ cup olive oil

½ teaspoon freshly ground black pepper

1 tablespoon salt

1 clove garlic, minced

1 teaspoon chopped fresh sage

1 tablespoon dried basil

1 tablespoon dried rosemary

¼ cup orange juice

¼ cup white wine

¼ cup soy sauce

4 duck-breast halves, boned and skinned

RELISH:

2 cups chopped raspberries

½ cup chopped Vidalia onion

4 teaspoons raspberry vinegar

2 teaspoons lemon juice

1 tablespoon chopped fresh sage

½ teaspoon crushed red-pepper flakes

3 tablespoons crème de cassis

½ cup whole raspberries

Fresh mint sprigs

Mix marinade ingredients in a sealable container and marinate the duck breasts in the refrigerator overnight. Soak two handfuls of wood chips (hickory, mesquite, alderwood, apple or cherry) for 45 minutes in a pot of water. Light about 12 to 15 charcoal briquettes in a grill or brazier. Allow briquettes to burn past their hottest stage. Layer the coals with some of the damp wood chips (if you don't have wood, use fresh herbs or tea as a source of smoke), place the breasts on the grill, and cover. After 30 minutes, add more wood chips and turn the breasts. After 30 minutes more, test for doneness and flavor. If the smoke flavor is too mild for your taste, add more wood chips and cook for another 20 minutes.

In a glass bowl, make relish by mixing all ingredients except whole raspberries and mint. Remove duck breasts from grill, slice and arrange on plates with a dollop of relish; garnish with raspberries and mint sprigs. Serve with polenta and wild mushrooms.

SERVES 4.

(This recipe is adapted from *American Game Cooking*, whose authors adapted it from the dish prepared at Patrick O'Connell's Inn at Little Washington, in Virginia.)

THIGHS AND
WHISPERS

In everyday life, the worst questions Miss F. can ask me concern her appearance. Depending on a set of variables (mood, context, time, place, effort), I think she is stunningly gorgeous, classically beautiful, stylishly pretty, or comfortably ordinary. The range here seems to me realistic and natural. But if I come upon her standing unclothed in front of a full-length mirror, examining front, back, and side views with a doubtful expression, I reverse my direction. She has a firm, athletic body, but what does that matter? If I don't get away in time, she snares me with the question: "Am I fat?" You'd think there's only one answer, but there's not. There are plenty of them, and she's going to solicit them all. "No," I say. "You're not fat."

"What about here?" Miss F. asks, pinching the insignificant, Botticellian swell of her abdomen.

"Only an anorexic would call that fat."

"I've always hated it," she says.

A group of her friends has recently discovered liposuction.

"Go get it vacuumed off if it bothers you that much," I say.

"So you think I'm fat?"

Pampering is really an acquiescence to silliness, and I refuse its strategy. A man cannot possibly pacify a woman's insecurity about body image in a reliable, enduring fashion, anyway.

"Yes," I say, losing patience. "You are a sloth and a hog. Exercise more, eat less." She exercises regularly and picks wistfully at pasta and greens.

"Screw you," Miss F. says, fire in her eyes.

"Not only are you becoming a paleolithic Venus," I continue bravely. "But you are unspeakably vain. Your values are shallow, you have body odor, and your teeth are getting crooked as you age. Not only that, but I've slept with all your friends and most of your enemies, men and women alike, and we make fun of you behind your back. Plus," I say, winding up, "your intelligence is not what I once imagined it to be when you were young and attractive."

We are on the floor now, wrestling. "And still, *still*," she demands, laughing, "you love me?"

Despite all that, I say.

I guess it's just one of those things, and no getting over it.

Now, let's do a little work on those thighs.

COCONUT-CREAM PIE, ISLAND-STYLE

½ cup sugar

¼ cup cornstarch

¼ teaspoon salt

2 ¼ cups milk, scalded

4 egg yolks, slightly beaten

1 teaspoon vanilla extract

1 tablespoon dark rum

2 cups freshly grated coconut (or flaked, unsweetened coconut)

1 tablespoon butter

1 cup heavy cream

Mix sugar, cornstarch, and salt in a large saucepan. Stir in scalded milk until mixture is smooth. Stirring constantly, cook over medium heat until mixture thickens. Stir 4 tablespoons of the hot-milk mixture into beaten egg yolks until well blended. Add this mixture to the remaining hot milk and cook over low heat, stirring constantly, until custard is smooth and thick. Remove from heat and add vanilla, rum, coconut, and butter. Pour custard into a baked pie shell (see recipe for piecrust, below) and refrigerate until set.

Whip heavy cream until stiff. Cover pie with whipped cream, chill until ready to serve.

MAKES ONE 9-INCH PIE.

BING'S KEY-LIME PIE

FOR THE FILLING:

1 14-ounce can sweetened condensed milk

⅓ cup Key-lime juice

1 egg, separated

FOR THE MERINGUE:

5 egg whites

¼ teaspoon cream of tartar

6 tablespoons sugar

Mix sweetened condensed milk, Key-lime juice and egg yolk in a medium-size bowl, beat egg white until nearly stiff. Fold into lime mixture. Pour into a baked pie shell (see recipe below).

To make the meringue, beat egg whites with cream of tartar until fluffy. Continue beating, and very slowly add sugar. Beat until stiff and glossy peaks form, about 8 minutes. Smooth meringue over top of pie, making sure to cover filling completely. Bake in a preheated oven at 375 degrees for approximately 8 to 10 minutes, or until the meringue is golden brown. Serve pie at room temperature.

MAKES ONE 8-INCH PIE.

BASIC PIECRUST

2 ¼ cups all-purpose flour

1 teaspoon salt

1 teaspoon sugar (optional)

¾ cup cold butter, cut into small pieces

4 to 5 tablespoons ice water

In a large bowl, stir together flour, salt and sugar. With a pastry blender or two table knives, cut butter into flour until pieces are about the size of small peas. Measure water into cup. While stirring flour mixture lightly and quickly with a fork, sprinkle in water 1 tablespoon at a time (up to 4 tablespoons), just until flour is moistened. (If mixture seems too dry and crumbly, sprinkle with another tablespoon of water. Mixture should not be wet or sticky.) Continue to stir with a fork until dough starts to form a ball and sides of bowl are nearly clean.

Form dough into a ball with your hands. Divide dough in half and flatten each half into a 4-inch round. Cover with plastic wrap and place in refrigerator for 1 hour. Roll dough until it is approximately 2 inches larger than pie pan and about ⅛ inch thick. Wrap lightly around rolling pin, and unroll into pie pan. Trim dough, leaving about 1-inch overhang. Fold edge of crust under so it is even with rim of pan; flute edge by pinching between thumb and forefinger. Prick bottom and sides of shell with a fork and bake in a preheated oven at 450 degrees for 10 minutes, or until lightly browned. Cool completely before filling.

MAKES TWO SINGLE-CRUST PIES OR ONE DOUBLE-CRUST.

INDEX

BOB SHACOCHIS is a novelist, essayist, journalist, and educator. A former contributing editor for *Harper's* and *Outside*, Shacochis currently teaches in the graduate writing programs at Bennington College and Florida State University. Among his works are the short story collections *Easy in the Islands* and *The Next New World*; the novel *Swimming in the Volcano*, a finalist for the National Book Award; *Domesticity*, a collection of essays about food and love; *Between Heaven and Hell*, a travel memoir of his journeys in the Himalaya; and, most recently, the novel *The Woman Who Lost Her Soul*. *The Immaculate Invasion*, about the 1994 military intervention in Haiti, was a finalist for the New Yorker Magazine Literary Awards and a New York Times Notable Book. Shacochis's work has received a National Book Award for First Fiction, the Rome Prize in Literature from the American Academy of Arts and Letters, and a National Endowment for the Arts Fellowship. His op-ed commentaries on the U.S. military, Haiti, and Florida politics have appeared in the *New York Times*, the *Washington Post*, and the *Wall Street Journal*. He lives in Florida and New Mexico with Ms. F. They have been together for thirty-eight years.